WHAT IS A POET?

WHAT IS A POET?

*Essays from The Eleventh
Alabama Symposium
on English and
American Literature*

Edited by HANK LAZER

The University of Alabama Press

Tuscaloosa and London

Copyright © 1987 by
The University of Alabama Press
Tuscaloosa, Alabama 35487
All rights reserved
Manufactured in the United States of America

Library of Congress Cataloging-in-Publication Data

Alabama Symposium on English and American Literature
(11th : 1984 : University of Alabama)
What is a poet?

Bibliography: p.
Includes index.
1. American poetry—20th century—History and
criticism—Congresses.   2. Poetry—Congresses.
3. English poetry—History and criticism—Congresses.
I. Lazer, Hank.   II. Title.
PS325.A34   1987   811'.5'09   86-19234
ISBN 0-8173-0325-1 (alk. paper)
ISBN 0-8173-0326- X(pbk. : alk. paper)

British Library Cataloguing-in-Publication Data is available.
Book and jacket designed by Courtney Stewart Delaney

To Kenneth Burke

Contents

Illustrations

Acknowledgments

The Eleventh Alabama Symposium on English and American Literature: What Is a Poet?, where most of the essays in this volume were first presented, was in large part made possible through a grant from the Committee for the Humanities in Alabama, a state program of the National Endowment for the Humanities. In addition, encouragement, assistance, and financial support for the symposium were provided by The University of Alabama's Department of English, College of Arts and Sciences, College of Continuing Studies, and Office for Academic Affairs. I wish to thank a number of administrators for their support and participation: Claudia Johnson, Richard Peck, Dennis Prisk, and Roger Sayers. I especially wish to thank Joab Thomas, President of The University of Alabama, for his support of and active participation in the symposium.

I also wish to thank James Ramer, Dean of the Graduate School of Library Science, and Gabriel Rummonds, Director of the Institute for the Book Arts, for their support, courage, and guidance in the publication of *On Equal Terms,* a deluxe limited-edition book with two poems each by Charles Bernstein, David Ignatow, Denise Levertov, Louis Simpson, and Gerald Stern.

The symposium itself took nearly two years to plan. Many of the English Department's graduate students, through their diligent efforts, made it possible for the event to run smoothly. I especially wish to thank Janet McAdams and Paul Johnson for their help, and the students in my "What Is a Poet?" seminar for their interest, comments, and friendship. The symposium would not have taken place if not for the patient and expert assistance of Susan Motes and Joe Ann Slact from the College of Continuing Studies. In the English Department, my colleague George Wolfe offered helpful advice, historical perspective, and a needed sense of poise and humor. Christel Bell made the financial records and paperwork both bear-

ACKNOWLEDGMENTS

able and accurate, as did Patton Seals, the University's Assistant Comptroller for Contracts and Grants. Shelton Waldrep and Catherine Davis provided valuable assistance in preparing the book manuscript and in transcribing the panel discussion. At The University of Alabama Press, I have benefited from the advice and expertise of Director Malcolm MacDonald.

But my greatest debt of gratitude is to the participants themselves, who presented excellent talks, and who took the necessary time to write and revise the essays which constitute this book. I especially wish to thank them for their active participation in the concluding panel discussion, an event of considerable heat and light.

Finally, I dedicate this book to Kenneth Burke, writer *extraordinaire* and practitioner of the counter-gridlock method, whose seventy years of writing crosses and cross-pollinates the genres under consideration in this book, and whose belated contribution to the book is deeply appreciated.

HANK LAZER

WHAT IS A POET?

Hank Lazer

INTRODUCTION

What is poetry? is so nearly the same question with, what is a poet?
that the answer to the one is involved in the solution of the other.

—Samuel Taylor Coleridge, *Biographia Literaria*

The Eleventh Alabama Symposium: What Is a Poet? took place
October 18–20, 1984, at The University of Alabama. In late 1982
when I began to plan the symposium, my main intent was to gather
together a distinguished group of poets and critics to discuss the
nature of poetry. From the outset, I hoped that I would be able to
assemble a group of critics and poets who represented at least a
fairly wide portion of the spectrum available today for a discussion
of contemporary American poetry. I did not want nor hope for a
symposium of backslapping, mutual admiration, and easy consensus. I hoped that the differences in aesthetics and writing practice would lead not only to disagreement but also to clarification of
the reasons for differently held views of poetry. Also, I was just plain
curious to see what would happen when poets and critics *together*
took part in a program of this kind. Often, poets scorn the work of
critics as overly theoretical, abstract, and out of touch with the
practice of writing, while critics bemoan the lack of intellectual
rigor or ambition and the absence of serious self-questioning in
much contemporary poetry. I had already attended plenty of poetry
festivals and literature conferences where one group quite self-
satisfyingly describes the failings of the other.

1

I also had a dim awareness that, once again, American poetry was beginning a period of upheaval and renewed questioning. After all, the well-documented[1] poetic revolt of the late fifties and early sixties had become rather comfortably (and institutionally) entrenched. I had read Robert Pinsky's grumblings in *The Situation of Modern Poetry* (1976) but had dismissed them as the rather predictable complaints of a neo-Winters sensibility, a conservative bemoaning directed at an accomplished American mysticism, which was incompatible with Pinsky's own more discursive ramblings. Then, Charles Altieri's essays, especially "From Experience to Discourse: American Poetry and Poetics in the Seventies" (published in *Contemporary Literature* in 1980), began more seriously to chip away at the habits and assumptions of what had become the dominant poetry of the seventies and eighties. In my own essay in this volume, an essay written a year or so prior to the symposium, I tried to refute Altieri's criticisms. I have since found myself to be in greater and greater agreement with Altieri's fundamental criticisms,[2] points which he developed at length in *Self and Sensibility in Contemporary American Poetry* (1984).

In addition to creating a topic—"What Is a Poet?"—that would give the speakers at the symposium the freedom to approach such a nebulous subject in whatever manner they deemed appropriate, I also had in mind an earlier effort to ask and answer such a question: Heidegger's "What Are Poets For?" Heidegger's essay, which was first delivered as a lecture to a small group in 1946 commemorating the twentieth anniversary of Rilke's death, prompted me to wonder what the function of our best poets might be in our own "destitute" time. For his own era, Heidegger turned back to Hölderlin's poetry and concluded:

> Poets are the mortals who, singing earnestly of the wine-god, sense the trace of the fugitive gods, stay on the gods' tracks, and so trace for their kindred mortals the way toward the turning. . . .To be a poet in a destitute time means: to attend, singing, to the trace of the fugitive gods. This is why the poet in the time of the world's night utters the holy.
>
> It is a necessary part of the poet's nature that, before he can be truly a poet in such an age, the time's destitution must have made the whole being and vocation of the poet a poetic question for him. Hence "poets in a destitute time" must especially gather in poetry the nature of poetry.[3]

2

I hoped that by putting in question the vocation and nature of the poet, the writers gathered for the Alabama symposium might offer their own descriptions and definitions.

◆

The format for the symposium was, to a great extent, one that I inherited. That is, as with the previous ten symposia, the major event would be a series of lectures by the principal speakers. Several speakers—Czesław Miłosz, John Ashbery, John Hollander, Donald Hall, Gary Snyder, Harold Bloom, Robert Bly, and Allen Ginsberg among them—were, for various reasons, unable to attend. Other than the celebrity status (with schedules booked well in advance) of many American poets and critics, one other "problem" began to crop up. Many of the poets I considered either simply did not write essays, or they were quite leery of writing a substantial lecture for presentation and publication. Considering that many of these same poets hold established teaching positions, I found such a distancing from discursive activity to be especially odd.

The nine speakers—Charles Altieri, Charles Bernstein, Kenneth Burke, David Ignatow, Denise Levertov, Marjorie Perloff, Louis Simpson, Gerald Stern, and Helen Vendler—each presented a lecture, and Bernstein, Ignatow, Levertov, Simpson, and Stern each gave a poetry reading (as well as contributing two poems to *On Equal Terms,* a deluxe limited-edition book printed under the supervision of Gabriel Rummonds, cofounder of Plain Wrapper Press and Director of The University of Alabama's Institute for the Book Arts). The concluding event of the symposium was a two-hour panel discussion, held Saturday, October 20, 1984. All nine speakers participated in the panel discussion, and Gregory Jay (author of *T. S. Eliot and the Poetics of Literary History* and coeditor of *After Strange Texts: The Role of Theory in the Study of Literature*) and I served as moderators. The complete panel transcript is included in this present volume.

In transcribing the panel discussion I have tried to keep my editorial activities to a minimum. Whenever possible, I have opted for a verbatim transcription, while occasionally eliminating repetitious phrases. It has been my intent to retain, as much as was practical, the flavor of actual speech. I hope that the transcript gives some indication of the intensity, anger, impatience, humor, and seriousness of the discussion which took place.

3

The discussion was an extremely valuable airing of differences and stating of positions, especially since the issues being argued will not go away. Immediately after the discussion, I thought that the general mood was one of exhaustion, mixed with a sense that an opportunity of some sort had been missed. Certain topics, questions, and perspectives remained unexplored. For example, Greg Jay's opening questions about the nature of poetic thinking were, to a great degree, ignored. These questions, I contend, remain both unanswered and of interest. Perhaps the opportunity missed, though, was not the chance to answer a specific question, but the occasion to use this assembled talent *collectively* (to think as a group about issues common to our involvement with poetry). During the discussion, there were attempts to establish such a common base: Helen Vendler's assertion of a genetic similarity between poets and critics, Charles Bernstein's advocacy of the term *writer* (instead of the polarizing terms *poet* and *critic*). But such suggestions were bypassed. Instead, we spent much of our time struggling to draw boundaries between poetic and critical activity, and then arguing against the validity of such boundary lines. And, of course, much of the discussion was devoted to an articulation of differences in tastes and principle.

I would call attention, however, to several issues from the panel discussion, which, in all likelihood, will remain central to arguments about poetry. The first is Helen Vendler's distinction between reviewing and criticism. To ignore this distinction would be to blur the (often hidden) reasons for disagreement. Often the panelists, as with other readers and critics of contemporary poetry, while seeming to argue over more general principles of criticism, were in fact arguing over matters of evaluation and taste, i.e., reviewing. Second, I would direct attention to the exchange between Greg Jay and Louis Simpson over the relationship between language and experience. In part, their disagreement may be seen as generational: a younger generation whose reading habits are more theoretically inclined is much more apt to grant to language itself a formative role in shaping our versions of experience and of our world. Simpson counters with a defense of the primacy of experience over language and of a writing practice which strives to represent (not produce) that primary world. Third is the sporadic but repeated concern in the discussion with poetry's uneasy institu-

4

tional accommodations. What effects do English departments, critical theory institutes, M.F.A. programs, and workshops have on our reading and writing habits? (Such questions are taken up quite directly in a supplemental essay to this volume, Donald Hall's "Poetry and Ambition.") What kinds of writing are allowed to be heard (accepted, assigned, awarded, and sponsored), and what approaches are rendered inaudible by our current institutional practices? I predict further inquiry into and serious fighting about such matters. Finally, while the panel seemed to agree that poetry and politics are not divorced, there was considerable disagreement over *how* poetry and political considerations can be most effectively meshed.

While a two-hour panel discussion could not be expected to resolve major differences, I do think that the discussion accomplished what Louis Simpson asserted, in the symposium's opening lecture, had *not* been happening for nearly twenty years in America: a heated exchange of ideas. For a rare time in recent American literary history, a relatively diverse group of poets *and* critics, writers, took part in that exchange.

One particularly painful irony of the panel discussion was that the participant who was nearly overlooked, Kenneth Burke, was the one who by the example of his seventy years of writing could have best assisted us in extracting ourselves from our least productive moments of divisiveness. Burke's entire career rebukes our usual habits of categorizing and partitioning thinking. Charles Bernstein, from what seems to me a Burkean perspective, argues in "Writing and Method":

> For what makes poetry poetry and philosophy philosophy is largely a tradition of thinking and writing, a social matrix of publications, professional associations, audience; more, indeed facts of history and social convention than intrinsic necessities of the "medium" or "idea" of either one.[4]

While for my own purposes I would like to think of Burke as a writer who practices a thorough disregard of boundary lines, that is an inaccurate picture of his viewpoint. Instead, Burke argues:

> Critical and imaginative works are answers to questions posed by the situation in which they arose. They are not merely answers, they

5

are *strategic* answers, *stylized* answers. For there is a difference in style or strategy, if one says "yes" in tonalities that imply "thank God" or in tonalities that imply "alas!" So I should propose an initial working distinction between strategies and "situations," whereby we think of poetry (I here use the term to include any work of critical or imaginative cast) as the adopting of various strategies for the encompassing of situations.[5]

While I would like to seize on Burke's parenthetical definition as absolute, he also, as in his essay included in this book, draws distinctions between poetic and critical activities. In Burke's conception, the activities of poet and critic overlap, complement, and complete one another, though I'm still not at all sure that either is *necessary* to the other. The two activities (for Burke) are certainly not the same, but their relationship might still be described as constituting a kind of off-rhyme, with both resembling and differing from each other. At his most conciliatory, Burke concludes:

> As poet-plus-critic, one both acts and observes his act. By this faculty of observation, he matures his acts with relation to other people. . . . And we all, as poet-and-critics working together, win somewhat by developing poetic symbols and critical formulation that enable us to size up the important factors of reality (particularly by recourse to the comic critique of social relationships) and to adopt workable attitudes toward them.[6]

I discuss Burke's work at length in this introduction because he anticipates (and encompasses) so many of the problems and conflicts that were essential to our symposium. His notion of counter-gridlock may, in fact, be an apt metaphor for the variety of approaches taken to poetry at the symposium. In "The Philosophy of Literary Form" (1941), Burke equates "dramatic" with "didactic" and applies such a definition of drama to conversation and argumentation:

> Where does the drama get its materials? From the "unending conversation" that is going on at the point in history where we are born. born. Imagine that you enter a parlor. You come late. When you arrive, others have long preceded you, and they are engaged in a heated discussion, a discussion too heated for them to pause and tell you exactly what it is about. In fact, the discussion had already begun

long before any of them got there, so that no one present is qualified to retrace for you all the steps that had gone before. You listen for a while, until you decide that you have caught the tenor of the argument; then you put in your oar. Someone answers; you answer him; another comes to your defense; another aligns himself against you, to either the embarrassment or gratification of your opponent, depending upon the quality of your ally's assistance. However, the discussion is interminable. The hour grows late, and you must depart. And you do depart, with the discussion still vigorously in progress.[7]

Within this discussion, Burke sees each speaker as departing from some "rock-bottom fact." Burke hastens to point out that such "facts" are, of course, not the special possession of the speakers, but representative stances taken at a given historical moment: "Actually, the very selection of his 'rock-bottom fact' derives its true grounding from the current state of the conversation, and assumes quite a different place in the 'hierarchy of facts' when the locus of discussion has shifted."[8]

Thus, I had expected there to be conflict, but not at the level at which it took place. For example, during the talk by Charles Altieri, two poets in the audience, after cracking a few jokes, got up and left, encouraging their friends and students to do likewise. One said, "Who can understand *this* . . . ?" Charles Bernstein, the writer least known to the audience, and the most experimental of the writers present, was also the focal point for a fair amount of hostility by the audience, and even by certain symposium participants. In the opening lecture, Louis Simpson delivered a very thinly veiled attack on Helen Vendler. While not attacking Vendler by name, Simpson derided two of Vendler's favorites: Wallace Stevens and Amy Clampitt.

At stake in such an exchange of views, as I have become increasingly aware, is power. While Shelley's notion of the poet as "the unacknowledged legislator of the world" may sound to us almost comically self-serving and out of touch with American (or British) political life, the last twenty years in America have seen a proliferation of university writing programs, creative writing grants, well-paying academic positions for poets (and critics), and poetry prizes. When Charles Bernstein defines "official verse culture" (in "The Academy in Peril: William Carlos Williams Meets the MLA," a talk delivered at the 1983 MLA convention), both his tone and his definition point us toward some of the sources of conflict at the Alabama symposium:

> Let me be specific as to what I mean by "official verse culture"—I am referring to the poetry publishing and reviewing practices of *The New York Times, The Nation, American Poetry Review, New York Review of Books, The New Yorker, Poetry* (Chicago), *Antaeus, Parnassus,* Atheneum Press, all the major trade publishers, the poetry series of almost all of the major university presses (the University of California Press being a significant exception at present). Add to this the ideologically-motivated selection of the vast majority of poets teaching in university writing and literature programs and of poets taught in such programs as well as the interlocking accreditation of these selections through prizes and awards judged by these same individuals. Finally, there are the self-appointed keepers of the gate who actively put forward biased, narrowly-focused and frequently shrill and contentious accounts of American poetry, while claiming, like all disinformation propaganda, to be giving historical or non-partisan views.[9]

Given the radically divergent affinities for poetry present at the Alabama symposium, predictably, antagonisms would arise from deep-seated opinions about what constituted "good," "interesting," "major," "significant," and "vital" poetry.

One year after the symposium, Helen Vendler offered the following argument about the question of the literary canon's formation:

> . . . canons are not made by governments, anthologists, publishers, editors, or professors, but by writers. The canon, in any language, is composed of the writers that other writers admire, and have admired for generations. The acclamations of governments, the civic pieties of anthologists, the hyperboles of marketing, the devotion of dons, have never kept a writer alive for three or four hundred years. It is because Virgil admired Homer, and Milton Virgil, and Keats Milton, and Stevens Keats that those writers turn up in classrooms and anthologies. And writers admire writers not because of their topics (Blake and Keats thought Milton quite mistaken in his attitudes) but because of their writing. And writers admire writing not because it keeps up some schoolmasterly "standard" but because it is "simple, sensuous, and passionate" (as Milton said)—strenuous,

imaginative, vivid, new. The canon is always in motion (as Eliot reminded us, and as formalists have always known) because new structures are always being added to it by subsequent writers, thereby reshaping the possibilities of writing and of taste; but the evolving canon is not the creation of critics, but of poets.[10]

For the poets, the critics have too much power and influence. For critics such as Vendler, it is ultimately the poets who will determine what is read. And thus no one seems to want to acknowledge his or her own power in the process of judgment and recognition.

◆

Included in this book then are the nine lectures presented at the symposium, some of them revised quite significantly. I have included as well my own thoughts on the relationship between poetry and criticism in "Critical Theory and Contemporary American Poetry," an essay written prior to the symposium. In addition, I have included Donald Hall's "Poetry and Ambition," in part because that essay informs some of the questions which arose in the panel discussion, but also because Hall's essay touches directly on the issue of poetry's relationship to institutional settings.[11]

I leave it to the readers of this book to describe for themselves the "rock-bottom facts" for each speaker/writer in this book. It is hoped that the reader of this present collection of essays and a panel discussion will grapple and argue with the viewpoints articulated here, and thus each reader's response will further extend this conversation.

NOTES

1. Three examples come to mind: Charles Altieri's *Enlarging the Temple: Ontological Themes in American Poetry of the 1960s*, James E. B. Breslin's *From Modern to Contemporary: American Poetry, 1945–1965*, and Robert Von Hallberg's *American Poetry and Culture: 1945–1980*.

2. See my "Criticism and the Crisis in American Poetry," *The Missouri Review*, Vol. IX, No. 1 (1986), especially pp. 213–15.

3. Martin Heidegger, "What Are Poets For?," *Poetry, Language, Thought* (New York: Harper & Row, 1971), p. 94.

4. Charles Bernstein, *Content's Dream: Essays 1975–1984* (Los Angeles: Sun & Moon Press, 1986), p. 217.

9

5. Kenneth Burke, *The Philosophy of Literary Form* (Berkeley: University of California Press, 1973), 3rd edition, p. 1.

6. Kenneth Burke, *Attitudes Toward History* (Berkeley: University of California Press, 1984), 3rd edition, pp. 213–14.

7. Burke, *The Philosophy of Literary Form*, pp. 110–11.

8. Ibid, p. 111.

9. Charles Bernstein, manuscript version of *Content's Dream*, pp. 247–48.

10. Helen Vendler, *The New York Review of Books,* Nov. 7, 1985, p. 59.

11. For two divergent reactions to Hall's essay, see Sherod Santos, "Notes Toward a Defense of Contemporary Poetry," *New England Review*, Summer 1985, pp. 284–96, and my "Criticism and the Crisis in American Poetry."

THE SYMPOSIUM

Louis Simpson

THE CHARACTER
OF THE POET

For twenty years American poets have not discussed the nature of poetry. There has not been the exchange of ideas there used to be. The polemics of the Beat, the Black Mountain, the Sixties Poets, and the New York Poets are a thing of the past. The resistance to the war in Vietnam brought poets of different groups together on the same platform, and since that time they have ceased to argue—perhaps because arguing over poetry seems trivial when we are living under the shadow of nuclear annihilation.

Another reason is the ascendancy of criticism. If poets do not speak for themselves others will speak for them, and when poets vacated the platform critics rushed to take their place. Those who have no great liking for poetry like to explain it. The poets have been willing to see this happen—they are workers and not given to abstract thinking. They believe that the best literary criticism and the only kind that's likely to last is a poem.

When the theory of an art is divorced from the practice it becomes absurd. And when it acquires authority it can do considerable harm. The young people who we hope will read our poems are likely to attend a university, and there they will be exposed to

13

the teachings of fashionable schools of criticism. Suppose such a young person were to read this poem by Wordsworth:

> A slumber did my spirit seal;
>   I had no human fears:
> She seemed a thing that could not feel
>   The touch of earthly years.
>
> No motion has she now, no force;
>   She neither hears nor sees;
> Rolled round in earth's diurnal course,
>   With rocks, and stones, and trees.

Here is the kind of explanation the young reader might be given. "'A Slumber Did My Spirit Seal' . . . enacts one version of a constantly repeated Occidental drama of the lost sun. Lucy's name of course means light. To possess her would be a means of rejoining the lost light, the father sun as *logos,* as head power and fount of meaning. . . . The death of Lucy is the loss of the *logos,* leaving the poet and his words groundless."[1]

This is not a parody but the work of a respected literary critic. His interpretation does not take into account the effect of the poem upon the reader, the poem as drama, a thing experienced. That is to say, his interpretation has nothing to do with poetry. The reflection, however, would not deter the kind of critic who reads poetry in this way. On the contrary, as such critics are not slow to admit, they think that interpretations are more important than poems.

The poet works to create an image, rhythm, and sound that will carry his thought to the heart and mind of the reader. The critic interposes to say that there is no such thing as meaning. Writing is a series of verbal signs. In writing we resort to key metaphors, and "such metaphors are self-conflicting . . . any attempt to explicate one of them proliferates into further metaphors without the possibility of coming to a halt in a literal, or 'proper' meaning."[2]

You will recall these lines by Yeats:

> What shall I do with this absurdity—
> O heart, O troubled heart—this caricature,
> Decrepit age that has been tied to me
> As to a dog's tail.

Imagine, if you can, telling Yeats that these words have no literal or proper meaning, that they are merely metaphorical. But this is what such scholars teach and, as Robert Burns said:

> A set o' dull conceited hashes
> Confuse their brains in college classes!

In the face of such misleading it is necessary, as perhaps never before, for poets to reaffirm the primacy of feeling, to say that poetry is not a game played with words, that it is in earnest. At the end of every idea lies a life . . . someone has paid for it. There is an end to metaphor, an angel in the gate with a fiery sword who says, "Thus far and no farther." The meanings in poems were written in blood—damn their misreadings!

We need to speak again about common life, that life people in universities appear to have put behind them. As poets this is our concern—as William Carlos Williams said, "The first thing that stands eternally in the way of really good writing is always one: the virtual impossibility of lifting to the imagination those things which lie under the direct scrutiny of the senses."

Can we make poetry out of such things? Can we write about offices and the people who work in them? About factories and the people who live in mean streets? Can we write about those large tracts between cities lined with houses, where so many people live? If we cannot bring these into poetry then something is missing— the life most people know.

Poets have come to think that they are different from the common man and woman, and to think that because the common man and woman do not read poetry, poetry can exclude the common man and woman. This is the fallacy that has made so much poetry in our time empty and unimportant. Suppose Chaucer had said to himself, "The ordinary man doesn't care for poetry, so I won't write about him." This is how many poets think—consequently they write of matters that are of no concern.

How can we lift to the imagination those things which lie under the direct scrutiny of the senses? By lifting ourselves—there is no other way. We know what the poet does—she absorbs what she sees and transforms it. Whitman has described the process of absorbing:

15

> There was a child went forth every day,
> And the first object he look'd upon, that object he became.

But this does not explain the transforming. The poet has to be the kind of person who transforms what she sees and hears into poetry—writing poetry requires no less.

Yeats was right, there is no singing school. But I think that if we look into the lives of poets we shall find there was a time of withdrawal from the world, of silence and meditation. We tend to think of poetry as making something out of nothing, as having original ideas and fetching images from afar. But does poetry have no power in itself? No reality? What would happen if instead of trying to write poetry one allowed silence to speak?

Dante has told us how he became a poet. For nine years love had ruled his soul—the image of Beatrice was always present in his mind. Then one day he saw her walking in the street between two older women of distinguished bearing. She greeted him—he experienced the height of bliss and his senses reeled.[3]

He returned to his lonely room where, thinking of Beatrice, he fell asleep and had a vision of a lordly figure, "frightening to behold," says the poet, "yet in himself, it seemed to me, he was filled with a marvellous joy." The figure said many things of which he understood only a few, among them the words, *"Ego dominus tuus,"* "I am your master." The figure held Beatrice in his arms; she was asleep, naked, wrapped in a crimson cloth. In one hand he held a fiery object, and he seemed to say, *"Vide cor tuum,"* "Behold your heart." It seemed that he wakened the sleeping Beatrice and prevailed upon her to eat the glowing object in his hand. Reluctantly and hesitantly she did so. A few moments later his happiness turned to bitter grief and, weeping, he gathered Beatrice in his arms and together they seemed to ascend into the heavens.

The poet felt such anguish at their departure that he woke. It was, he tells us, the first of the last nine hours of the night. Pondering what he had seen in his dream, he decided to make it known to a number of poets who were famous at the time. "As I had already tried my hand at composing in rhyme, I decided to write a sonnet in which I would greet all Love's faithful servants; and so, requesting them to interpret my dream, I described what I had seen. This was the sonnet beginning, 'To every captive soul.'"

With the passing of the old religious world poets no longer thought of themselves as inspired by a god, but still they felt prompted to write by a power outside themselves. For Wordsworth this power spoke through nature. He tells how he first became aware that he was to be a poet. He was returning home at dawn from a night spent in "dancing, gaiety, and mirth," with "slight shocks of young love-liking interspersed," when

> Magnificent
> The morning rose, in memorable pomp,
> Glorious as e'er I had beheld—in front,
> The sea lay laughing at a distance; near,
> The solid mountains shone . . . [4]

The scene before him included laborers going out to till the fields. "Ah! need I say, dear Friend," he says, addressing Coleridge:

> that to the brim
> My heart was full; I made no vows, but vows
> Were then made for me; bond unknown to me
> Was given, that I should be, else sinning greatly,
> A dedicated Spirit. On I walked
> In thankful blessedness, which yet survives.

I believe that all true poets feel a sense of dedication, and that this comes to them in solitude and silence. The silence of which Pascal spoke, the silence of infinite spaces, is terrifying, and most avoid it, but poetry feeds on silence. To apprehend the silence of the universe is to wish to break it, to speak to those who are in the same boat with ourselves.

The measure of a man, said Ortega, is the amount of solitude he can stand, and great poets are those who have listened greatly. Rilke speaks of this:

> Voices. Voices. Listen, my heart, as only
> saints have listened: until the gigantic call lifted them
> off the ground; yet they kept on, impossibly,
> kneeling and didn't notice at all:
> so complete was their listening. Not that you could endure

17

> *God's* voice—far from it. But listen to the voice of the wind
> and the ceaseless message that forms itself out of silence.[5]

The task of the poet is to put into words the message that formed itself out of silence.

"What is a poet?" Wordsworth asks and answers the question himself:

> He is a man speaking to men [he might have said a man or woman speaking to men and women] . . . a man, it is true, endowed with more lively sensibility, more enthusiasm and tenderness, who has a greater knowledge of human nature, and a more comprehensive soul, than are supposed to be common among mankind: a man pleased with his own passions and volitions, and who rejoices more than other men in the spirit of life that is in him; delighting to contemplate similar volitions and passions as manifested in the goings-on of the Universe, and habitually impelled to create them where he does not find them.[6]

Amen to that! I am pleased by the pleasure Wordsworth takes in his own passions and volitions. It is good to have him come right out and say so. I also like the sentence about feeling impelled to create them where he does not find them.

The idea of the poet as having a greater knowledge of human nature than the ordinary person, and a vitality he wishes to impart, has dwindled since Wordsworth wrote. The poet's conviction that he has something important to say, some god- or wind-given message, has almost disappeared. Must we then talk only of ourselves and be reduced to writing confessions? In recent years it has seemed so—the poet as alienated man or woman, this has been the subject of much contemporary verse. I need hardly point out how uninteresting the subject finally is. It has dwindled into this kind of writing:

> Most of us, though white,
> Belonged to no country clubs
> And had perfectly reasonable ideas.
> I drove my parents' third car, the Toyota . . . [7]

In poetry-writing workshops all over the country, writers, having been told that they must describe things accurately and be sin-

cere—and if you asked them who said so, they might say
Williams—are writing these dreary little exercises in futility:

> I learned to write ninety words a minute.
> I quit the band because I wasn't stupid.
> At concerts no one sat with me;
> They called me bad names and didn't like me.

The idea behind such writing is that if you are sincere it will be
poetry. But it isn't—it doesn't lift anything to the imagination. One
could, in fact, expatiate on the positive dislike of imagination that
lies behind such writing—it is the form Puritanism takes in our
time. The obsession with one's personal history, one's body, one's
parents—American poetry has been going round and round the
self like a squirrel in a cage. There is no way to break out except by
regaining the idea of poetry as a force, a reality. I am not saying that
poetry should not speak with feeling—I have said that it must—but
confessional writing is a dead end. If poetry is to be important it
must regain Dante's and Wordsworth's sense of the importance of
what they were saying. Poetry must be conceived as a force beyond
the self, and the poet as the medium of this force.

I do not see how this can be felt unless one has the vision of a
community. For a long time I tried to describe the essential quality
of a poet, that which makes the poet different from the mere writer
of verse, some vibrancy of emotion in his language. I have come to
think that this proceeds from his sense of being a part in the
scheme of things, and from this only. All other matters having to do
with poetry are secondary to this. There is no word or phrase to
describe this quality in a poet. We speak of the poet's style or
voice—we may examine his choice of words and use of syntax. But
from what does the voice proceed? From his sense that his
thoughts count for something with his fellow human beings, that
they are helping to build a community.

The poets we call great express such a sense through their
works. It is true of Dante, Wordsworth, Akhmatova . . . any memora-
ble poet you can name. When we read them we feel not only, as
Whitman said, that we are touching flesh and blood, but that the life
in the words is far-reaching and significant. That the poets felt this
themselves there can be no doubt—it was the ground of their
proceeding. Wordsworth, in the lines I have quoted, knew that he

19

had been dedicated to carry out a task and that if he refused he would be "sinning greatly." In *The Prelude* he says that the love of nature leads to the love of man. Similar passages are to be found in the lives of all poets whose words have power to move us.

One does not live to oneself, and in order to write poetry one must believe in something. The old gods are dead or sleeping, and the nineteenth-century ideal of Beauty expressed through Art is of no comfort to twentieth-century men and women who face the prospect of the destruction of everything in some nuclear holocaust. What then can the poet hope for? A community of hearts and minds that will extend across nations and leap the barriers erected by governments. Poets may represent the millions who have no voice of their own. Poets may speak to other poets and through them to all who are filled with the same hopes and fears. Through poetry there may be an exchange of the best thoughts of people around the world. If this is called visionary I would like to know what practical alternative is proposed? What else can poets believe if they do not believe in this?

Am I asking for poets to be political? In the largest and deepest sense, yes. I am asking for poetry that represents the lives we really have and makes our thoughts and feelings known. I am not asking for propaganda. Poets are free men and women—they cannot serve an ideology, for to do so is not to be free.

Are you a poet? Is your thinking real? Does it touch hearts and minds? If so, your writing is political.

There may still be some who think that I am asking for some crude, propagandistic kind of writing. Then let me read a passage from a writer I admire greatly, Joseph Conrad. He is a novelist, but no matter—on this point the concerns of the poet and the writer of prose are the same. Many are familiar with Conrad's statement of his method: "My task which I am trying to achieve is, by the power of the written word to make you hear, to make you feel—it is before all, to make you see."[8] What many readers have not noticed is the larger statement that follows:

> To snatch in a moment of courage, from the remorseless rush of time, a passing phase of life, is only the beginning of the task. The task approached in tenderness and faith is to hold up unques- tioningly, without choice and without fear, the rescued fragment

20

before all eyes in the light of a sincere mood. It is to show its vibration, its colour, its form; and through its movement, its form, and its colour, reveal the substance of its truth—disclose its inspiring secret: the stress and passion within the core of each convincing moment. In a single-minded attempt of that kind, if one be deserving and fortunate, one may perchance attain to such clearness of sincerity that at last the presented vision of regret or pity, of terror or mirth, shall awake in the hearts of the beholders that feeling of unavoidable solidarity in mysterious origin, in toil, in uncertain fate, which binds men to each other and all mankind to the visible world.

Thus the author of *The Shadow Line* . . . With such a sense of purpose a poet could go far. Though imagination may not reach to another world as it did centuries ago, still, the common road leads somewhere.

◆

For a hundred years lyric poetry has been placed on a pedestal. Can it be only coincidence that this has been accompanied by a general decline of interest in poetry? It is the nature of the lyric to express a subjective mood and ignore the outer reality. It is to be expected that such writing will interest very few.

The separation of the lyric from narrative and discursive writing began with Poe and was adopted by the Symbolists as an absolute principle. Mallarmé wished to reduce to a minimum all elements but the lyric, so as to arrive at "pure poetry." He placed narrative and discursive poetry in an inferior category. A critic has described the reason behind this kind of thinking as "a revulsion from crass reality and an ardent inspiration towards a finer life. The poet," says this critic, "denounces with searing scorn the revolting happiness of those gross appetites that are so easily satisfied."[9] Among the gross appetites, however, Mallarmé did not include his own for tobacco:

> All the soul summarized
> when slowly we exhale
> smoke-rings that arise
> and other rings annul
>
> attests some cigar . . . [10]

21

The smoke of Mallarmé's cigar was not pure. Words do have meanings, unavoidably, and "pure poetry" is no purer than the other kind, it is only less substantial. If the Symbolists had carried to the logical conclusion their program for poetry that would approach "the condition of music," they would have given up writing. For why have words when one can have music itself?

The wish for "pure poetry" has brought about writing that is as far from meaning as one can get without lapsing into nonsense, and frequently it crosses the line. Here is a passage from Wallace Stevens's "Notes Toward a Supreme Fiction":

> The romantic intoning, the declaimed clairvoyance
> Are parts of apotheosis, appropriate
> And of its nature, the idiom thereof.
>
> They differ from reason's click-clack, its applied
> Enflashings. But apotheosis is not
> The origin of the major man. He comes,
>
> Compact in invincible foils, from reason,
> Lighted at midnight by the studious eye,
> Swaddled in revery, the object of
>
> The hum of thoughts evaded in the mind,
> Hidden from other thoughts, he that reposes
> On a breast forever precious to the touch . . .

This sounds like a man philosophizing, and if one studies the passage one can make sense of it. But this writing is either sound and no sense, or sense without sound, for in disassembling the phrases to find what they mean, one loses their effect as sound. The later poetry of Wallace Stevens is a case of the disassociation of sensibility Eliot pointed to years ago as a defect of Milton's verse and a besetting defect of Victorian verse. Stevens's poetry is not philosophy and his philosophy is not poetry.

With us, however, the wish to be pure has not expressed itself as music—more commonly it has led to imagistic writing, poems that consist only of images.

If poetry is to matter we must put in our poems those elements that have been excluded as impure. This means breaking with the standards set by the academy, by those who have made emptiness a virtue—who have elevated Stevens above Frost, above Williams and Pound and Eliot; who have praised to the skies James Merrill's musing over a Ouija board and have told us that Amy Clampitt is a poet.

I came across the following lines in *The New Yorker.* The subject is some pigeons that keep returning to perch on a building that no longer exists—it has been knocked down. The pigeons are described as:

> descending yet again the roofless
> staircase of outmoded custom, the
> soon-to-be-obliterated stations
> of nostalgia—as though the air
> itself might wince at the stigmata
> of the dispossessed, the razed,
> the *triste,* the unaccounted for.[11]

The pigeons are said to be descending as though the air might wince. This is perfect nonsense. Then consider the word "stigmata," the offensiveness of using it in this connection. C. H. Sisson, writing about Herbert Read, says that "it is as if the facility of Read's discursive mind was such that the barriers to expression, the sense of which is often a preliminary to poetry, did not exist."[12] The same might by said of Amy Clampitt: her mind, facile and discursive, encounters no barriers. And where are the stigmata located? On the wings of the pigeons? Their feet and sides? Are the stigmata to be seen on the building that is no longer there? The word "razed" in the phrase, "the stigmata / of the dispossessed, the razed," indicates that there are stigmata on a nonexistent building. The word *"triste"* adds the final touch of silly affectation.

This is what comes of straining to be poetic. But poetry is not something one has to invent—it is there in the object, waiting to be seen. As Pound said, "The natural object is always the adequate symbol." Williams said it also: "No ideas but in things."

The similarities between objects, that is, metaphors, don't have to be invented—they are there if you look for them. And the more they rise of their own accord, the more striking they will be, affecting the reader with the power of a natural force.

23

No sooner does an American set up as a poet than he begins to suffer from what a friend of Whitman's called the "beauty disease." He thinks that poetry has to be written in a special language and that subjects have to be far-fetched. This brings on the inanity of which I have given examples, a kind of anorexia nervosa, so that poetry becomes thin to the point of disappearing. There is no cure but immersion in the common life and the language, as Wordsworth said, really used by men.

Common life since the Industrial Revolution has been increasingly antipoetic. Baudelaire found a sordid enchantment in the city, comparing it to an ant heap that at dusk disgorged prostitutes, crooks, and thieves. Whitman found a grandeur in the streets of Brooklyn and Manhattan:

> Burn high your fires, foundry chimneys! cast black shadows at
>   nightfall! cast red and yellow light over the tops of the houses!

In our time the poetry of cities has become more elusive—how is one to find poetry in an office where secretaries sit typing or in the aisle of a supermarket? Yet it is imperative for poetry to deal with such material—it is all around us. Not only urban scenes but the minds of the people need to be represented, and I don't mean some programmatic literature about the working man or woman such as Socialist Realism produced—I mean poetry about the people you actually meet and the ideas they have, including the banal, foolish ones.

This is the step that has to be taken, and some poets have already taken it, though you won't find them in *The New Yorker.* The following poem by Toi Derricotte is titled "Fears of the Eighth Grade":

> when i ask what things they fear,
> their arms raise like soldiers volunteering for battle:
> fear to go into a dark room, my murderer is waiting;
> fear of taking a shower, someone will stab me;
> fear of being kidnapped, raped;
> fear of dying in war.
> when i ask how many fear this,
> all the children raise their hands.
>
> i think of this little box of consecrated land,
> the bombs somewhere else,

the dead children in their mothers' arms,
women crying at the gates of the palace.

how thin the veneer!
the paper towels, napkins, toilet paper—everything
burned up in a day.

these children see the city after armageddon;
the demons stand visible in the air
between their friends talking;
they see fire in a spring day
the instant before conflagration:
they feel blood through closed faucets
& touch sharks crawling at the bottom of the sea.

Yes, the poet "has a greater knowledge of human nature, and a more comprehensive soul, than are supposed to be common among mankind." She has lifted herself, and so she is able to carry things with her into thought, transform experience into significant thought.

The city is antipoetic, the suburbs are antipoetic, but turn to the people, and subjects for poetry abound. This is the solution to our present difficulty, the emptiness and unimportance of American verse. We need a poetry of human situations. Imagination does not consist in thinking of surrealist imagery—one could write like that forever, as Dr. Johnson remarked, if one abandoned one's mind to it. Imagination shows us the possibilities in human nature—it says, like the dwarf in the tale by Grimm, "Something human is dearer to me than the wealth of all the world."

There is a poem by Thomas Hardy, "Neutral Tones," that presents a scene: a pond, a white sun, gray leaves scattered under a tree. This is the setting for a meeting between a man and woman who have been lovers and are no longer so. They are having a sad, bitter discussion about, as Hardy puts it, "Which lost the more by our love":

The smile on your mouth was the deadest thing
Alive enough to have strength to die;
And a grin of bitterness swept thereby
    Like an ominous bird a-wing . . .

25

The remarkable thing is the amount of passion Hardy gets into his neutral tones, the amount of volition. He bleaches all color out of the scene to go with the bleaching out of love. Then, as if to show what poetry can do, he injects the scene with his own interest, fixes in memory the "God-curst" sun, tree, and pond edged with grayish leaves. The scene has become emblematic—it might be hung as a picture to illustrate the ending of love and the tears of things.

Hardy certainly seems to have been impelled to create volitions and passions where he did not find them. At the passage of this small man things were charged with energy and assumed a significance. As he says, he was a man who used to notice such things, and in return they have noticed him. The slightest poem of Hardy's vibrates with the life that was in him.

One must have that kind of energy, that interest. One must have a theme. It is the theme in a narrative by Hardy that makes it live as the narrative poems of other Victorians do not. Hardy's character as a poet is expressed in his theme—he has chosen to tell this story as no other out of some inner necessity. The necessity returns in poem after poem—it has to do with the gaining and losing of love between men and women. The theme is of vital concern to Hardy—it animates not only his characters but their surroundings.

Robert Frost, referring to some contemporary poets, said that they were not much troubled by anything that was in them. And Yeats has a speaker in a poem say, "What, be a singer born and lack a theme?" It is the theme that gives poetry is authenticity. I have spoken of the poet's training in solitude and silence. What he discovers there, the messages the wind delivers to him, are the themes of his writing. He emerges from solitude as the Indian woke from the dream that gave him a name and a place in the tribe.

The art of poetry consists in discovering the themes that are proper to oneself. There can be no formulas for such discoveries. Keats said that the world was a vale of soul-making. For the poet it is the vale where he makes his theme. The poet's theme is his true self.

It is to be differentiated from the merely personal life, as the Indian's big dream was different from little dreams. In our time there has been an appetite for biographies of poets, but with a few exceptions—the life of Keats by Gittings, of Johnson by Bate—they are beside the point. Proust said it once and for all:

By failing to see the gulf that separates the writer from the man of the world, by failing to understand that the writer's true self is manifested in his books alone, and that what he shows to men of the world . . . is merely a man of the world like themselves, Sainte-Beuve came to set up that celebrated Method which, according to Taine, Bourget, and the rest of them, is his title to fame, and which consists, if you would understand a poet or writer, in greedily catechising those who knew him, who saw quite a lot of him, who can tell us how he conducted himself in regard to women, etc.—precisely, that is, at every point where the poet's true self is not involved.

The method Proust describes, is that not exactly the way biographers have gone about describing the lives of our poets—how one has written the life of Delmore Schwartz, another the life of Robert Lowell, and another the life of John Berryman? What did one learn from these books? That the men suffered from vanity, from drink, from mental illness. What did one learn about the nature of poetry? Practically nothing.

The theme is the man. "You want," says Conrad's storyteller, "a deliberate belief"—another way of describing the writer's theme. Conrad distinguishes this from principles, by which he seems to mean morality. "Principles won't do. Acquisitions, pretty rags—rags that would fly off at the first good shake."[13]

The poet may be helped to discover his true self or theme by looking at pictures and statues and reading books—what Yeats called "monuments of unageing intellect," though they need not be so monumental—Yeats himself read Madame Blavatsky. The book that nourishes one's theme may as well be some simple book read in childhood as Dante or the *Book of Job.*

The poet can only speak of his theme, that which is proper to him. The mere writer of verse can speak of anything with equanimity. "A rhymer, and a *poet,* are two things."

"With talent," said Ingres, "you do what you like. With genius, you do what you can."

◆

Those who have followed me so far may wonder why, feeling as I do about a poetry of human situations, I have not spoken about prose fiction rather than verse. There is a great difference between verse and prose, and I would not give up the one thing verse has in its favor: an absolute form. We do not know why certain people who are called poets feel compelled to write in lines—this is a great mystery. If the poet were a dancer she would dance; a musician, she would compose music; but she is a poet and so she writes . . . in lines. Lines are the form of her soul. The movement of the poem corresponds to a movement of the poet's soul.

There is something demonic about the writing of poetry, some power the poet wishes to exact over the reader's emotions. The rhythm and breaking of the line determines that the reader shall respond in a certain way and no other. Measure compels. It is different with prose—the reader is allowed to get loose of the writer's emotion and drift into reverie.

Writing in lines appears to establish an absolute order of language—though of course it only appears to do so. It is the poet's task to make us feel that the order is absolute, but any poet who has done thirty or forty drafts of a poem knows the uncertainty of such things. We aim at perfection knowing that we can never hit it. We do not finish, we leave off.

Not only does the line compel, every syllable does. As Coleridge said, poetry proposes to itself "such delight from the *whole,* as is compatible with a distinct gratification from each component part."[14] We take pleasure in each syllable, word, and phrase as it occurs. There is a pleasure in fine sentences too, the prose of Flaubert, but as a rule prose does not give the effect of an absolute order of language.

Now that I have brought my subject down to the actual writing I would like to step back and speak once more of poetry as an act of communion. "The Poet," says Wordsworth, "binds together by passion and knowledge the vast empire of human society, as it is spread over the whole earth, over all time."

There are those who would reject this idea. W. H. Auden was such a one—poetry, he said emphatically, does nothing, it is a purely gratuitous activity. Others who might admit that poetry can change the individual would deny that it can bring a community into being. Statements such as Wordsworth's, and the longer statement by Conrad I quoted earlier, they would say are orective and conative in nature—"orective because [the author's] view of the ultimate function of literature is a matter of what is desired rather than what they thought to be a fact; conative because they are really talking about the creative direction which they themselves are trying to take as writers."[15]

Solidarity, then, is only an idea. But so was the republic we live under, and a dozen actions we perform every day originated with an idea. I have never understood the kind of person who, dressed in a suit that came from an idea in the mind of a tailor, and having dined on a meal that was an idea in the mind of a cook, will talk scornfully of ideas and idealism.

The physicist has a theory about the atom without the supporting facts. He proceeds on the assumption that his theory is true, and lo, the suspected particle swims into our ken, where he said it would be. It is the same with poetry. The poet believes that people will sympathize with her ideas, and this enables her to write with an emotion that moves them to sympathize. The poet's faith then stands on accomplished fact—she has created passions and volitions where she did not find them. If poets are the liars Plato said they are, poems are not—they become part of our thinking and we see the world by the light of poetry.

If it be said that binding hearts and minds is only an idea, a feeling we have when we are reading poems or hearing them, far from this being an argument against the social effectiveness of poetry, it is a powerful argument in its favor. If it is in poetry, and only there, that human sympathy is found, such writing must have a unique, irreplaceable value. It is not the expression of a faith but the community we are seeking, the thing itself.

NOTES

1. Hillis Miller, in *Theories of Criticism: Essays in Literature and Art,* ed. M. H. Abrams and James Ackerman (Washington, D.C.: Library of Congress, 1984), 28.

2. Ibid., 22–23.

3. Dante Alighieri, *La Vita Nuova,* trans. Barbara Reynolds (Middlesex, U.K.: Penguin Books, 1969), 31–32.

4. William Wordsworth, *The Prelude,* Book Fourth.

5. *The Collected Poetry of Rainer Maria Rilke,* ed. and trans. Stephen Mitchell (New York: Random House, 1982), 153.

6. Preface to the *Lyrical Ballads,* 1800.

7. Laurie Henry, "Downtown Newberry Destroyed by Tornado," *The American Poetry Review* (May/June 1984), 48.

8. Preface to *The Nigger of the "Narcissus."*

9. Lloyd James Austin, "Presence and Poetry of Stéphane Mallarmé: International Reputation and Intellectual Impact," 1973. In *The Symbolist Movement in the Literature of European Languages,* ed. Anna Balakian (Budapest: Akadémiai Kiadó, 1982), 45.

10. "Autres Poèmes et Sonnets," Stéphane Mallarmé, *Selected Poems,* trans. C. F. MacIntyre (Berkeley: University of California Press, 1957), 101.

11. Amy Clampitt, "Vacant Lot with Tumbleweed and Pigeons," *The New Yorker,* 30 January 1984, 32.

12. *English Poetry 1900–1950: An Assessment* (Manchester, U.K.: Carcanet New Press, 1981), 186.

13. *Heart of Darkness.*

14. Samuel Taylor Coleridge, *Biographia Literaria,* Chapter 14.

15. Ian Watt, *Conrad in the Nineteenth Century* (Berkeley: University of California Press, 1979), 80–81.

Charles Altieri

WHAT MODERNISM OFFERS THE CONTEMPORARY POET

I

Contemporary poetry grows increasingly divided between those who seek to continue the experimental spirit fostered by Modernism and those who seek as a new postmodern an alternative to the entire constructivist edifice so that poetry may return to the social roles it once served.[1] I want here to defend the Modernist line, indeed to use the postmodern alternative as a contrast for dramatizing the possible powers we now tend to overlook in Modernist poetry. Doing that, however, requires that I make clear the stakes involved in the alternatives, so I shall spend considerable time narrating an academic melodrama involving my departmental search for a young poet whom we would invite to apply for a position. Here one can still find the passionate intensity about poetry one might hope to locate in less contentious and self-interested situations. Because the aim was to hire, our most cherished self-representations came into play—about status, about expressing our values to the public, and about selecting someone who should represent for our students and faculty the vital energies in contemporary poetry. Whom we choose was inseparable from who we thought we were. But the deep investments involved did not all come out clearly or directly. So even if I could, or dared to, there would be no point to reproducing our debates. Instead I shall concentrate on two poems which focused our differences (at least the literary ones) and which determined our ultimate decision. The wounds are deep enough that I shall avoid a purely reportorial role in order to make in this imaginary space the arguments I wish I had made at the time. Then if I prove ineffectual I can once again sulk in self-righteousness.

This was the popular choice, Richard Kenney's "Speed of Light":

> The radium in luminescent numbers
> painted on my watch face fades—no time,
> and no things in the closed-in cosmos now
> but these: the massive plow looming ahead,
> the soft churn of chains in snow, eccentric
> scything of his hazard lights like amber
> helicopter blades above, the close
> cones of headlamps pressed against the blizzard's
> high wall. I've followed him for miles now,
> watched the spume combing off his cutwater,
> the great V-plow, speeding, sparks spurting
> underneath its tempered edge and drifting
> up the windscreen now in strange and unfamiliar
> constellations, changing . . .
>   A universe
> in one dimension only, love, this road,
> the black trace reeling off his rear wheels here
> like new creation dragging off its spool—
> this is the limiting velocity:
> I thread this white cloud chamber as I can,
> I etch this line across what curvature
> of space and time still separates us now,
> and night dilates, all night, all night the plow
> grinds the stone roadbed like my heart
> grinding through this last bad month alone
> without you, in the dark or in the light.

If one asks what images of poetry, of persons, and of values would lead people to support such a poem, there seem obvious answers.

This is simply a very talented poet, soon in fact to win a Guggenheim at a very early point in his career. Kenney's ear is superb, his facility for lively images and intricate figures striking, and his structural ability to develop complicated shifts in tone and affect masterful. "Speed of Light" renders the state of consciousness of a lover at once anxiously and bemusedly spinning metaphors to while away the frustration as he follows a snowplow to the house of a woman from whom he has been separated for a month. Structurally the poem follows a delightful curve from an initial anxious glance at his watch, a figure for his cloud in cosmos, through expanding twists on that metaphor as the plow becomes a kind of *demiourgos* whose sparks are constellations, back to a more inward version of the cloud in cosmos as the plow allows an equation for his heart. Here the play on constellations also swerves inward, offering a measure of both the intensity of his love and the honesty about himself he wrings from his playful beginnings. At the conclusion he recognizes just what the person he loves means to him as the principle for a cosmos so profound and comprehensive that it controls and makes contingent even the fundamental archetypal alternations between darkness and light. No physical or metaphorical constellation can make the kind of difference the beloved's presence and absence does.

I remain nonetheless extremely suspicious of those who preferred this poem. My glib reason is probably also my best: there is a whole lot of grinding going on, too much for the sparks of understanding that get generated. Kenney is too intelligent and too contemporary to be lugubrious about his pain. But it is perhaps the very effort to displace it into a kind of witty charm that I find most limiting. For Kenney seems to want to project the best of two worlds without taking responsibility for either. There is first the playful poet spinning metaphors to while away the time. Then from this distance, he can shift to the sensitive, vulnerable, yet masculine and direct lover of the last lines whose bearing his pain draws all the turnings of the poem into a badge of personal authenticity. This triumph of crafted tone subordinates all understanding of love— and of the energies poetry can mobilize—to the melodramatic heart's grinding out its rueful state of need by self-satisfied flashes of insight. The poem devotes its linguistic energies primarily to the scene's capacity for manipulating feelings, so that little is done to understand them or clarify their sources and consequences. Kenney creates a rich sense of the difference love makes, but the poem's desire for dramatic effect seems to me to evade the paradox on which the themes are based. The pangs of loneliness become the perverse source of poetic exuberance, and love calls us to the things language makes. Our pleasures in our own lyricism depend on our so staging our dependences on the beloved. Kenney's heroism is not the blind narcissism of self-glorifying sensitivity to loss one finds in Kinnell or Strand. But his self-awareness seems to me even more disturbing because it can live again, softened by charm and by style, the melodramatic staging of the self as made noble by one's repeating standard lyric emotions without reflecting upon their claims and their limits. Charming melodramatic realizations may be our most insidious means for preserving forms of ethos in poetry, which parallel a culture committed to emotional hot tubs, trapped into treating sensitivity and sincerity as our only measure of human worth, and increasingly blind to the duplicities and banalities that accompany our preferred, wistful forms of poetic insight.

For now the best criticism I can make of Kenney's stance is to compare it with its rival, Donald Revell's "Motel View":

> It is conceivable in fact that waves
> and lustre work in such a way, in such
> a mannered disproportion, that the sea
> becomes an architectural conceit
> with which to play upon the measure of
> a liquid give and take, a weathering. Wave
> and the measurement of it can therefore do
> but little to intensify the spume
> of water in the sun. Cape Ann today
> is seascape, rock, and a freezing wind. The moon
> is nearly full, but risen far too soon
> to have its proper place in the postcard sun—
> light being quite the thing for photographs,
> the elderly, and a decent view of the gulls.
> (When thinking back, it is the elderly
> that one remembers most, enclosed by gulls
> and glaring eastward like the benches.) Wave
> and lustre mannered to a fault, the cold
> vacationland in April, all combine

into a law of things, an intellect
of various disproportions, which, by day,
can sometimes contradict the weather, give
one's time a fiction, or as water does,
an elemental dullness, an expanse.

Here the situation is all too obviously not exploited for its possible
dramatic resonance, leaving in its stead what my colleagues delicately termed "academic sterility." Instead of concentrating on the
specific condition of a concrete persona, Revell's poem focuses
most of its attention on the linguistic situation of a reflective, writing presence. What affect there is derives not from the rendering of
lifelike situations (an emphasis that had become truly academic in
painting by 1880) but from the construction of scenic materials into
an elaborate composition. Revell's affective appeal depends not on
echoes of our loves but on the work's self-reflexive confrontation
with the sterility perhaps inherent in pure description.

The most pronounced difference between the poets may be
their ways of using scenic analogies. Revell's scene is not primarily
dramatic and illusionistic. Rather his opening lines immediately
place all the concrete elements in the realm of the conceivable: the
poem will ultimately be "about" the relation of waves and light to
the workings of a mind that weaves from them "mannered dis-
proportion" and "architectural conceits." Weathering and measuring then constitute the thematic poles. Time-ridden pleasures and
the pressure of nature's otherness confront the imagination's
power to reorganize the world so that our contemplative and affective energies find a satisfying external home. The dramatic focus
for this resistance is the parenthesis because it defines sharp breaks
with the illusionary surface, thereby linking the thematic situation
to the literal energies marshaled by this act of writing. Within the
illusionary structure of the poem as a contemplation at Cape Ann,
the parenthesis creates a frame for thinking back against the forces
in nature that impose "today" upon us, dazzling the senses but also
blinding the mind to all the destructive effects of the sun's glare.
The parenthesis is the syntactic equivalent to a life of motel views,
situatings of the mind on the shifting margins of the scenes it
confronts (so that within it, it is the elderly who glare, rather than
the sun).

This self-reflexive insistence on the writing as the poem's literal

35

subject transforms the whole idea of landscape. Now memory is not merely an element described by the poem. It becomes an active character, figurative in its literalness, which provides actual evidence for the concluding sentence. That sentence then exists both within and without the scene, making visible an actual "intellect of various disproportions" and establishing the powers one can claim for such an intellect. The poem becomes testimony by taking responsibility for how it can handle analogy. So the dramatic movement of "Speed of Light" to a climactic rhetorical theater of self-control can give way to an intellectual climax allowing control to justify itself as it interprets the very powers it demonstrates.

Let me spend a few moments unpacking the poem's last sentence so that we recognize just how fully Revell at once makes good on his abstract claim and then makes the abstraction itself the basis for the emotional resonance of the concluding metaphor. If this is academic, it is as emotionally comprehensive as academicism gets. The mannered wave and lustre become a law of things in two ways—as a description or metaphor for time and change, and as a physical emblem or, more accurately, a projected physical equivalent, for the very workings of mind as it composes disproportions. The law then is at once a mirror of the sea and a contradiction of its temporality, a measuring of its weather that literally gives time a fiction. That fiction, however, is not simply an abstract concept. We have just seen it take the form of the double-edged metaphor of "wave and lustre mannered to a fault," so that even here, in summary, the poem can continue the physical analogies of sea and metaphor that it has been working out. This final sentence brilliantly conjoins the inescapable materiality of flesh and time with a sense of the reflective and the physical spaciousness expanded by the act of thinking, by this play of metaphoric transfers. Revell's version of melodramatic surprise consists in his making this intricate statement suddenly come right as it balances dullness and expansiveness, the scene perceived, and recoveries made possible by the mind's power to place our parenthetical differences from nature themselves within a physical, contemplative parenthesis. Our humanity requires no personal pronouns, no theatrical emotions, and almost no swerve from the elemental dullness that constitutes the basic ground for our coming to work out the powers and obligations of our thinking. Expansiveness and dullness feed on and ground one another. Despite its apparent difficulties, Revell's poem is in fact discursive, a plain statement energized simply by the intelligence that controls it and a clear grasp of elemental aspects of what it means to be human.

I am tempted to say (and should have said at our meetings) that this is a cosmos for poetry which does not require the duplicity of the lyrical ego or the equation of authenticity with life on an emotional roller coaster. It does, however, require the reader to imagine a definition of organizing intelligence sharply opposed to the sense of agency dominating Kenney's melodrama. This, after all, is a "Motel View," a process of the mind reconciling itself to its own parenthetical marginality in relation to the natural order. It is the form of synthesizing activity, not the typicality of the dramatic scene, that makes the poem representative. To know the self in this kind of flux means to replace lyrical theatrics with what I shall later try to describe as the adventure of impersonality. Only by viewing the self from the cold distance that takes it as an object among objects do we restore a firm sense of what makes the "I" different from other objects—precisely its capacity to synthesize objective states and distribute itself among them by mannered metaphors. The poem itself must be the key to what it seeks, an embodiment of our differences as constructive minds within a dullness all physical being shares. Thus analogy does not collapse into the needs of the desiring subject but forms an actual equivalent between objectivity and the writing presence as it displays the capacity of metaphor to align the desiring self to time and to change.

II

My own rhetoric also grinds too hard. First of all Revell's poem is not quite typical of the best work inspired by Ashbery because it prefers hard edges to the looser, evocative syntax that attempts to generate mystery by playing off the exuberance of periodic structures against a deliberate refusal of clear semantic sense. And Revell's poem has flaws we might expect of even the best young poet, primarily in its insistent architecture, while poems like "Speed of Light" do serve important functions, since charm and the melodramatic imagination may be the basic means for keeping the imaginary and imaginative lives alive in resistance to society's demands for a lucid calculating consciousness. We need a range of imaginative stances. Yet we also must recognize what is at stake when we come to prefer any one by identifying with the specific structures of emotion and forms of sensibility the style cultivates. Let us call Kenney's way the model of dramatic lyricism devoted to the powers of identification, empathy, and tonal richness sustained by a rhetoric that controls the evocative power of speech situations. Revell's way, on the other hand, is constructivist. Minimizing plot, character, and scene, it pursues what David Lehman calls "a radical re-definition of nature" within which the mimetic object becomes "the writer's consciousness," and the basic scene becomes the sentence or the abstract figures a poem makes.[2]

Such oppositions do not exhaust the range of contemporary poetry. But they did all too accurately encompass the taste of my committee. So I think the two poets I have discussed provide a representative sample on which to focus two general questions— how our poetry responds to or reflects certain features of contemporary culture, and how that response defines and is defined by the poets' understanding of their Modernist progenitors. In each case I shall try to defend the powers Revell's mode exemplifies in preference to those offered by Kenney.

Questions about an art's relationship to its culture depend on our being able to posit a distinctive role for the art within social life. When the art is poetry we must confine ourselves to a small segment of the culture. But there may well be a significant compensation for this narrowness since poetry has such force. Poems wield a form of emotional authority because readers expect poems to produce exalted moments of feeling, which allow them to make provisional identifications with the imaginative stances enacted. Some of these identifications are intense and momentary. Others are more diffuse, aligning us not only with specific states but also with the general ethos or image of authentic sensibility, which seems to provide access to the intense emotions. We become what we read regularly and devotedly because our imaginary investments bind us to certain myths, encourage us to represent ourselves to ourselves as certain kinds of agents, and compose overall emotional contours dictating which feelings are compatible, which opposed to each other.

Poems like Kenney's are so dangerous because they elicit identifications with values of sensitivity, vulnerability, charming capacities for self-mockery, and dignified self-possession, which are all tightly woven into our therapeutic society's ideal of maturity and adaption to limits. Yet all this self-awareness does not produce a deep sense of our banality or of the Romantic dream informing our pathos-ridden images of maturity. Moreover the poem itself pivots on a fundamental cultural duplicity that somehow our strength and dignity lie not in what we project of a future but how we compose ourselves toward loss, so the poetry, the exaltation of feeling and liberation of linguistic energies, comes to depend on a self all too bound to some basic cultural myths. Foremost among these is what I take to be a terrifying constriction of all values to the realm of personal psychology—as if the source of most of our problems had also to be the ground for their resolution. We no longer treat that personal sphere in the purely egoistic terms of confessional poetry. The eighties are the epoch of networks, support systems, and returns to the family. But the glue for these networks remains a narrow anti-intellectual reliance on emotional bonds—"Dover Beach" in a snowstorm—which I think will prove all too flexible in hard times and perhaps dangerously narrow or unpolitical in the best of times. In Kenney's poem the relevant emblem is his frustration behind the snowplow, as if everything in life were a deferral blocking him from the immediate, direct object of his desire. As the poem turns to its dramatic climax, all thought leads back to private desires, all the energy takes the form of a personal melodrama, and all the poetry concentrates on a single analogical moment. The dark and the light must compose a single narrow constellation that can at any moment become a black hole.

Are there real alternatives, genuine possibilities for locating within poetry powers that are not equally symptomatic of specific cultural configurations? I am not sure I have adequate answers, but I will only find out if I test the following claims. I see Kenney's poem as an aspect of a significant literary revolution, which has been taking form over the past twenty years. The revolution consists essentially in a conviction that high Modernism offers a road not worth taking because it confines poetry to an arid, formalistic set of abstract concerns, which separate the work from the interests of a literate populace and deprive it of its traditional cultivating roles. It is only by confronting these assumptions and showing the dangers they produce that I can hope to demonstrate that there are within poetry powers capable of resisting all the seductions of dramatic personality, so that it becomes possible to establish alternative values for whatever audience is willing to make the necessary breaks or finds itself already having made them.

The anti-Modernist case is by now so sufficiently familiar that I need only offer a brief summary, relying primarily on Jonathan Holden's "Postmodern Poetic Form."[3]

1. Modernist, anti-Romantic versions of organicism reduced that concept to a formalist concentration on the medium itself as the subject matter of poetry. This emphasis leads to an exotic, experimental spirit that sets poets in an adversary relation to the rest of culture.

2. The formalism generates and reinforces a radical impersonality that deprives poetry of recognizable human presences and the forms of representativeness for an audience, which can be created by a dramatic poetry based on speech situations.

3. Impersonality generates two fundamental yet problematic shifts in the values poetry can affirm or powers it can exemplify: *(a)* As Charles Newman puts it, "the history of Modernism is the history of a failure to affect the moral life of the culture by aesthetic means alone," and *(b)* as Jonathan Holden puts it, the author intends to become passive or thinglike because "the presence of a central consciousness all but disappears."

4. Distance from the social self breeds the elitist denials of sympathetic consciousness, which make it possible to hold the appalling political positions that most of the Modernists embraced.

I cannot quite refute these charges. They identify crucial themes and point to some damaging consequences of Modernist ideas. But I can suggest other ways of viewing the phenomena that at the very least take Modernism as a stance serious human beings might continue to work within and hope to modify—especially because the possibilities it offers directly address pressing cultural problems. Modernist poetry demonstrates the capacity of impersonal, constructivist strategies to create models of the person less prone than Kenney's mode to narcissistic self-staging and more responsive to the demands contemporary intellectual life puts on our sense of what persons are and how values can be articulated. In so doing it directly confronts the desire of poetry's traditional audience to have values reinforced, which become increasingly difficult to defend if one takes responsibility for addressing the best that is being thought and said in other disciplines.

III

In order to make good on my generalizations I shall elaborate four claims in defense of what Modernist impersonality made possible for poetry: (1) that Eliot's famous statement contains an important critique of the narcissism inherent in the dramatic-rhetorical lyric; (2) that the positive force of impersonality consists in recasting the ways we imagine the boundaries of the personal and the basic powers the mind has to reflect on its own duplicities; (3) that the means to this new sense of agency is a set of presentational, anti-dramatic strategies whereby formal dimensions of the poem take on semantic content for which the presentational strategies serve as direct testimony, so poets can finesse the invitations to infinite irony, which Paul de Man shows haunt the dramatic lyric; (4) that these explorations of agency participate in a philosophical project best articulated in the work of early Wittgenstein on the nature of thinking and willing subjects.

Eliot's praise of impersonality has as its target all Romantic ideals of self-recuperating dramatic subjectivity. The aim is to bring poetry to the "frontiers of metaphysics" (11):

> The point of view which I am struggling to attack is perhaps related to the metaphysical theory of the substantial unity of the soul: for my meaning is, that the poet has, not a "personality" to express, but a particular medium, which is only a medium and not a personality, in which impressions and experiences combine in peculiar and unexpected ways. . . . Poetry is not a turning loose of emotion, but an escape from emotion; it is not the expression of personality but an escape from personality. But, of course, only those who have personality and emotions know what it means to want to escape from these things. (9–11)

How difficult these frontiers are to reach is all too evident in the embarrassing traces of sensibility that this passage revels in. But

41

these symptomatic effects also show how much the infinite seductions of the ego require the very efforts Eliot expends. Thus it seems absurdly reductive to treat the ideal of impersonality as simply a passive or escapist one. For Eliot, active terms like concentration must prevail because impersonality must play the role of Arnold's or Babbitt's "best self." It must provide a construct capable of distancing us from the imperatives of the contingent or empirical self spoken through by its culture and environment. But Eliot cannot assume his predecessor's ethical righteousness, which only adapts the "substantial unity of the soul" to another, ideal plane where all the same self-serving invitations to rhetoric can be repeated. If there is a best self, it must be made present by poetry, not alluded to through some suspect cultural doctrine. Yet even so chastened a model of the best self had to face up to the position Wilhelm Worringer was making popular—that Western art since the Renaissance had trapped itself by a narcissistic and narrow pursuit of "objectified self-enjoyment." To those influenced by Worringer or sharing his view it is impossible to rely on what one shares with an audience because that may well be what is contaminated by the history of emphasizing the narcissistic in art. Work claiming such affiliations tends to emphasize the closure of the imagined world without giving full play to the energies, tensions, and duplicities that enter into the artist's constructive acts. And a similar limit plagues the world constructed because it takes its reality conditions from what Kant would call the logic of the understanding, thus repressing all those factors that might be said to engage the daimonic or present directly transpersonal states of mind. The dramatic lyric can sing and its images dazzle, but the formal elements are allowed little independent significance or even meaningful tension because everything must be subordinated to the psyche of an individualized speaker and dramatic ideals of emotive closure. Such poetry keeps us in the center of psychic or social life, far from the metaphysical frontiers that begin to emerge as the medium comes to take on an independent sensuality or to suggest in the clash of its surfaces strange intervals and connections where new forms of sense may abide. Under a new dispensation, art could try to stand outside the typical positions subjects take within experience, instead proposing a new emotional economy. Poems can suspend or fracture the "I," putting on stage instead forms of consciousness that can belong to anyone, simply by virtue of one's having a language. Thus a *Waste Land* so constructs a narrative voice that it appears virtually transpersonal, presenting literally the psyche of a generation and mapping that psyche's strange powers to maintain states of mind that weave together the deep privacy of pure obsession with glimpses of a mythic world one enters through the terror. Modernism, then, posits as the basis of its diverse projects the ethical imperative to stand outside the romance ambitions of the lyrical ego and to derive from this critical distance new ways to imagine the links consciousness forges between agents, bodies, and the energies preserved in imaginative traditions capable of resisting the positivities stemming from the historical moment and the rhetoricians' understanding of community.

The slogan for such an enterprise was that form must become content. In itself this is sufficiently vague to justify the impatience Holden obviously has with it. Yet we can see from contemporaries like Revell the continuing impact of the slogan, so we must try to understand it sympathetically. The shortest way is to see what the radical literalness of Modernist painting made available in this vein—most emphatically in figures like Mondrian, whose work is based on a total critique of the lyrical ego.[4] Form becomes content in large part because any other content traps the artist into conceiving his work as a window responsive to whatever it can replicate from the real. If there is only a set of actual, presentational relations establishing the subject matter, art can make these immediate relations and the energies they organize its basic metaphoric vehicle. Then the work's scope and depth depend on how the mind actually displays and disposes powers that are physically present— for example in Mondrian's capacity to capture intricate forms of dynamic balance. Significance is not a matter of inferring the capacities of a given dramatic individual; rather it resides in the transpersonal properties that must be experienced by the viewers as concrete physical actions if the work is to come alive at all. The art is primarily presentational rather than illusionary because these actual powers in effect constitute a world and permutations of the self, which cannot be cogently described within the logic of Renaissance representationalism.

Poetry probably cannot fully elaborate its medium if it ties itself too closely to these visual models. But it can locate there suggestions for new experiments in verbal structure. A quick return to Revell will clarify that and prepare the way for our seeing how Modernist abstraction can be a fertile source for the contemporary. Notice first how Revell's insistent refusal of lyric song calls attention to other physical properties of the medium, which the poem can then name and in naming create as the poem's basic metaphorical substance. The poem begins in a flat, prosaic, discursive mode. And it emphasizes throughout a carefully etched metrical regularity. Language aspires not toward the condition of music but toward an elemental lawfulness, a sense of time as a pressure and a structure. That provides a physical correlate for the reflection, which does not entail an illusionary drama. When the poem speaks of "the conceivable in fact" it names its own condition and provides the necessary ground for the concluding metaphoric equations of dullness and expansiveness. Similarly the parenthesis then becomes an evocatively literal incursion into time, law, and the elements, actually producing for consciousness what the sense of mannered metaphor does for the relation of sea to sense. Lyrical form becomes literal testimony to powers of mind.

Ultimately the relation of literal properties to the projected acts of mind creates a new sense of analogy, which Holden recognizes in Ashbery but does not understand. Analogy is not a form of socialization. Rather it allows the poet to assert crucial differences between life and the site of mind art occupies. For analogy in Revell cannot be resolved into scene. Rather it holds firm the reality of mannered metaphor by making irreducible the expanse of mind or space writing creates, so that seas share properties with minds and establish a perspective within which time and space, metaphor and perception, isolation and identification coexist as dynamic contraries. By refusing any elaborate metaphoric constellations within the poem Revell allows the literal properties to constitute a single metaphor similar to those created by abstract painting. In this space, finally, it would make little sense to concentrate on the motives or plight of an individual speaker. This world is too elemental for the contingencies of subjective contexts, and it is too ontologically complex in its dense relations to elicit the forms of empathy required for drama. Here identification is not a matter of feeling for someone else's plight but of recognizing how one actually participates with others in the model of mental and affective agency, which the poem literally constitutes. The expanse within and as dullness is an actual site we make real in the reading. Our reading is more than projected empathy, since it enacts what the poem claims and thus becomes literal testimony to properties and powers that extend beyond the fictive constellations of traditional art.

But why do such sites and properties matter? Granted that Modernism is inventive, why should someone care about the inventions or think they are necessary for the spirit rather than simply elitist exercises in constructivist ingenuity? We have already begun to work out an answer, which now de Man and Wittgenstein can help us elaborate. Modernism, we know, begins in the exploration of infinite irony but, in Anglo-American poetry at least, soon leads to a range of efforts at forms of writing with claims to resist those corrosive effects and to engage a fuller range of human energies than ironic roles can satisfy. De Man provides the best general account I know of the rationale compelling the irony, so he also establishes a useful measure of whether the proposed "impersonal" alternatives have any claims to succeed. Thinkers have tried in a variety of ways, de Man argues, to distinguish the descriptive or grammatical features of a discourse from its performative or rhetorical properties so that one can isolate the propositional elements, which can refer and be assessed in terms of truth conditions. Even when philosophers become painfully aware of the distorting traces of the individual subject inherent in performative dimensions of the discourse, they hope for "a grammatization of rhetoric" enabling them to locate and isolate the disruptive parasite. But such desires are evasions of actuality. All utterance teeters over an infinite regress of intentions attempting to understand intentions, or interpreters trying to fix into the nonpersonal what inevitably carries the effects of the specific desires that put each performative act in motion.[5] As our example, take the Sartrean problem of sincerity which plagues contemporary poetry: How can a rhetorical act claim sincerity when it both consciously and unconsciously stages that which should be immediate? At best the rhetorician can try to recapture sincerity. But that obviously introduces infinite gaps between the actual experiences one purports to be sincere about and the various inducements to seducing the self and others that occur as one rhetorically manipulates the medium.

These duplicities of description are basic to Modernist irony, since self-consciousness must protect the self from being betrayed by expressions that invite a scrutiny responsive to features not deliberately intended by the author. Once a culture cannot mediate between descriptions and idealizations, or prosaic objectivity and projections of value, personality becomes contaminated by the very excess which had for four hundred years been the source of its power to generate values. Imagination is our undoing. Art can respond by what Alan Wilde calls the "anironic impulse," which consists in projecting totalizing states of consciousness able to hold in balance all that in practice would prove incompatible and self-destructive. But that may serve only to replace self-contradiction by an absolute idealism radically separating art from life. The line of inquiry here suggests another, more positive route. So long as art is personal or represents personal quests it is very difficult to take intellectual responsibility for the conditions of will in the work. These conditions elicit the need to produce substantial unities of the soul, so they remain always other, always at odds with any integrative or descriptive impulse attempting to define them. But an impersonal art has no such obligations to dramatic coherence. Eliot's *Waste Land* clearly has a pathological dimension, yet that is part of the poem, inseparable from its juxtapositional structure and even from the moments of transcendent ritual it postulates. On simpler levels, the will need not displace reference so long as the force of will is transparent, as it is when the basic semantic features of the work are its constituent elements. Then the foreground of the work is simply its capacity to exemplify certain forces. There is no description apart from the relations the work embodies. What will can be is part of what the poem's structural units try to project.

Will must be redefined by art because of what it had become in life. By 1914 European culture was confronted with the consequences of nineteenth-century perspectivism and its nationalist corollaries. A liberal pluralism like Mill's could believe that diversity would never become so extreme as to challenge all possibilities of consensus, and national differences seemed to offer a vital range of cultural possibilities in the place of bland Enlightenment hierarchies. But the dream of mutually affirming plurality became the monstrous reality of irreconcilable differences. So artists and philosophers saw the need for a counterrevolution re-establishing within subjectivity some principles for a shareable human identity grounding performative differences. Thus we have Husserl's *Ideas,* Bradley's Absolute, the Marburg school's symbolic forms, and Russell's theory of types all sharing what one might call the impersonal but nonreductive stance on the personal, which the poets tried to elaborate. None of these, however, is as responsive to the depth, mobility, and transpersonality of subjective life as the Wittgenstein of the *Tractatus,* so I shall use it to identify themes for which poetry turns out to be the best testimony.[6]

Wittgenstein saw that to the extent language has meaning, which for early Wittgenstein entails having truth value, there is simply no point to speaking about perspectival differences (cf. TLP, 5.631 ff.). Meaning is inherently transpersonal, whatever the supplementary features that may engage subjective differences. And if that is the case, defenses of the humane, say against empiricist reductionism, become extremely vulnerable if they rely on powers of imagination or engagement produced by perspectivist themes. For these are not fundamental; the world can go on without them and, more importantly, they do not locate what really matters about individual persons. The "I" that carries basic human values occupies a site beyond the entire domain of discursive thought or specifiable "perspectives": "The subject does not belong to the world; rather, it is a limit of the world. . . . what brings the self into philosophy is the fact that the world is my world" (TLP, 5.632;1 5.641). What the world is or what belongs to it are matters for descriptive thought. How the world is, whether it makes me happy or unhappy, is a question no description can handle. Establishing that is the role (and the curse) of the deep subject, the "I" definable by no thought because it in effect constitutes the weather or modality within which we experience the contents of thought. Hence this subject is always on the margin of the world. It cannot be accessible to reflection or empirical analysis because such stances must be continually driven and modified by the very investments they hope to find.

The best brief way to get a rough sense of what Wittgenstein is after is to observe some of the consequences of his nondramatic way of locating the deep subject. First, value is sharply distinguished from fact, just as the willing self is divided from the thinking subject: "If there is any value that does have value, it must lie outside the whole sphere of what happens and is the case. For all that happens and is the case is accidental" (TLP, 6.41). Second, the realm of values, of ethics, is one that cannot be developed by propositions or explanations (TLP, 6.42) because these discursive modes depend on what is the case. Ethics can only be a matter of examples or models, of unrationalizable ways of responding to what is the case. Third, the ontological correlate of this sense of ethics is a profound role given to silence. There is a "mystical" because there can be a sense of the whole that leads one to identify oneself within it and accept what becomes in effect an eternal present (TLP, 6.4311; 6.45). There cannot, however, be any determinate route to this vision: enlightenment is a matter of accepting silence and using it to attach ourselves to the mystical as things "make themselves manifest" (TLP, 6.522; 7). Finally, ethics and aesthetics must be "one" because they each involve an attitude toward the whole, allowing one to align oneself to it simply by virtue of the form of presence that one's vision correlates with the will. Both disciplines require an overcoming of the illusions that thinking provides power and that selves are fulfilled by a process of expressing their needs and triumphs. The triumphs that matter are those which reflexively position the will so that it can assume an attitude toward phenomena responsive to a whole—that is to something with claims to suffice as an eternal present without the kind of dependencies and substitutions which prevent us from taking complete responsibility for the world we inhabit at any moment. So long as "I" have excuses or think that "I" matter by virtue of some individual properties, I fail to come to terms with the basic parameters where will in fact makes a difference. Paradoxically the "I" is at once too private ever to be manifest and too shareable in its essential functions to warrant our attributing significant specific content to that privacy.

IV

I cannot here defend or even extend Wittgenstein's thinking on these matters. I mention them primarily to indicate the range of issues and possibilities that constitute a new Modernist model of the nondramatic subject to be located as the "other" of all descriptions and images. No poet I know strictly follows Wittgenstein (although late Stevens often comes pretty close). But the best Modernists all see that in positing impersonality as a principle they embark on a philosophical adventure requiring them to take up the same questions and to imagine forms of satisfaction for something like this inescapable and indefinable self, who is only cheapened by dramatic contexts intended to explain its plight or its exaltations. Instead of the dramatic rendering of personal situations, they would have to find ways of dealing with subjectivity as a function perhaps identical for all persons and with images as perhaps inevitable distortions of the life those functions reveal. They would have to generate styles that could project a sense of engaging the world as a whole while cutting through the contingencies of social life, so that whatever ultimately determines happiness or unhappiness could manifest its force. Situations would have to yield to the foregrounding of the constitutive structures shaping the needs and powers we bring to a variety of contexts. Three particular Modernist stances—represented by Eliot, Williams, and Stevens—will flesh out the permissions impersonality affords for exploring these structures and the ways each of the traits I have described combine to give significance to those explorations.

Eliot's were the founding moves in this new poetic. For it was he who most deeply experienced the limitations of the lyrical personae elaborated in Victorian poetry and he who saw how *Symboliste* poetics could be adapted to the philosophical project of testing alternatives to the fiction of "the substantial unity of the soul." That poetics gave Eliot access to a distinctive site—a realm of the imaginary—where one could explore those features of experience that seem at once to resist description and to mock any purely subjective efforts to appropriate them. Were one to treat Eliot's "Preludes" (1910–11) dramatically, it would appear as a late Victorian mood piece. Like Wilde's "Impression" poems or Symons's "City Nights" sequence (or half the poems in last year's *New Yorker*), sensibility has given way to a weary lucidity content with refined impressions that language teases from a hostile world. But Eliot's peculiar self-consciousness introduces a new era by insisting on structural parallels that play against the lyric mood. Lyric intensity remains, now dependent on two basic processes of abstraction. First Eliot escapes the mood lyric by making the scene considerably more than an evocative moment. Style so calls attention to itself that it in effect becomes the subject matter, transforming the poem into an exploration of the general epistemological issues which had formed the central implicit tension in Victorian poetry—the struggle between the imperatives to lyricism and to lucidity. Lyricism consists in the desire to continue for a secular culture the forms of romance sustained by our imaginative traditions, while Enlightenment lucidity requires that all romance submit to the authority of principles of reasoning sanctioned by the sciences. Eliot's style evokes these issues primarily by echoing the "dark house" motif in Tennyson's *In Memoriam,* where spiritual loss takes the form of experiencing one's world as a series of metonymic fragments, each insisting on a hostile sensual presence, which mocks all sacramental desires that objects of perception carry some kind of positive meaning or grace.

Eliot's quest to transcend pure description breeds a voice so self-conscious of its desire to delude itself that, like Arnold's, it must keep itself under very tight restraint—the pathos all in what cannot be said and the pressure that that entails on the psyche. The poet becomes a cultural diagnostician. But for Arnold that role justified a virtually endless melodramatic rhetoric. Diagnostics produces an abstract subject matter only to free the diagnostician into a very general space for soulful laments. So Eliot must develop a second strategy, which produces a speaking mode as abstract and spare as the scene to which the poet is reduced. Now impersonality does its stuff. It eliminates the poetic ego torn between cries and prayers, and it requires the poet to locate his basic lyric effects in the conceptual force generated primarily by the formal relations. For it is there that the impersonal expands into the transpersonal, into the drama of powers and plights available to us all simply by virtue of our capacity to engage ourselves in what the language does.[7]

"Preludes" becomes a meditation on its own modes of presenting experience within a juxtapositional logic that art can graft on to the real. The poet's drama consists primarily in the unfolding tension between the demonic impersonality of the descriptions and the pathos of a performative space reduced to a few embedded pronouns.

50

In the poem's first section the logic is radically scenic, with all action the provenance of inanimate objects. The closest we come to human affective energies is the pathos of "the lonely cab horse." Other than this pathetic fallacy there are only metonymic masquerades of human desire culminating in the brilliant tautology, "the lighting of the lamps." Here light appears not by any human agency but as a result of an abstract necessity as mechanical and repetitive as the return of morning. Yet the depersonalizing is so completely and incisively rendered that we feel an intelligence we cannot locate in the semantic content. Its presence, we soon see, is structural, not directly interpretive or expressive. For buried in the first poem is a pronominal adjective that connects it to the forms of thinking dramatized in the other "Preludes." Here the simple reference to "your feet" creates the only moment of explicit human presence, the syntactic equivalent of the "lonely cab horse." In relation to the other sections, we find ourselves facing a minimal condition of human subjectivity. The world of objects allows only the feeling of human consciousness as an adjective, a qualitative pressure that introduces needs without producing any corresponding resources for action. "Your feet" ends the seventh of thirteen lines, a pathetic center of this turning world.

As the morning comes to consciousness in the second section, it allows the transformation of adjectives into the impersonal "one," the universal shifter given the role of the thinking subject, which can only register metonymies of its own paralyzed state. Thinking here gets equated with the hands that can at most let morning light disclose private lives, which all repeat one another because they are trapped within a common environment. But even this much consciousness allows the third "Prelude" to let us inside the room, inside the agent's own view of his or her life. Such an imposition entails second-person address, the infinite division of the self as subject from the object it begins actively to observe. Even the tense then is in the past, always a remove from the mind that watches. And the watching doubles its own self-division in the tension it produces between finding its psychic state absorbed by the "thousand sordid images of which your soul was constituted" and positing a self completely beyond what the street can understand. The "you" is both distanced from the act of thinking and too intimate to be captured as an object of thought.

To posit that intimate self in the present is to experience the finer tensions of the third-person stance that begins the fourth "Prelude." Here verbs and adjectival participles become indistinguishable ("Stretched tight") and the self becomes one with what the eye sees, little more than an adjectival intrusion on a world of facts. However, once it goes through this cycle, consciousness cannot avoid the traces of itself that accrue around the images—at once a sign of their insufficiency and the basis for the indefinable, imaginary plenitude that comprises the structure of investments that we call the "I." The "I" enters, in and as "fancies that are curled / Around these images, and cling: the notion of some infinitely gentle. / infinitely suffering thing." But because its imaginary status requires it to be maintained by acts of negation, this "I" is tremendously vulnerable, breeding by the gaps it causes and the wistfulness it sustains a constant temptation to expunge it and restore life to its impersonal equanimity. So the poem ironically comes to its emotional climax by shifting to the imperative mood, whose form for the subject is a chillingly profound blend of second and third persons. The spirit of lucidity attempts to sacrifice the subjective "I" to the empty generality of a destiny whose banal image of recurrence carries strange overtones of dark Greek forces:

> Wipe your hands across your mouth and laugh;
> The worlds revolve like ancient women
> Gathering fuel in vacant lots.
> [15]

Irony frees the poem's voice from the seductive consolations of lyricism—but at a substantial price. It invokes such distance from subjective energies that it allows only an infinitely repetitious revolution of worlds, with all psychic life reduced to a horrifying otherness. Close attention to the logic of the subject's emergence only confirms its prison and makes one wish one could reduce the self to that initial adjectival place within a turning world.

Irony, however, is not the poem's ultimate form of self-reference. Because the poem resists the temptation to provide a dramatic center as a force for empathy, it can free its organizing patterns to become a form of testimony in their own right. Reading the poem is less a matter of "interpreting" its positions than it is a process of occupying them, because we too must struggle with the poem's needs to find stances that allow human presence within a world of metonymic images. The result is not empathy with some other person but a literal sharing of states of mind that do not depend on individual differences. In this sharing the poem as an experience takes on a unique philosophical status as an irreducible analogy for the complex duality embodied in the closing passages. So in reading we win from the pressure of a world reduced to sensations a gradual sense of the fragile "I," which the sensations negate but in negating reproduce. As our own investments become evanescent and difficult to fix, we are asked to turn on ourselves with the dismissive arrogance of the demand for disillusioned lucidity, which is the modern myth of authenticity. Yet curled around this imperative are fancies that cling, fancies like the very myth of authenticity, the echoes of tragic submissions to destiny, and the need to overcompensate for vulnerability by resorting to the poem's closing ironic attitude. If we so need irony, the poem reminds us, our efforts to dismiss the fragile "I" prove deeply dependent on the very investments this form of self-consciousness would deny in the name of lucidity. Instead of pure negation, we have the poem. We have an irreducible analogical structure for the insubstantial yet persistent lyric "I" poised within and against forces of objectification in nature as well as those in the mind's second- and third-person positions.

Poems as presentational acts, in other words, become something like physical correlates for the nature of consciousness. The patterned elements which create an allegorical space themselves become its substance because the very force of the patterning creates the power of the diffused yet insistent tension among personal positions, which at once comprises and defines lyrical investments, perhaps intrinsic to self-reflexive activity. The poem's juxtapositional relations, the sensual qualities by which it renders the pressure of its sensations, the intelligence manifest in the economy, precision, and delicacy of the language, and, most importantly, the remarkable feelings of pressure and of contradiction all become testimony to the pathos and power of an "infinitely gentle, infinitely suffering thing" curled about our self-denying efforts to treat the world simply in terms of the images we reproduce for it.

V

Eliot's deep will, like Wittgenstein's, is a bleak one, ultimately to be satisfied by nothing less than everything, by God. But Eliot's strategies need not lead only to this metaphysics. Similarly, an anti-dramatic poetics blending pure denotation with the indirect presence of a will so deep it only appears in the impersonal writing self need not produce only the dry monotone of Eliotic reflection. The deep will might prove as varied, even as playful, as the dramatic subject it must replace. Modernism depends on Eliot's experimentalist imperative to treat form as a philosophical principle rather than as a rhetorical means for implicating actual themes or structures of social life. But having opened that space, Eliot's Protestant rigors of self-consciousness had the depth, precision, and bleakness to inspire, even to require, other competing stances. Once he had reduced exile to its elemental social, epistemological, and metaphysical poetic constituents, Eliot in effect demanded the creation of opposing presentational styles which could adapt impersonality and Wittgensteinian imperatives to constrasting principles of plenitude. An Eliot must generate a William Carlos Williams, whose quintessentially abstract "Poem" presents in pure form the possibilities within Modernism of making the impersonal a vehicle for lucid acts of lyrical celebration:

> Poem
>
> As the cat
> climbed over
> the top of
>
> the jam closet
> first the right
> forefoot
>
> carefully
> then the hind
> stepped down
>
> into the pit of
> the empty
> flowerpot

On one level this poem is pure denotation, a particular description that should satisfy the most ardent of positivists. Here Williams completely eschews metaphor violations of the cat that interpret it as a symbol of anything else. As a result there is absolutely no overt personal stance, and not even metaphysical traces of melodrama. Where there is no effort to interpret an X as a Y there may be no possibility of subjectivity because there are no signs of a distinctive history imposing choices on what can otherwise be described in truth-functional terms. But—and here is Williams's genius—the expulsion of personality in no way eliminates the vitality and pressure of a personal presence—now defined by the density of the analogical relationship between meanings and physical actions. The affirmative will resides in the way the artifice composes details and then offers the compositional act itself as constituting the analogy, giving the poem metaphoric representativeness.

Syntax achieves here what structure did as the mark of intelligence in Eliot's poem. While Williams's language denotes a cat's movements, the poem as presentational act transforms denotation into exuberant construction. Self-consciously artful, coped to a taut edging yet intricately supple and fluid, the sentence becomes a literal analogue for the cat.[8] Notice how each sentence unit comes to a temporary pause, gathers its strength, and then carefully continues its movement. Most good readers in fact recognize this; most good readers even feel the remarkable sense of expansiveness this control of language creates. But because the poem has no grand theatrics or thematic assertiveness its significance is rarely appreciated. Let us here try to address that lack by asking what possible semantic force results from imposing this syntactic echo on the poem's mimetic level. I propose two closely related achievements. First, the sentence deserves its self-delight because it gives the "philosophical self" the capacity to affirm the facts of the world without displacing them into dramas inquiring about the terms for affirmation. Williams's poem is as self-conscious as the most radical of Romantic or Eliotic lyrics. But instead of worrying about the terms its uses, the poem simply makes its compositional act testimony to what cats mean to the mind and what the mind affords for our capacity to appreciate cats.

Second, Williams understands the careful movement of the sentence as a warrant for an anti-Platonic model of form. Williams connects awe at the tensile intricacy of sentences and of cats with a radically physical sense of what minds and cats do. It is crucial here that the poem need not interpret cats. For that refusal calls attention to the analogy between cats and sentences as something irreducible, something that perhaps captures a locus of spirit on the other side of interpretation, where sentences are ways of physically stretching outselves out among what language denotes. Sentences do not substitute for things but offer ways of inhabiting their vital relations. Thus a dullness of the sea and an expansiveness of mind can define one another. Ultimately this sentence becomes inextricable from Williams's version of Modernist analogies that stay analogies. Although the semantic level of the poem contains no metaphor and no drama, the presentational level becomes all metaphor. While the cat is simply referred to, the sentence that does the referring is inextricably wound into analogies with the cat it describes. Strictly literal properties of the sentence qua sentence ground that analogical level as a distinct site where cats move like sentences and sentences have all the sinuous physicality and power to focus attention which we find fascinating in cats. The vehicle of the poem becomes the tenor concretely grounding its metaphoric implications in properties the language actually possesses.

Such intricacies require commentary, but not interpretation in the traditional sense. There is nothing hidden and no dramatic intentions to be hypothesized. The human core of Williams's poem is elemental and transpersonal—a sentence anyone or everyone could speak and a form of expression which denies any need to inquire into deep motives or repressed desires. Yet this transparency takes on considerable depth simply because the reference outward is duplicated by the self-defining physicality of the poem as testimony to the power of sentences. All that it claims about cats and about sentences it literally presents in the composed energies its sentence makes available. The concrete sentence virtually becomes a transpersonal mind capable both of accurate depiction and articulate, nondiscursive celebration of that capacity as our condition for there being a world at all.

For Eliot and Williams, impersonal, compositional poetics provides access to functions and powers deeper and more abiding than the contingencies necessary to situate a dramatized self. Stevens takes the opposite tack. In his later poetry there is a crucial level on which the dramatic is not contingent enough. Dramatic and scenic poems rely for their coherence on the culture's assumptions about character and social determinants. For Stevens this cannot be sufficiently perspectival, cannot capture the constantly shifting relations produced by the play of metaphor and by the various positions our investments create. From the romance of tropes to the ecstasies of rendering some condition in a lucid transparent language, Stevens's poetry turns Williams's intentional structures into the perennial revolutions of a deep self seeking to know its energies in the varied pressures and possibilities it projects on and as the real. Similar concerns transform Eliot's sense of personality as a medium "in which impressions and experiences combine in particular and unexpected ways" into a form of celebratory precision which in Ashbery and Merrill becomes the pursuit of the transparent yet elegant and emotionally supple phrase uniting the gay materiality of language with the delicacies of sense.

My claims about Stevens cannot easily be illustrated by any one example. But I can at least give some concrete indication of what the claims respond to if I concentrate on his work at its most schematic and general. The compositional act must become something more ambitious than Williams's analogical parallel to the energies the act celebrates. Instead the writing must carry forms of investment capable of complementing efforts at denotation by producing "in the imagination a universal iridescence, a dithering of presences and, say, a complex of differences" (OP, 192). As we negotiate these differences we can glimpse at play among them a single central figure of desire, which seems inseparable from the very form of our fascination. We enter an "enormous a priori" and recognize on the margin or threshold of appearance "as poetic a concept as the idea of the infinity of the world" (OP, 194).

For our purposes the best example is a summary passage like the final canto of "It must be abstract," where Stevens tries to make as explicit as possible the consequences of this extended meditation on the mind's powers. What matters is the presentational force by which the language becomes testimony to what it plainly propounds:

The major abstraction is the idea of man
And major man is its exponent, abler
In the abstract than in his singular,

More fecund as principle than particle,
Happy fecundity, flor-abundant force,
In being more than an exception, part,

Though an heroic part, of the commonal.
The major abstraction is the commonal.
The inanimate, difficult visage. Who is it? . . .

It is of him, ephebe, to make, to confect
The final elegance, not to console
Nor sanctify, but plainly to propound.
[388–89]

The genius here lies in fusing the elegance and the propounding so that abstraction takes form as an exponential process of self-consciousness based on actual denotation rather than the staging of a dramatically situated lyrical ego. This relation between the abstract and the exponential has two basic features. First we see that anything which can expound supreme fictions must itself be abstract because it must try to describe something like a *Symboliste* ground only partially glimpsed in the individual lyrics. Then, more importantly, we see that the very process of naming becomes exponential in the mathematical sense. In reading we follow a course of increasing abstraction, which we experience as a literal direct exponential growth in our understanding of major man. Now the *Symboliste* ground takes on a content as we see the initial direct assertion breeding an apposition, which grows into more elaborate appositions. We watch a plain diction become fecund with its own "flor-abundant force." And we participate in a remarkable expansion from bold generalized abstraction, to a question whose answer can only lie in the imagination, to the remarkable directness of the final imperative. That imperative, moreover, has its origin and authority within a process that is as intensely personal as meditation, yet its terms have nothing to do with the contingencies of personal identity.

This is not to say that Stevens's poetry has nothing to do with personal identity. Rather it is to insist that there are aspects of identity that require such exponential abstractions if we are to recognize the possibilities language affords for our making identifications with other persons. By calling attention to the poem as testimony Stevens asks us to reflect on our participation as a form of action in which we take on parts enabling us to make identifications that do not depend on names or images but seek fecundity in principles. In "Notes" the appropriate expounding takes place at the climax of the next section, "it must change":

> There is a month, a year, there is a time
> In which majesty is a mirror of the self:
> I have not but I am and as I am, I am.
>
> These external regions, what do we fill them with
> Except reflections, the escapades of death,
> Cinderella fulfilling herself beneath the roof?
> [405]

On the one hand the "as" is a figure of constant change because the reading and writing selves must adjust to all that the investments of our expoundings make evident. The inescapable "as" of our tropes suggests a constant openness to identification. Then as we reflect on this flexible, radically personal "I", living in change becomes something impersonal or transpersonal—a figure for what all "I's" share in the very process of constructing provisional identities. Instead of images we enter the level of pure activity where it makes sense to speak of "the commonal."

These abstractions will become relatively concrete if we return to the example of reading a difficult imaginative construct. As is indicated in Dante's closing image projecting God as a book we enter, the more fully we relate the parts, the more we come to envision the possibility of a whole—not a specific unity by a stage of comprehension transcendental because it is an exponent of its parts. As the reader understands the assertions, she also gains access to the conditions of desire generating them and creating an atmosphere within which the parts take on resonant tonalities. Beyond the test there is "an inanimate difficult visage" we create as we reflect on our very participation in the energies the propounding elicits. Propounding fixes a world; confecting constitutes the chorales for a commonal by staging description as a part of desires all readers can share. That sharing, moreover, is quite literal, yet because it does not depend on reflected images it shows poetry a way not so bound to the "escapades of death." Understanding depends only on our recognizing how in the absence of dramatic images it is we who become both the subject and object of a final elegance, like "rubies reddened by rubies reddening" (346). Compared to this, traditional religious and rhetorical roles would be pompous parodies.

VI

Contemporary critics and poets have on the whole not proved good exponents of the modern. Instead we may be in the process of selling our birthright for a mess of rhetorical pottage. The willingness for such a sacrifice is not difficult to understand: any plausible claims to poetry's social relevance appear worth pursuing in a time when all serious reading seems anachronistic. But desperate attempts at restoring poetry's social role may risk more than they secure, especially if they tie poetry too closely to the demands of a narcissistic society. If we pander to conceptually outmoded forms of lyrical sensibility, we may deprive poetry of the critical intelligence and constructive force capable of partially changing the basic emotional commitments of those who become suspicious of that society. And we may even be able to show how poetry holds out very different models of value and of agency.

The problems critics face take sharply focused form in the conclusion of Stanley Cavell's *The Claim of Reason*. Cavell's overriding concern is to take the problem of scepticism out of epistemology into the broader realm of human relations. Scepticism becomes a matter of failed trust, and philosophy becomes involved with therapeutic concerns that have increasingly shaped Cavell's work (and would, I think, have appalled Wittgenstein because of the lush self-stagings they allow Cavell). Yet Cavell is too good a thinker not to see the possible cost of his enterprises. So he ends his book on this question: granted that the final actions in Othello define the source and price of scepticism, can philosophy accept such emblems from "the hands of poetry"? "Perhaps it would if it could itself become literature. But can philosophy become literature and still know itself?" (496). Implicit here are the alternatives facing contemporary poetry. One way is the anti-Modernist. It rejects inquiry into grounds and first principles in order to shore against the ruins of our efforts to know ourselves a set of dramatic images or self-representations that finesse all such demands. The emotional states and social bonds they create become ends in themselves. In my view, however, such stances usually leave us back in post-Victorian expressions of mood and sensibility, on the brink of the collapse of rhetoric into the all-corroding irony requiring Modernist solutions. It is no accident that so many dramatic personal lyrics have as their recurrent theme the pressures of frustrated desires and the collapse of metaphoric constellations, however playfully held. Against these tendencies, poetry can try to arrogate to itself on the level of art what philosophy increasingly despairs of on the level of description, its only claim to truth. What might be called the constitutive-reflexive dimension of Modernism embarks on a new spiritual adventure in which poetry resides precisely in the capacity of poetic testimony to offer itself as a form of self-knowledge. Poems display an enacting of powers whereby we are allowed to reflect on the impersonal core of our various personal acts and desires. As we get increasingly suspicious of what and how sentences describe, the Modernist tradition asks us simply to see what our sentences speak for, or speak as, in their capacity to constitute new senses for the world.

NOTES

1. The most explicit claims for a return to pre-Modernist poetics is offered by Christopher Clausen. Related arguments may be found in influential work by Donald Davie, Gerald Graff, Charles Newman, and Jonathan Holden. Finally, among younger American poets Robert Pinsky attacks Modernist experimentalism and Stanley Plumly offers a good example of the new insistence on poetry as a rhetoric. For the rear guard avant-garde, in whose ranks I enlist, see Robert Kern's thoughtful critique of Holden. Even this, however, proves somewhat limited because its primary defense of Modernism consists not in defining the powers it affords but in asserting its historical authenticity in a post-Nietzschean culture. I am afraid this kind of argument is easily countered by the argument that historical myths

projecting the necessity of Modernist principles need to be assessed on independent, functional grounds which do not beg the historicist answer. I try to describe contemporary society as requiring these Modernist strategies in my *Self and Sensibility in Contemporary American Poetry.*

2. I take the Lehman statement from a very interesting collection of remarks, mostly by younger poets under the influence of Ashbery, on the idea of form. I quote from p. 37.

3. The core of Holden's account is a rich defense of analogical rather than organic notions of form. This approach (17–22) produces a better rhetorical typology than I do in *Self and Sensibility*, although his rhetorical categories beg the question of describing the actual qualities of vision or imagined goals informing the forms he catalogs. For links between this position and what I attribute to the implicit poetics of Kenney's text consider the following passage:

> Poems in the so called post-modern*ist* mode, for example many of Ashbery's poems which are asserted as objects and whose forms depend *entirely* on analogues, in that they passively recapitulate all the possible models of discourse, literary or otherwise, . . . reveal in stark outline the fundamental choice confronting the poet working in America today. It is a choice between analogues, between forms which . . . range from the communal to the impersonal. Curiously enough, this choice ends up being not an epistemological one but an ethical one: whether to trust the self and presume to impose upon the world, by sheer force of character, an individual aesthetic and ethical order or to continue the modernist hegemony of Eliot and Pound, to retreat in an elitist disgust from modern civilization and indulge in the facile despair of the parodist, recapitulating all the bad languages that comprise our environment, holding our own civilization up before us as if the sad facts could only speak for themselves.(22)

4. A representative sample of Mondrian's prose will demonstrate the intensity and intelligence of his distrust of the dramatic:

> Abstract art is therefore opposed to a natural representation of things. But it is not opposed to nature as is generally thought. It is opposed to the raw primitive animal nature of man, but it is one with true human nature. It is opposed to the conventional laws created during the culture of the particular form but it is one with the laws of the culture of pure relationships. First and foremost there is the fundamental law of dynamic equilibrium which is opposed to the

static equilibrium necessitated by the particular form . . . (122) That which is regarded as a system is nothing but constant obedience to the laws of pure plastics, to necessity, which art demands from him . . . In this way he is in his creation sufficiently neutral, that nothing of himself or outside of him can prevent him from establishing that which is universal. Certainly his art is art for art's sake . . . for the sake of the art which is form and content at one and the same time. (130)

5. The most direct statements in de Man of the themes I recount may be found in the essays "Semiology and Rhetoric" and "Action and Identity in Nietzsche," both in his *Allegories of Reading.*

6. Wittgenstein's fullest reflections on the opposition between the willing and the thinking subject occur in his *Notebooks 1914–1916,* pp. 71–91, and his *Blue Book,* pp. 61–74 (where the alternative to the thinking subject is no longer explicitly a willing subject).

7. My approach here is intended partially as a critique of Ronald Bush's deep and sensitive reading of the poems primarily as expressions of Eliot's psychic life. Bush teaches us a lot, but he deprives the early poems of a good deal of their power, intelligence, and strangeness. As is obvious I take Bush's reading as symptomatic of literary directions in our culture, which gain in popularity as the only apparent alternative to the depersonalizing effects of deconstruction and critical historicism.

8. Hugh Kenner is very good on how the sentence is an active agent for Williams (59) and on the objectivist desire for denotation. But he does not see the importance of constructive style as a way of connecting agency to denotation. Ironically, Kenney's *The Evolution of the Flightless Bird* (which does not include "Speed of Light") turns out to offer a very rich abstract sense of how a way of reading landscape projects a strange model of the mind's agency. While I think I am right about Kenney's poem, I fear I am quite wrong about the limitations of the poet.

BIBLIOGRAPHY:
Works Cited

Altieri, Charles. "Arnold and Tennyson: The Plight of Victorian Lyricism as Context of Modernism." *Criticism* 20 (1978), 281–306.
———. "Representation, Representativeness, and Non-Representational Art." *Journal of Comparative Literature and Aesthetics* 5 (1982), 1–21.

————. *Self and Sensibility in Contemporary American Poetry*. New York: Cambridge University Press, 1984.

Bush, Ronald. *T. S. Eliot, A Study in Character and Style*. New York: Oxford University Press, 1984.

Cavell, Stanley, *The Claim of Reason*. Oxford: Clarendon Press, 1979.

Clausen, Christopher. *The Place of Poetry*. Lexington: University Press of Kentucky, 1981.

Davie, Donald. *Thomas Hardy and British Poetry*. New York: Oxford University Press, 1972.

De Man, Paul. *Allegories of Reading*. New Haven: Yale University Press, 1979.

Eliot, T. S. *Collected Poems 1909–62*. New York: Harcourt, Brace and World, 1963.

————. *Selected Essays*. New York: Harcourt, Brace and Co., 1950.

Graff, Gerald. *Literature Against Itself*. Chicago: University of Chicago Press, 1979.

Holden, Jonathan. "Postmodern Poetic Form: A Theory." *New England Review* (Fall 1983), 1–22.

Kenner, Hugh. *A Homemade World: The American Modernist Writers*. New York: William Morrow and Co., 1975.

Kenney, Richard. "Speed of Light." *The New Yorker* (1983), 50.

Kern, Robert. "Form and Ethos in Postmodern Poetry." *New England Review* (Fall 1983), 23–24.

Lehman, David. "Ecstatic Occasions, Expedient Forms" [A Symposium], *Epoch* 33, No. 1 (Fall–Winter 1983), 33–97.

Mondrian, Piet. *Plastic Art and Pure Plastic Art*. Reprinted in Robert L. Herbert, *Modern Artists on Art*. Englewood Cliffs: Prentice Hall, 1964.

Newman, Charles. *The Post-modern Aura*. Evanston: Northwestern University Press, 1985.

Plumly, Stanley. "Chapter and Verse," *American Poetry Review* (January–February 1978), 21–35, and (May–June 1978), 19–32.

Revell, Donald. *From the Abandoned Cities*. New York: Harper and Row, 1983.

Stevens, Wallace. *The Collected Poems of Wallace Stevens*. New York: Alfred Knopf, 1955.

————. *Opus Posthumous*. Ed. Samuel French Morse. New York: Alfred Knopf, 1957.

Williams, W. C. *The Collected Earlier Poems*. New York: New Directions, 1951.

Wittgenstein, Ludwig. *The Blue and Brown Books*. New York: Harper and Row, 1958.

————. *Notebooks 1914–1916*. Translated by G. E. M. Anscombe. New York: Harper and Row, 1961.

————. *Tractatus Logico Philosophicus*. Translated by D. F. Pears and B. F. McGuiness. London: Routledge and Kegan Paul, 1961.

Worringer, Wilhelm. *Abstraction and Empathy*. Translated by Michael Bullock. Cleveland: Meridian Books, 1967.

Helen Vendler

KEATS AND
THE USE
OF POETRY

Heidegger asked, "What is the poet for in a destitute time?" I want to depart today from Heidegger's premises, though not from his question: What can we say is the use of poetry? Heidegger's premises are those of nineteenth-century nostalgia, a nostalgia for the presence of God in the universe. He writes as one deprived of theological reassurance, seeing emptiness about him, and longing for presence. He suggests that the poet exists to restore presence, to testify to its possibility—or at least, like Hölderlin, to testify to felt absence.

There are premises of a particular moment—the moment of Götterdämmerung. But Heidegger's plangent lamentation offers only one response to that moment; readers will remember Nietzsche's far more athletic and exulting response to the same moment, and some will recall Wallace Stevens's remark, in "Two or Three Ideas," that:

> to see the gods dispelled in mid-air and dissolve like clouds is one of the great human experiences. It is not as if they had gone over the horizon to disappear for a time; nor as if they had been overcome by

other gods of greater power and profounder knowledge. It is simply that they came to nothing. . . . It was their annihilation, not ours, and yet it left us feeling that in a measure, we too had been annihilated. . . . At the same time, no man ever muttered a petition in his heart for the restoration of those unreal shapes. There was in every man the increasingly human self, which instead of remaining the observer, the non-participant, the delinquent, became constantly more and more all there was or so it seemed; and whether it was so or merely seemed so still left it for him to resolve life and the world in his own terms. (OP, 206–207)

Perhaps we can consider a response like Heidegger's as one dictated not by the facts of the case but by a certain temperament in Heidegger himself. Another temperament, other premises. And in the confidence that the use of the poet, in human terms, remains constant even through the vicissitudes of cultural change, I want to take up today the ideas on the social function of poetry expressed by John Keats.

Keats, a resolute nonbeliever and political radical, came into a post-Enlightenment world, it is true, but it was still a world which felt some of those pangs of loss later expressed by Heidegger. Keats too felt a religious nostalgia, and it entered into many of his own meditations on the function of the poet; but he did not confine himself within that framework. I take the case of Keats to be an exemplary one of a modern poet seeking to define his own worth; Keats seems to me to have thought more deeply about the use of poetry than any subsequent modern poet. And although Keats will be my example, I want to close by bringing the topic into the present day, by quoting two contemporary poets who have reflected profoundly and long on it, the Polish poet Czesław Miłosz and the Irish poet Seamus Heaney—both of them compelled by their history to inquire into their own social function. But I will begin with Keats as a modern posttheological poet, a forerunner to others contemplating the question of the use of secular poetry.

Keats had hoped, originally, that literary creation could confer therapeutic benefits on its audience. Admirable as the desire is that art could "beguile" Dido from her grief, or "rob from aged Lear his bitter teen" ("Imitation of Spenser"), this concept of art bars it from participation in human grief. Keats later brought this idea of art to its apogee in the "Nightingale" ode, where the poet-speaker hopes that the purely musical art of bird notes will enable him to fly away from the world of the dying young, the palsied old, fading Beauty, and faithless Love. We must distinguish Keats's "escapism" (as it has sometimes been called) from an escapism that does not promise a therapeutic result, such as comforting Dido or Lear or Ruth in grief, "charming the mind from the trammels of pain" ("On Receiving a Curious Shell").

Other ends of art early proposed by Keats include the civilizing psychological one of "attuning . . . the soul to tenderness" (" To Lord Byron") and the educative one of expanding the soul, as, by vicarious experience, it strays in Spenser's halls and flies "with daring Milton through the fields of air" ("Written on the Day That Mr. Leigh Hunt Left Prison"), a view of art given its classical Keatsian expression in the sonnet on Chapman's Homer. Keats's concept of the *utile* here is far from the usual didactic one, which emphasizes social responsibility and moral action. To become tender, to expand one's sense of imaginative possibility are early recommendations consistent with Keats's later program of turning the blank intelligence into a human "soul"; the difference we notice here is the absence of that "world of pains and troubles" that will become the chief schooling agent of the heart in the letter on soul-making.

Keats, in his early poetry, enumerates four social functions of poetry: a historical one, as epic poetry recorded history of an exalted sort, written by "bards, that erst sublimely told heroic deeds"; a representational (if allegorical) one, as Shakespeare gave, in his dramatic poetry, an incarnation of the passions; a didactic one, as in Spenser's "hymn in praise of spotless Chastity" ("Ode to Apollo"); and a linguistically preservative one, which can "revive" for our day "the dying tones of minstrelsy" ("Specimen of an Induction to a Poem"). And yet, Keats perhaps sensed that these functions—historical, allegorically representational, didactic, and linguistically preservative—were not to be his own: these claims for the social functions of poetry are, in his early work, asserted merely, not enacted. A fair example of the feebleness of the early work comes in Keats's epistle to his brother George, where, after describing the living joys of the bard, Keats passes to "posterity's award," the function of the poet's work after he has died, as society makes use of his verse:

> ... The patriot shall feel
> My stern alarum, and unsheathe his steel ...
> The sage will mingle with each moral theme
> My happy thoughts sententious; ...
> Lays have I left of such a dear delight
> That maids will sing them on their bridal night.
>   ... To sweet rest
> Shall the dear babe, upon its mother's breast,
> Be lulled with songs of mine.

These uses of poetry are strictly ancillary; presumably the hero would still be heroic, the sage wise, the maids bridally delighted, and the baby sleepy, even without the help of the poet. In this conception, poetry is chiefly an intensifying accompaniment in life.

Keats's earliest notions of the power of art were concerned chiefly with the theme the poem may embody. The poet's pastoral tale will distract the grieving; his patriotic and moral sentiments will inspire hero and sage; and his love poems will wake an answering echo in the breast of the young. Poems exist to charm the fair daughters of the earth with love tales, and to warm earth's sons with patriotic sententious ideas.

It is to be expected that a poet of Keats's honesty would soon perceive that the embodying of a thematic and didactic intent was not his own sole motive in composing verse. He eventually admitted that in venturing on "the stream of rhyme" he himself sailed "scarce knowing my intent," but rather exploring "the sweets of song: / The grand, the sweet, the terse, the free, the fine; ... / Spenserian vowels that elope with ease ... / Miltonian storms, and more, Miltonian tenderness; ... / The sonnet ... / The ode ... / The epigram ... / The epic" ("To Charles Cowden Clarke"). This avowal of the aesthetic motives of creation, this picture of the artist investigating his medium—its vocal range, its prosodic inventions, its emotional tonalities, and its formal genres—sorts uneasily with Keats's former emphasis on the social service of poetry.

While the emphasis on social service always brings in, for Keats, the relief of pain, the emphasis in descriptions of art itself, in early Keats, dwells always on the pleasure principle, so that even woe must be, in literature, "pleasing woe" ("To Lord Byron"), and poetry must make "pleasing music, and not wild uproar" ("How Many

Bards") full of glorious tones and delicious endings ("On Leaving Some Friends"). In these early poems, Keats expresses the characteristic view of the youthful poet, to whom the aesthetic can be found only in the beautiful.

Keats's first attempt to reconcile his philosophical emphasis on social service and his instinctive commitment to those aesthetic interests proper to composition appears in "I stood tiptoe," where he proposes an ingenious reconciliation by suggesting that form allegorically represents content:

> In the calm grandeur of a sober line,
> We see the waving of the mountain pine;
> And when a tale is beautifully staid,
> We feel the safety of a hawthorn glade.

The myths of the gods are said, in "I stood tiptoe," to be formally allegorical renditions of man's life in nature: a poet seeing a flower bending over a pool invents the myth of Narcissus. This is a promising solution for Keats—that form, being an allegory for content, bears not a mimetic but an algebraic relation to life. But in "I stood tiptoe," this solution is conceptualized rather than formally enacted.

In his next manifesto, "Sleep and Poetry," Keats makes an advance on the thematic level, realizing that his former advocacy of a consoling thematic happiness to cure human sorrow cannot survive as a poetic program. Rather, he says, he must "pass the realm of Flora and old Pan" for a "nobler life" where he may encounter "the agonies, the strife / Of human hearts." With the thematic admission of tragic material, formal notions of power and strength can at last enter into Keats's aesthetic and fortify his former aesthetic values—beauty and mildness—with a new sculptural majesty:

> A drainless shower
> Of light is Poesy; 'tis the supreme power;
> 'Tis might half-slumbering on its own right arm.

Nonetheless, Keats is still critical of a poetry that "feeds upon the burrs, / And thorns of life," arguing rather for the therapeutic function of poetry, "that it should be a friend / To soothe the cares, and lift the thoughts of man"—an end still envisaged in the later "Ode on a Grecian Urn." The poet is simply to "to tell the most heart-easing things"; and the poetry of earth ranges only from the grasshopper's delight to the cricket's song "in warmth increasing ever."

A far sterner idea of poetry arises when Keats hopes that something will draw his "brain / Into a delphic labyrinth" ("On Receiving a Laurel Crown"). As soon as he admits thought, prophecy, and labyrinthine mystery into the realm of poetry, Keats becomes frightened at the interpretive responsibilities that lie before him, objectified for him in the example of the Elgin marbles. He cries out that he is too weak for such godlike hardship, that these "glories of the brain / Bring round the heart an undescribable feud."

But Keats obeys the Delphic imperative and writes his first tragic poem, a sonnet on the death of Leander, forcing his art to describe his worst personal specter, the image of a dying youth whom nothing can save. Keats's chief tragic adjective, "desolate," appears for the first time at this period (in his sonnet on the sea), to reappear in the "Hymn to Pan," the passage in "Endymion" on the Cave of Quietude, and the "Ode on a Grecian Urn." Henceforth, Keats can conceive of poetry as a mediating, oracular, and priestlike art, one which, by representation of the desolate in formal terms, can interpret the mysteries of existence to others.

The long romance "Endymion" marks Keats's first success in finding poetic embodiments for the principles he had so far been able merely to assert. The tale of Endymion is not socially mimetic, but rather, allegorical of human experiences; however, it is still a "pleasing tale," a pastoral, not a tragedy. Even so, Keats admits in "Endymion" two tragic principles that he will later elaborate: that in contrast to warm and moving nature, art must seem cold and carved or inscribed (a marble altar garlanded with a tress of flowers [90–91], the inscribed cloak of Glaucus); and that the action demanded of their devotees by Apollo and Pan is a sacrifice of the fruits of the earth. Art is admitted for the first time to be effortful: Pan is implored to be "the unimaginable lodge / For solitary thinkings; such as dodge / Conception to the very bourne of heaven, / Then leave the naked brain." These daring and difficult solitary thinkings and new concepts will become, says Keats, "the leaven, / That spreading in this dull and clodded earth / Gives it a touch ethereal—a new birth."

In one sense, this passage represents the end of Keats's theoretical thinking about the nature and social value of poetry. But he could not yet describe how solitary original thinkings become a leaven to resurrect society. The poem "Endymion," as it journeys between the transcendent Cynthia and the Indian maid, may be seen as a journeying to and from between the two elements of solitude and society, as Keats looks for a place where he can stand. He would like to avert his gaze from the misery of solitude, where those solitary thinkings take place, but he summons up the courage to confront the necessities of his own writing. Eventually, he arrives at two embodying symbols. The first is the cloak of Glaucus, "o'erwrought with symbols by . . . ambitious magic" (III, 198), wherein everything in the world is symbolized, not directly or mimetically, but in emblems and in miniaturizations. Gazed at, however, these printed reductions swell into mimetic reality:

> The gulfing whale was like a dot in the spell.
> Yet look upon it, and 'twould size and swell
> To its huge self, and the minutest fish
> Would pass the very hardest gazer's wish,
> And show his little eye's anatomy.

Keats faces up, here, to the symbolic nature of art. Art cannot, he sees, be directly mimetic; it must always bear an allegorical or emblematic relation to reality. Also, art is not a picture (he is speaking here of his own art of writing), but a hieroglyph much smaller than its original. However, by the cooperation of the gazer (and only by that cooperation), the hieroglyph "swells into reality." Without "the very hardest gazer's wish" the little fish could not manifest himself.

In this way, as later in the "Ode on a Grecian Urn," Keats declares that art requires a social cooperation between the encoder-artist and the decoder-beholder. The prescriptions written on the scroll carried by Glaucus announce Keats's new program for poetic immortality; the poet must "explore all forms and substances / Straight homeward to their symbol-essences": he must "pursue this task of joy and grief"; and enshrine all dead lovers. In the allegory that follows, all dead lovers are resurrected by having pieces of Glaucus's scroll sprinkled on them by Endymion. Endymion goes "onward . . . upon his high employ, / Showering those powerful fragments on the dead" (III, 784).

This allegory suggests that one of the social functions of poetry is to revive the erotic past of the race so that it lives again. But in the fourth book of "Endymion," as Keats admits to the poem the human maiden Phoebe and her companion Sorrow, the poem begins to refuse its own erotic idealizations and resurrections. At the allegorical center of Book IV, the narrator of "Endymion" finds at last his second major symbol of art, the solitary and desolate Cave of Quietude, a "dark Paradise" where "silence dreariest is most articulate; . . . / Where those eyes are the brightest far that keep / Their lids shut longest in a dreamless sleep." This is the place of deepest content, even though "a grievous feud" is said to have led Endymion to the Cave of Quietude.

Keats thought that this discovery of the tragic, hieroglyphic, and solitary center of art meant that he must bid farewell to creative imagination, to "cloudy phantasms . . . / And air of vision, and the monstrous swell / Of visionary seas":

> No, never more
> Shall airy voices cheat me to the shore
> Of tangled wonder, breathless and aghast.
> (IV, 651–55)

This farewall to "airy" imagination displays the choice that Keats at first felt compelled to make in deciding on a tragic and human art. He could not yet see a relation between the airy voices of visionary shores and human truth; and he felt obliged to choose truth. "I deem," says the narrator of "Endymion," "Truth the best music." "Endymion," uneasily balancing the visionary, the symbolic, and the truthful, had nonetheless brought Keats to his view of art as necessarily related, though in symbolic terms, to human reality; as necessarily hieroglyphic; as the locus of social cooperation by which the symbol regained mimetic force; and as a social resurrective power.

Shortly afterward, in a sudden leap of insight, Keats came upon his final symbol for the social function of art, a symbol not to find its ultimate elaboration, however, until Keats was able to write the ode "To Autumn." In his sonnet "When I have fears that I may cease to be," Keats summons up a rich gestalt:

> When I have fears that I may cease to be,
> Before my pen has glean'd my teeming brain,
> Before high-pilèd books, in charact'ry,
> Hold like rich garners the full-ripen'd grain. . . .

The poet's "teeming brain" is the field gleaned by his pen; the produce of his brain, "full-ripened grain," is then stored in the hieroglyphic charactery of books, which are like rich garners. Organic nature, after its transmutation into charactery (like that of Glaucus's magic symbols) becomes edible grain. By means of this gestalt, Keats asserts that the material sublime, the teeming fields of earth, can enter the brain and be hieroglyphically processed into print. Keats's aim is now to see the whole world with godlike range and power, with the seeing of Diana, "Queen of Earth, and Heaven, and Hell" ("To Homer") or that of Minos, the judge of all things ("On Visiting the Tomb of Burns").

Still, Keats has not yet enacted very far his convictions about the social function of art. The audience has been suggested as the consumer of the gleaned wheat that the poet had processed into grain; and the audience has been mentioned as the necessary cooperator in the reading of Glaucus's symbols, and as the resurrected beneficiaries of Glaucus's distributed scroll fragments. Now, in his greatest performative invention, Keats decides to play, in his own poetry, the role of audience and interpreter of symbols, not (as he so far had tended to do) the role of artist. This seems to me Keats's most successful aesthetic decision, one that distances him from his own investments (therapeutic and pleasurable alike) in creating. By playing the audience, he approaches his own art as one of its auditors, who may well want to know of what use this art will be to him.

In the odes on "Indolence" and to "Psyche," Keats had played the role of the creating artist; but in the "Ode to a Nightingale" and the "Ode on a Grecian Urn" he is respectively the listener to music and the beholder of sculpture. Each of these odes inquires what the recipient of art stands to receive from art. Keats here represents the audience for art as a single individual, rather than as a collective social group such as his Greek worshippers on the urn. In the absence of ideational content ("Nightingale"), no social collective audience can be postulated; and a modern beholder does not belong to the society that produced the urn. Keats seems to suggest that the social audience is, in the case of art, an aggregate of individual recipients, since the aesthetic experience is primarily a personal one; but what the individual receives, society, as a multiplication of individuals, also receives, as we conclude from the enumeration of listeners to the nightingale through the ages.

In the two "aesthetic odes" proper to the senses of hearing and sight, Keats begins to enact the theories of the social function of art that he had previously only asserted. As the listener to the nightingale, Keats enters a realm of wordless and nonconceptual, nonrepresentational song. He leaves behind the human pageant of sorrow and the griefs of consciousness; he forsakes the conceptual faculty, the perplexing and retarding brain. He offers himself up to beauty in the form of Sensation, as he becomes a blind ear, ravished by the consolations of sweet sounds articulated together by the composer-singer, the nightingale.

In the "Ode on a Grecian Urn," by contrast, Keats as audience opens his eyes to representational (if allegorical) art and readmits his brain, with all its perplexities and interrogations, to aesthetic experience. In this fiction, one function of art is still, as in the case of the "Nightingale" ode, to offer a delight of an aesthetic and sensuous sort—this time a delight to the eye rather than to the ear. But no longer does art, with consolatory intent, ravish its audience away from the human scene; instead, it draws its audience into its truthful representational and representative pictures carved in stone. The fiction of artistic creation as a spontaneous outpouring to an invisible audience—the fiction of the "Nightingale" ode—is jettisoned in favor of admitting the laborious nature of art, as sculpted artifice. And Keats, in the "Urn," establishes the fact that appreciation need not be coincident with creation; he is appreciating the urn now, even though it was sculpted centuries ago. The freshness and perpetuity of art is insisted on, as is its social service to many generations, each of whom brings its woe to the urn, each of whom finds itself solaced by the urn, a friend to man. The social function of art, Keats discovers here, is to remind its audience, by means of recognizable representative figures, of emotions and events common to all human life—here, lust, love, and sacrifice.

The Elgin marbles, recently installed in England, were Keats's example of his aesthetic ideal—an art that exerts a powerful aesthetic effect even though created long ago, even though the audience cannot ascribe historical or legendary names to the figures represented. This ode declares that art need not be historically based in order to be humanly meaningful; that art, although representationally mimetic, is not directly or historically mimetic; that art works in a symbolic or allegorical order, like that of Glaucus's cloak. It is wrong, therefore, to demand of an artist that he treat directly—autobiographically, journalistically, or historically—of events; his means are radically other than reportage. In fact, unless he pursues things to their "symbol-essences" he will not be able to communicate with ages later than his own.

Finally, in the ode "To Autumn," Keats finds his most comprehensive and adequate symbol for the social value of art. He does this by playing, in this ode, two roles at once. Once again, as in "Indolence" and "Psyche," he will play the role of the artist, the dreamer indolent in reverie on the bedded grass or the gardener Fancy engaged in touching the fruits of the earth into life. But he will also play the role of audience, of the one who seeks abroad to behold the creative goddess and sings hymns to her activity and her music.

In "Autumn," in his final understanding of the social function of art, Keats chooses nature and culture as the two poles of his symbolic system. He sees the work of the artist as the transformation of nature into culture, the transmutation of the teeming fields into garnered grain (the gleaning of the natural into books, as his earlier sonnet had described it). Since civilization itself arose from man's dominion over nature, the processing of nature by agriculture became the symbol in Greece of the most sacred mysteries. The vegetation goddess Demeter, with her sheaf of corn and her poppies, was honored in the Eleusinian rituals. And the two symbolic harvests, bread and wine, food and drink, remain transmuted even to this day in the Christian Eucharist.

Keats's "Autumn" ode takes as its allegory for art the making of nature into nurture. The artist, with reaping hook, gleaning basket, and cider press, denudes nature, we may say, but creates food. We cannot, so to speak, drink apples or eat wheat; we can only consume processed nature, apple juice and grain. Since the artist is his own teeming field, art, in this allegory, is a process of self-immolation. As life is processed into art by the gleaning pen or threshing flail, the artist's own life substance disappears, and where wheat was, only a stubble plain can be seen; but over the plain there rises a song. Song is produced by the steady rhythm of nature transmuted by self-sacrifice into culture. Art does not mimetically resemble nature, any more than cider mimetically resembles apples. But without apples there would be no cider; without life there would be no hieroglyphs of life. In this way, Keats insists again on the radically nonmimetic nature of art but yet argues for its intelligible relation to life in its representative symbolic order.

Keats is the audience for the artist-goddess's sacrifice of herself into food, as she passes from careless girl through ample maternity and into her own death vigil; when all the corn has been threshed, and all the apples pressed, she disappears; nature has become culture. As her beneficiary, Keats is full of an overflowing gratitude—for her generous omnipresence ("whoever seeks abroad / May find thee") and for her elegiac harmonies ("thou hast thy music too"). Her rhythms permeate the whole world until all visual, tactile, and kinetic presence is transubstantiated into Apollonian music for the ear.

We can now put Keats's view over against Heidegger's. Heidegger looks at the world and sees an absence; Keats looks at the world and sees, through the apparition of postharvest absence, a vision of past natural plenty—apples, nuts, grapevines, gourds, honey, and grain. For Keats, the task of the poet is to remember and re-create the immeasurable plenitude of the world and process it, by the pen, into something which draws from the sensual world but does not resemble it mimetically. The artist must find a charactery, or symbolic order, by which to turn presence into intellectual grain and cider, food and drink. The reaper's hook, the threshing flail, and the cider press are images of the mind at work, processing nature. The work of the mind in aesthetic production is not interrogative or proposition-making (as Keats had thought in the "Urn"), but rather "stationing"—composing symbolic items in a symbolic arrangement until that order bears an algebraic or indicative relation to the order of reality. Only in this way is a vision of reality made intelligible to other minds.

It is not by being a sage or a physician (two roles that appealed to Keats) that the artist produces his result in other minds; it is by his creation of symbolic equivalences arranged in a meaningful gestalt. Once the mind of the audience sees this vision of reality, this shadow of a magnitude, it shares its intelligibility, can "consume" it. The haphazard and unreadable texture of life becomes the interpreted and the stationed. We, as audience, may indeed find ourselves enlightened, solaced, or cured by art; but it cannot be the artist's chief *aim* to enlighten or solace or cure us; he must rather aim to transmute the natural into the hieroglyphic aesthetic, making his music part of a choral harmony contributed to by all his fellow artists. If his art is not music, it has not yet done its work of transsubstantiation but is still inert direct mimesis.

By putting the "airy voices" of his choir of creatures, and the "barred clouds," at the end of his ode, Keats places the imaginative (the quality he thought he might have to forfeit in his quest for reality and truth) in a harmonious relation to the natural. He thus displays the aesthetic principle of music as paramount over even the algebraic or symbolic principle of allegorical representation. Music resembles apples even less than cider does; and yet it is the music of autumn, which arises cotemporally with its transmutations and because of them, on which Keats insists as he closes his ode.

I believe that every poet of substance passes through a course of realization very like those of Keats. Judging from their juvenilia, artists all begin with an exquisite, almost painful, response to the beautiful, and an equal revulsion toward the ugly. In their youth, they often equate the tragic and the deformed with the ugly and attempt therefore to create an idyllic counterspace. This space is usually not a social one; at most it is occupied only by a narcissistically conceived other, the beloved. As soon as the social scene intrudes into the young artist's poetry—either in the form of history (mythological or actual) or in the form of current political or domestic struggle—the poem is forced into the world of human tragedy. This exemplary process leads to a new aesthetic, in which the dissonant, the mutable, and the ugly must find a place. Usually, a poet writes *about* such disagreeable subjects before he can write *within* them. Later, if the poet can do the requisite work of internalization and symbolizing, there comes the discovery of a virtual order, powerfully organized, through which the complex vision of tragic reality can express itself. The move into the symbolic order always angers those for whom the artist's duty is a historically mimetic one, and for whom the clarity of propaganda is preferable to the ambivalence of human response to the human world. "Art," Yeats said, "is but a vision of reality." In using the concessive "but" and the symbolic word "vision," Yeats argues for the algebraic or allegorical relation between art and reality. One who cannot recognize that algebraic relation, and bring it, by his own gaze, back into "swelling reality," is incompetent to read art.

Those poets who encounter particularly acute political stress, like Czesław Miłosz and Seamus Heaney, are always urged to be more socially specific in their poetry than poets can be. Poets resist this pressure by offering their own meditations of the social function of the artist, faced with the huge and varied questions of the world. Imagination, as Stevens says, presses back against the pressure of reality. I want to quote two poems, one by Miłosz, one by Heaney, which reaffirm the necessarily symbolic nature of the artist's work and yet repeat its equally necessary connection with social reality.

Miłosz's poem, "The Poor Poet," was written in Warsaw, in 1944, during the last horrors of the war. It recapitulates the passage that we have seen in the young poet from an aesthetic of joy to an aesthetic of tragedy; it is Modernist in its hatred of the mutually tormenting relation between the arranged symbolic order of art and the random tragic sense of life; and it sees the creating of the symbolic order as a form of revenge against the horrors of life. The poet as a man is deformed by the deformations he witnesses; and for all the beauty he creates he cannot himself be beautiful but must share the deformities of the world:

The Poor Poet

The first movement is singing,
A free voice, filling mountains and valleys.
The first movement is joy,
But it is taken away.

And now that the years have transformed my blood
And thousands of planetary systems have been born
     and died in my flesh,
I sit, a sly and angry poet
With malevolently squinted eyes,

And, weighing a pen in my hand,
I plot revenge.

I poise the pen and it puts forth twigs and leaves,
      it is covered with blossoms.
And the scent of that tree is impudent, for there,
      on the real earth,
Such trees do not grow, and like an insult
To suffering humanity is the scent of that tree.

Some take refuge in despair, which is sweet
Like strong tobacco, like a glass of vodka drunk
      in the hour of annihilation.
Others have the hope of fools, rosy as erotic
      dreams.

Still others find peace in the idolatry of country,
Which can last for a long time,
Although little longer than the nineteenth century
      lasts.

But to me a cynical hope is given,
For since I opened my eyes I have seen only the
      glow of fires, massacres,
Only injustice, humiliation, and the laughable
      shame of braggarts.
To me is given the hope of revenge on others
      and on myself.
For I was he who knew
And took from it no profit for myself.

Selected Poems (Ecco, 1980, 53–54)

Formally, this poem places its one moment of adult "beauty" in
one line, recounting the blossoming of the pen and alluding to
Aaron's rod. This Keatsian moment (with its promise of fruit to
come, following the blossoms), is encapsulated within Miłosz's two
mentions of revenge: "I plot revenge. . . . To me is given the hope
of revenge." It is also encapsulated within tragedy ("Joy . . . is taken
away") and the common responses to tragedy, whether despair,
hope, or idolatry. The poet's "cynical hope" is his penalty for his

creation of poetry, and his revenge is directed not only against others but against himself for daring to "insult" suffering humanity with the perfection of form. Miłosz's Manichaean spirit poses the problem of content and form in its most violent aspect, as the serenity of form (even here, in the concentric form of this lyric) tortures the anguish of content ("fires, massacres, . . . injustice, humiliation, . . . shame"). There can be, according to Miłosz, no political poetry that does not aim at the aesthetic equilibrium of form. Art, in its social function, thus enacts for us the paradox of our orderly symbolic capacity as it meets the disorder it symbolizes.

A poem by Seamus Heaney about Chekhov traces again the young poet's passage from sensuous pleasure to social obligation. The recognition of social obligation by the poet must pass, the poem suggests, not into social activism but rather into symbolic representation. In the poem, as in fact, Chekhov decides to leave his attractive life in Moscow to go to see the penal colony on the faraway island Sakhalin, off the east coast of Russia below Japan. Though Chekhov is a doctor, he does not go to Sakhalin to minister to the convicts, but rather to observe, and to write a book. He even forces himself to stay to watch a flogging in order to see the full reality of life in the colony. And then he has to find the right tone to write about what he has seen—"not tract, not thesis." Once he has admitted the colony to his consciousness, he will never be able to exorcise it; he will carry a second convict-self within him. The parallels with Northern Ireland need no describing; the poet has left Northern Ireland and lives in the Republic, but he writes about the reality he has left behind and must find a symbolic way to enact its truth.

Chekhov's biographer recounts that as he departed for Sakhalin, his friends came to see him off at the railway station and gave him a bottle of cognac to drink when he should have arrived (by rail and boat and troika) at Sakhalin, thousands of miles away. The cognac is Chekhov's last taste of uncomplicated sensual joy; henceforth he will be a symbolic convict:

Chekhov on Sakhalin

So, he would pay his "debt to medicine".
But first he drank cognac by the ocean

81

With his back to all he travelled north to face.
His head was swimming free as the troikas

Of Tyumin, he looked down from the rail
Of his thirty years and saw a mile
Into himself as if he were clear water:
Lake Baikhal from the deckrail of the steamer.

That far north, Siberia was south.
Should it have been an ulcer in the mouth,
The cognac that the Moscow literati
Packed off with him to a penal colony—

Him, born, you may say, under the counter?
At least that meant he knew its worth. No cantor
In full throat by the iconostasis
Got holier joy than he got from that glass

That shone and warmed like diamonds warming
On some pert young cleavage in a salon,
Inviolable and affronting.
He felt the glass go cold in the midnight sun.

When he staggered up and smashed it on the stones
It rang as clearly as the convict's chains
That haunted him. In the months to come
It rang on like the burden of his freedom

To try for the right tone—not tract, not thesis—
And walk away from floggings. He who thought to
     squeeze
His slave's blood out and waken the free man
Shadowed a convict guide through Sakhalin.

Station Island (Farrar, Straus, 1984)

Heaney's poem implies that the truest way to write about the condition of the poet in twentieth-century Ireland is to write about a nineteenth-century Russian incident. The indirection proper to art is reflected thematically here in the repudiation of religious tract and political thesis alike: Chekhov's book is detached, descriptive, the book of a novelist, not an evangelist or social reformer.

Heaney's formal insistence here on the suppression of Chekhov's audience enacts the one condition for socially effective art—that it be directed, not to the transformation of its putative audience, but to the transformation of the artist's own self. By acknowledging his own past as the grandson of a serf and the son of a grocer, Chekhov can enter the chains of the convict and write powerfully about them. At the same time, he drinks with full relish and intoxication the brandy of his Moscow self, before he turns to "all he travelled north to face." The self-transformation of Keats's goddess of the corn acknowledged a similar death in the self as the condition of an art that could nourish others.

In separate ways, Miłosz and Heaney have retraced the steps toward an analysis of art that we have seen in Keats. It is important to each of them to assert that poetry does perform a social function; it is equally important to them to remove it from a direct and journalistic mimesis. The poet witnesses, constructs, and records; but the creation of symbolic and musical form is the imperative, in the end, which he must serve if his witness is to be believed.

Marjorie Perloff

LUCENT AND INESCAPABLE RHYTHMS: METRICAL "CHOICE" AND HISTORICAL FORMATION

No good poetry is ever written
in a manner twenty years old.
—Ezra Pound

I

One of the most heated controversies concerning poetry today has to do with the question of "prose"—or what looks like "prose"—as a medium for poetry. In a recent book called *Poet's Prose: The Crisis in American Verse,* Stephen Fredman declares: "I have felt for a number of years that the most talented poets of my own postwar generation and an increasing number from previous generations have turned to prose as a form somehow most consonant with a creative figuration of our time"(1). Fredman proceeds to study the special kind of prose used by Williams in *Kora in Hell*, by Creeley in *Presences*, by Ashbery in *Three Poems*, and finally by such experimental contemporaries as David Antin and the younger Language Poets. At the same time, others have dismissed what we might call "the prose phenomenon" as merely beside the point. Denise Levertov, for example, sees the work of the Language Poets as no more than "re-hashed Gertrude Stein veneered with 70's semantics."[1]

In his *Free Verse: An Essay on Prosody* (1981), Charles O. Hartman takes what is surely the sensible position: he adopts Jeremy Bentham's practical definition that "when the lines run all the way to the right margin it is prose; when this fails to happen it is [verse]." Who can object to such good common sense? *"Verse,"* says Hartman, *"is language in lines.* This distinguishes it from prose. . . . This is not really a satisfying distinction, as it stands, but it is the only one that works absolutely. The fact that we can tell verse from prose on sight, with very few errors . . . indicates that the basic perceptual difference must be very simple. Only lineation fits the requirements"(11).

This definition is adequate enough if we bear in mind that it distinguishes between prose and *verse*, not between prose and *poetry*. But although Hartman himself does recognize that "'prose-poems' exist," most critics take the next step and equate poetry with verse, as Hartman defines it. Here is Richard A. Lanham's account in *Analyzing Prose* (1983):

> To print written utterance as prose amounts, in our time, to a funda-mental stylistic decision. In prose we expect not only a particular range of topics but a transparent style to express them clearly. . . . But with poetry, just the opposite—all the poetic virtues. The poet need not be grammatically correct, he'll talk about feeling not fact, and he'll do so in a self-conscious metaphorical way. We expect to look *through* prose, to the subject beneath, but *at* poetry where the language forms part of the subject. (79)

Lanham very sensibly points out that, as readers, we respond dif-ferently to the print format of "prose" than to that of "verse." But notice that the word "verse" is now, quite simply, replaced by the word "poetry," the implication being that the two are identical. It seems that, in a century in which "free verse" has largely super-seded all the traditional metrical forms, we must hold on to some-thing to give us a sense that poetry as a mode of discourse survives. Lineation, the creation of discourse that does not run all the way to the right margin, is the saving grace. Not that all lineated texts are good poems, but it is their status as lineated texts that allows them to be considered as poems in the first place.

So much for the common wisdom. A very different view is pre-sented in a monumental book called *Critique du Rythme: An-*

thropologie historique du Langage by the French Marxist poet-critic, Henri Meschonnic. The basic argument of this complex study is that "historically, poetically, and linguistically, the difference between forms of prose and verse are ones of degree, not of kind," and that, accordingly, all binary models (verse/prose; image-full language/non-image-full language; poetry as ordered language/prose as the absence of order; and so on) are wholly reductive. Even Bakhtin's famous distinction between lyric poetry as monologic, prose fiction as potentially dialogic, crumbles, so Meschonnic argues, when applied to, say, Pound's *Cantos* (448–55).

Meschonnic gives countless examples from around the world of discourse that may be construed as "prose" or "poetry," as the case may be. In the ninth century, the word *prose* was used to refer to a liturgical prose sequence structured by the assonance of *a*'s so as to prolong the sonority of the *Alleluia*. Eventually this *récitatif* was lineated and passed into the realm of "poetry." Or again, Boris Eikhenbaum, studying the "prose" of Gogol's *The Overcoat,* discovered that the ratio of accented syllables to total number of syllables was precisely that of contemporary iambic meter, as found in the poems of Mayakovsky.

Indeed, free verse à la Mayakovsky (a poet who echoed Pound in his declaration that "one must make verses with all of one's life and not by fishing for trochees and iambs") must, so Meschonnic argues, be construed historically. "Free verse is just a passage, a moment, not only of a cultural situation, but of the unity of discourse which contains it and which is the poem." For "it is the poem which makes the free-verse line, not the line which makes the poem" (Meschonnic, 605). Further, the prominence of free verse must be understood as part of the Modernist destabilization of the notion of the poem as object. But the poet is no more "free" vis-à-vis "free verse" than the seventeenth-century French poet was "free" vis-à-vis the alexandrine. These forms are, after all, inscribed by a particular culture; they are, so to speak, givens. As Anthony Easthope puts it, "Just as poetry is always a specific poetic discourse, so line organization [or nonlinear organization] always takes a specific historical form, and so is ideological" (24).

These are, I think, important reminders, for we tend to forget that the poet is, as Meschonnic puts it, inevitably "ventriloquized by his or her tradition." In this context, metrical choice becomes an important indicator of the historical and cultural formation in which it takes place. The question for us, as readers of contemporary poetry, is then not: "Is it a good thing for, say, Lyn Hejinian to have written *My Life* in prose?" but rather, "What does it mean that she chose to do so?"

What I propose to do here is to historicize this question by examining the status of four texts, each of which represents a particular moment in the history or, so to speak, the geography of poetic form: (1) Goethe's early Romantic lyric, "Wandrer's Nachtlied" ("Wanderer's Nightsong"), of 1780, (2) Rimbaud's prose poem "Les Ponts" ("The Bridges") of circa 1873, (3) Williams's 1916 free-verse poem, "Good Night," and (4) Beckett's 1972 composition called "Still." All four refer to what is roughly the same subject matter: a moment of silent contemplation when all the elements of the scene stand out in sudden sharp relief. But between Goethe's "Ruh" and Beckett's "Still" two centuries have intervened: by 1972, when Beckett was composing his text, the poet could not, in John Ashbery's words, "say it that way any more." How and why this is the case is my subject.

II

Goethe's "Wandrer's Nachtlied" ("Wanderer's Nightsong") was written on the night of 6 September 1780 in the mountains at Ilmenau above Weimar, where Goethe had accompanied his master, the young Duke Karl August. It was first recorded, evidently in a moment of inspiration, in pencil on the wall of the mountain hut on the Gickelhahn, where the poet spent the night. The same evening, Goethe wrote one of his nightly letters to his mistress Charlotte von Stein:

> On the Gickelhahn, the highest peak of the range . . . I have taken refuge, so as to escape from the turmoil of the town, the complaints, the demands, the hopeless confusion of mankind. If I could only record all the thoughts I have had today, there would be worthwhile things among them.
> My dearest, I descended into the Hermmansteiner Cave, to the place where you accompanied me, and found the S, which stands

> out as sharply as if it had been carved yesterday; I kissed it and kissed it so often that the porphyry seemed to give breath to the scent of the whole earth as if in response. I prayed to the hundred-headed god who has so greatly advanced and changed me and yet has preserved your love and this cliff for me, to let me continue to grow and to make me more worthy of your love.
>
> The sky is quite clear and I am going out to enjoy the sunset. The view is extensive but plain.
>
> The sun has set. It is the landscape of which I made a drawing for you when it was covered with rising mist. Now it is as clear and quiet as a large and beautiful Soul, at its calmest and most satisfied.
>
> If there weren't, here and there, some mists rising from the mines, the whole scene would be motionless.[2]

I shall come back to some key motifs in this letter in a moment. But first a few words about Goethe's situation in 1780. Let me remind you that the poet was twenty-six when he came to Weimar in 1775 at the invitation of the then eighteen-year-old duke. His attendance at the small court was a means of escape from the narrowly constricting life of Frankfurt and from his impending legal career.

The Weimar of the pre-Industrial period was a small walled Lutheran city of some seven thousand inhabitants, surrounded by the Thuringian forests and beyond these, the Harz Mountains. The city itself had neither modern amenities nor means of communication. The unpaved roads were unlit at night, there were no sewers, and coach travel was so precarious that Goethe and his friends generally traveled on horseback. When Frederick the Great died, the news did not reach his niece, the Dowager Duchess Amalia, until a week later. The court circle in what was a strictly stratified society spent its time in theatricals, skating parties, and balls; the model was the French Rococo court even though the Weimar version was much cruder, less sophisticated. In the evenings the writers-in-residence, like Von Knebel, Herder, and Goethe himself, might read to the company or entertain them with dramatic pieces.

In his early Weimar years, Goethe spent much time with the young duke on hunting trips and wild evening parties in the Harz Mountains. The pleasure-loving duke also had a real concern for his people, and one of his accomplishments was the reopening of the stagnant Ilmenau mines, to which the poet refers in his letter to his mistress. The Harz expeditions thus gave Goethe a chance to escape the social routine of Weimar and to dwell in what was still an unspoiled natural world. Yet even in the mountains there were difficult human problems to be encountered: the "turmoil of the town" to which Goethe refers in the letter is not that of Weimar but of the village of Ilmenau, where Goethe had to help the duke in various judicial and financial matters. The mountain retreat, moreover, kept the poet away from his adored mistress at a time when their affair was at its most intense: in this particular week he often wrote her two or three times a day.

This is the setting of the poem called "Wandrer's Nachtlied":

Über allen Gipfeln
Ist Ruh,
In allen Wipfeln
Spürest du
Kaum einen Hauch;
Die Vögelein schweigen im Walde.
Warte nur, balde
Ruhest du auch.

Above all the peaks
There is quiet,
In all the tree-tops
You feel
Hardly a breath;
The little birds keep silent in the forest.
Just wait, soon
You too shall rest.[3]

In this seemingly simple little song, which German schoolchildren learn by heart, the rhythm of recurrence is obviously predominant: the short, predominantly trochaic lines alternate masculine and feminine rhymes, and the vowel harmony of *u, a, i, u,* and the diphthongs *au* and *ei* creates an intricate echo structure, which is supported by the alliteration of liquids and nasals. "The Wanderer's Nightsong"—it might almost be a folk song.

But not quite. Goethe's poem presents a harmony marked by difference. The very rhyme scheme is irregular, the pattern of the first quatrain, *a b a b,* not being repeated by the second, *c d d c.* More importantly, the lines are uneven:

> Über allen Gipfeln
> Ist Ruh

where the falling rhythm of the first suspended line receives an answer from the single iamb of the second, the *u* sound being thus prolonged. The third line, "In allen Wipfeln," would be parallel to the first were it not foreshortened, and the fourth, "Spurest du," begins with a stress and surprisingly rhymes a pronoun with the noun "Ruh," the line being enjambed so that the reader must take a short breath before pronouncing the word "Kaum." The fifth line, "Kaum einen Hauch," is an amphibrach as is the eighth, "Ruhest du auch," which rhymes with it, although again the rhyming partners are different parts of speech. But the most peculiar echo effect is reserved for lines 6–7:

> Die Vögelein schweigen im Walde
> Warte nur,‖ balde

A nine-syllable line, predominantly dactylic, is complemented by the broken five-syllable line, the chiming "Walde"/"balde" being again suspended since meaning is deferred (what will happen "balde"?) until the final line.

The "nightsong" thus consists of a series of metrical suspensions and vocalic echoes that move toward the resolution of the final rhyme in one extended breath unit. The key to this echo structure is found, I think, in the use of the familiar second person: substitute "Spüre ich" for the fourth line or "Ruhe ich" in the eighth and the difference becomes clear. The "song" is the poet-wanderer's and he addresses himself, or is it Nature that addresses him, Nature that tells him, "Warte nur, balde / Ruhest du auch"? Or again, the use of "du" may imply that the wanderer's song is for everyone, for all those who find themselves, as he does, alone in the mountains preparing for the night's rest. The very birds are silent: "schweigen," a verb more properly applied to persons, suggests that the birds are part of the wanderer's world. And further, the syntax

90

points to a moment of future rest for mankind in general, perhaps to the final resting place.

Now consider the role in the poem of the speaking subject. The unnamed "I" here is presented as what is now called the transcendental ego; his account of what he sees and feels is authoritative, the implication being that it *is* possible to record such sensations as breathlessness and the absence of birdsong. Further, the "I" (or "you") is himself at one with the natural world; Nature, for Goethe, always wears the color of spirit or, in this case, the imprint of the hundred-headed god (Vishnu) to whom Goethe refers in the letter to his mistress. We do not need to inform ourselves about Goethe's botanic or anatomic studies, his gradually evolving nature philosophy, to see that here, as in the other poems of this period, the poet is positing the relation of the Many to the One, of microcosm to macrocosm, of the "I" to the "Other." In the letter, we recall, he speaks of kissing the porphyry stone in the cave until it seemed to give of the very breath of the earth; even so, the poet feels ("Spürest du") the slightest breath that emanates from the treetops. Again, in the letter, Goethe describes the landscape as a "large, beautiful soul at harmony with itself," an image conveyed in the poem by the very verse structure with its vowel harmonies and echoes.

Yet Goethe's is not an innocent vision of a harmonious universe. The cautionary imperative "Warte nur" ("Just wait") suggests that "Ruh" ("rest," "peace," "quiet") is not always possible, that the "Wandrer" is not always alone in his mountain retreat, that the silence is welcome precisely because it is not the norm. On the other side of the forest are the mines at Ilmenau and, beyond the mines, the descent into Weimar. Three days after writing "Wandrer's Nachtlied" and still in his mountain retreat near Ilmenau, Goethe writes Charlotte von Stein:

> This morning we had all the murderers, thieves, and smugglers brought forward and we questioned and confronted them all. At first I didn't want to go, since I shun that which is unclean. . . . (*Briefe,* 317)

In this context the "Wanderer's Nightsong" can be read as something of a prayer, a song of longing for escape from that which is unclean.

All these tensions are expressed in the sound structure of the poem. Goethe's central conviction that the landscape is man's natural habitat, his sense of himself as at once unique and yet representative, his view of poetry as the fruit of a particular experience, an experience to be "objectified" and universalized by purging it of the merely personal and by re-creating it in accord with fixed metrical laws—all these work naturally to create a text that calls attention to itself as a "poem," specifically a "song," by foregrounding sound repetition and stanzaic structure. The stress on the natural is an indirect comment on the artificialities of German Rococo poetry of the mid-eighteenth century; at the same time, Goethe's own lyric is, as I have argued, a sophisticated poem that reflects its author's social role and his manifold literary and scientific interests. The rhythm of recurrence is defamiliarized even as the very title, "Wandrer's Nachtlied," is self-conscious in its assumption of rusticity. For, despite its eventual popularity, Goethe's poem is hardly intended as a folk song to be recited or sung by the miners and peasants of Ilmenau. Rather, in what will be a characteristically Romantic gesture, "the natural" is transformed into "the poetic" by the equation of the "du" with the poem's reader and by the creation of a formal structure that enacts the "Ruh" of the opening line.

III

My second text, Rimbaud's prose poem "Les Ponts" ("The Bridges") was written in the early 1870s. We have no hard information about the circumstances of composition of the *Illuminations,* but Rimbaud's editors suggest that "Les Ponts" was inspired by a vision of London, which the poet had visited with Verlaine in the autumn of 1872 and again in the spring of 1873, before the fatal quarrel that led to Verlaine's shooting of Rimbaud (and two-year imprisonment) and to Rimbaud's famous renunciation of poetry at the age of nineteen (Bernard, liv–lxii).

The landscape of "Les Ponts" inevitably reflects a very different world from that of Goethe's Harz Mountains. For one thing, the relation of nature to the city had totally changed. Charleville, Rimbaud's birthplace near the Belgian border (and hence a battleground during the Franco-Prussian War) was a provincial and unattractive village. The child of small *propriétaires,* mean-spirited, narrow-minded, and pious Catholics, Rimbaud could hardly wait to escape to the City of Light. Yet the Paris of mid-century had become the locus of industrialization, poverty, and pollution as well as of art and culture. In one of his maxims, Goethe writes, "Nature: we are surrounded and wrapped about by her—unable to break loose from her"; by the time of the Paris Commune in 1870 (an event in which the sixteen-year-old Rimbaud participated), Nature had withdrawn in the face of what Engels called, with reference to London, "This colossal centralization, this heaping together of two and a half millions of human beings at one point . . . the hundreds of thousands of all classes and ranks crowding past each other. . . . The brutal indifference, the unfeeling isolation of each in his private interest" (239).

The dialectic of the urban and the natural is one of Baudelaire's great themes; for Rimbaud, however, the city becomes unreal, at once beautiful and ugly, mysterious and terrifying, a created world whose "reality" exists only in the self-sufficient language-field of the poem. It does not really matter, then, whether the site of "Les Ponts" is London Bridge, whether the "domes" are those of St. Paul, or whether the body of water, "as large as an arm of the sea," is the Thames. For in the semiabstract verbal composition which is "Les Ponts," all these locales shed their "realistic" identity. Here is the prose poem:

> Des ciels gris de cristal. Un bizarre dessin de ponts, ceux-ci droits, ceux-là bombés, d'autres descendant ou obliquant en angles sur les premiers, et ces figures se renouvelant dans les autres circuits éclairés due canal, mais tous tellement longs et légers que les rives, chargées de dômes, s'abaissent et s'amoindrissent. Quelques-uns de ces ponts sont encore chargés de masures. D'autres soutiennent des mâts, des signaux, de frêles parapets. Des accords mineurs se croisent et filent, des cordes montent des berges. On distingue une veste rouge, peut-être d'autres costumes et des instruments de musique. Sont-ce des airs populaires, des bouts de concerts seigneuriaux, des restant d'hymnes publics? L'eau est grise et bleue, large comme un bras de mer.—Un rayon blanc, tombant du haut du ciel, anéantit cette comédie.

> Crystal gray skies. A bizarre design of bridges, some straight, some arched, others descending or obliquing at angles to the first ones, and these figures renewed in the other lighted circuits of the canal, but all so long and light that the banks, laden with domes, sink and diminish. Some of these bridges are still encumbered with hovels. Others support masts, signals, frail parapets. Minor chords criss-cross and flow away, ropes rise from the banks. One makes out a red jacket, perhaps other costumes and musical instruments. Are these popular airs, scraps of manorial concerts, remnants of public hymns? The water is gray and blue, wide as an arm of the sea.—A white ray, falling from the top of the sky, annihilates this comedy.[4]

I have discussed, in *The Poetics of Indeterminacy* (Perloff 1981, Ch. 2), the semantic undecidability of Rimbaud's prose poems, the contradictory connotations of images and word groups that make it all but impossible to specify what it is that is being described. Here, therefore, let me merely point to such particulars as the instability of the angle of vision from which this scene is recorded. Such phrases as "on distingue" ("one makes out") or "peut-être" ("perhaps") imply that the speaker is trying to report faithfully what it is he sees. But the "bizarre design of bridges," at once advancing and receding, is all but impossible to locate in space. The reference to "masures" ("hovels"), for example, suggests that the observer is close to a particular bridge; yet the references to crystal gray skies, the "design" of arches and angles, and to the "rives chargées de dômes" ("banks, laden with domes"), place him at a great distance. The landscape, for that matter, is less that of reality than of a work of art, a proto-Cubist painting, say, by Marin, even as phrases like "accords mineurs" ("minor chords") suggest a musical composition.

The theatrical scene, in any case, dissolves when "Un rayon blanc, tombant du haut du ciel, anéantit cette comédie" ("A white ray, falling from the top of the sky, annihilates this comedy"). The magical landscape of curves and domes, frail parapets and hovels, crisscrossed by minor chords and scraps of manorial concerts, collapses in a lightning flash; the vision or waking dream is over.

But why did Rimbaud choose to present these visions, these "illuminations," in the form of the prose poem? Again, the verse form must be understood intertextually. If the rules of French versification were not as rigid as they are, the nineteenth-century prose poem, whose first great exemplar is found in Baudelaire's *Spleen de Paris,* might not have come into being. As stress-languages, English and German allow for great flexibility in the formation of lines; the French alexandrine, however, is based on syllable count, and so effective versification becomes a matter of observing certain norms: the caesura dividing the two hemistichs, the avoidance of hiatus, the alternation of masculine and feminine rhymes, and so on.

In his early poetry, Rimbaud, like Baudelaire before him, observed these rules carefully: LeRoy Breunig cites the lines:

> La chambre est pleine d'ombre; on entend vaguement
> De deux enfants le triste et doux chuchotement, . . .

where the first-line caesura follows "ombre" and the twelve-syllable count includes the mute *e*'s of "pleine" and "vaguement" but not of "ombre," which is followed by a vowel. Beginning with "Le Dormeur du val," however, Rimbaud, as Breunig has shown, began to dismember the alexandrine by introducing repeated enjambments and misplaced caesuras and by ignoring the prescribed alternation of rhymes. By the time of "Mémoire" and "Ô Saisons, ô châteaux," his poems were barely recognizable as verse, so that the "leap into prose" was a logical, indeed, almost an imperceptible step (7–11).

Rimbaud's prose poems should not, however, be construed as emblematic of the poet's renunciation of lyric. If the poet substitutes linear progression for the rhythm of recurrence provided by meter and rhyme, his formal structure is nevertheless "free" only vis-à-vis "les premiers romantiques" like Lamartine and especially Musset, whose work is dismissed in the "Lettres du Voyant" of 1871: "Musset is fourteen times loathsome to us. . . . O! the insipid tales and proverbs! O the *Nuits O Rolla*. . . . it is all French, namely detestable to the highest degree; French, not Parisian!"[5] Not Parisian, which is to say not like the first great Parisian poet, Baudelaire, "the first seer, king of poets, *a real god!*" And yet Baudelaire too is criticized for having lived in "too artistic a milieu" and for lacking the courage to invent new forms.

The "Lettres du Voyant" were written by a provincial seventeen-year-old "paysan" who fought to clear a poetic space for himself, to escape from the anxiety of influence by being more Parisian than the sophisticated Parisian dandy, Baudelaire. "Trouver une langue" ("To find a language") in this context meant to write a prose poem, not narrative or parabolic like Baudelaire's, but visionary.

"Prose" was, moreover, in Rimbaud's day the vehicle for patient and "realistic" description—one thinks immediately of the prose of Flaubert. To present the visionary, the magical, the artificial in prose was thus to explode the medium in a way that suited the young poet's need to shock, to be outrageous. And indeed one starts to read a text like "Les Ponts" with the expectations that it will provide a "picture" of something. "Des ciels gris de cristal"—the noun phrase promises a kind of exposition, a coherent visual image, that the text will purposely deflate. Not that the syntax is unusual: the typical unit is the simple declarative sentence: "D'autres soutiennent des mâts, des signaux, de frêles parapets" ("Others support masts, signals, frail parapets"). But within these "normal" syntactic slots, we find references that make no sense: what riverbanks, for example, are "laden with domes"?

Yet—and this is the curious aspect of Rimbaud's prosody—the *Illuminations* don't really violate the norms of nineteenth-century lyric. As Albert Sonnenfeld puts it:

> It would be plausible and tempting to deduce that the prose poem would, as the enactment of freedom from the formal constraints of prosody, aver itself as resolutely antiteleological or anticlosural. . . . But . . . the *prose poem,* though it may have thrown off the shackles of a caducous tradition of rhyme and meter, is formally a profoundly conservative and traditional structure in its ceremonials of entrance and exit; that no matter how radical its content, how relentless its striving for apparent or real incoherence, the prose poem undergoes the secondary elaboration of syntactical coherence and its boundaries most often are clearly defined and marked. (200–201)

This is an important point. The meaning of the poet's vision in "Les Ponts" may be undecidable, but formally, the syntactically ordered series of sentences ends with the strongly closural statement: "Un rayon blanc, tombant du haut du ciel, anéantit cette comédie." Those who know the *Illuminations* will recognize this as a typical ending: "Aube" ("Dawn") ends with the sentence "Au reveil il était midi" ("At waking, it was noon"), "Nocturne vulgaire," with "Un souffle disperse les limites du foyer" ("One breath disperses the limits of the hearth"), and "Parade," with the assertion, "J'ai seul la clef de cette parade sauvage" ("I alone have the key for this wild show").

What does this drive toward syntactical coherence and closure tell us? The Rimbaldian prose poem, we might say, is still governed by Romantic and Symbolist norms in that it posits: (1) that poetic language is inherently different from "ordinary" language; (2) that a poem is the site of lyric vision, of the sacred moment; and (3) that a "poem," whether in verse or in prose, is a framed discourse, an object separable and distinct from the encroaching discourses that surround it. In Michel Beaujour's words, "A prose poem is a text where the verse density approaches that of regular metrical forms, while eschewing the anaphoric servitudes of prosody." Its insistence on "an absolute distinction between journalistic cacography and artful writing is purely ideological and does not stand up to linguistic and rhetorical scrutiny: it is all a question of taste, and should ideology so decree, *bad* taste might become axiological king of the castle" (55–56).

Both Sonnenfeld and Beaujour suggest that the nineteenth-century French prose poem was thus a more conservative form than it is generally held to be, conservative, at least, when read in the light of such later developments as Dada. Perhaps it would be fairer to say that Rimbaud's brilliant prose poetry, revolutionary as it conceives itself to be, and as it is with respect to its ways of signifying, also bears the inscription of the culture in which it was created, a culture that no longer looks to Nature as the guardian of its soul, and for whom Art is, accordingly, as distinct from Life as possible. The poem, in other words, is regarded as an artifact, whether it is written in the dense verse of the *Symbolistes* or in prose. It was the free-verse poetry of Apollinaire and Cendrars, of Pound and Williams, of Mayakovsky and Klebnikhov that was to challenge this "object" status.

IV

Williams was thirty years old when he began, primarily under the influence of Pound, to write in free verse, but he seems never to have quite understood his own composing processes. In 1913, when the Imagist movement was at its height, he wrote an essay called "Speech Rhythm," in which he insisted:

> I do not believe in *vers libre,* this contradiction in terms. Either the motion continues or it does not continue, either there is rhythm or no rhythm. *Vers libre* is prose. In the hands of Whitman it was a good tool. . . . [He] did all that was necessary with it. . . .
>
> Each piece of work, rhythmic in whole, is then in essence an assembly of tides, waves, ripples. . . . for me the unit is of a convenient length, such as may be appreciated at one stroke of the attention. . . .
>
> The rhythm unit is simply any repeated sequence of lengths and heights. Upon this ether the sounds are strung in their variety. . . .[6]

Here we must read between the lines, or I should say, the sentences. *Vers libre* was a term first used by Gustave Kahn and his Symbolist cenacle in the 1880s; the early *vers librists,* such as Kahn himself, Jules Laforgue, Jean Moreas, and Henri de Regnier, wrote a slow, stately verse, characterized by phrasal and clausal repetition and heavily end-stopped lines. It is this form of free verse that was adopted by the British Imagists of the 1910s, a form undoubtedly too formal, too restrained, and too "foreign" for a poet like Williams, whose verse was to be more fluid, its "waves" and "ripples" being less a matter of sound repetition or even of speech rhythm than of sight. "Stanzas you can't quite *hear,"* as Hugh Kenner put it (58). Here is the first such stanza of a poem called "Good Night," originally published in the New York magazine *Others* in 1916:

> In brilliant gas light
> I turn the kitchen spigot
> and watch the water plash
> into the clean white sink.
> On the grooved drain-board
> to one side is
> a glass filled with parsley—
> crisped green.
>   Waiting
> for the water to freshen—
> I glance at the spotless floor—:
> a pair of rubber sandals

lie side by side
under the wall-table
all is in order for the night.

[*Poems,* 145–46]

Since this poem is paradigmatic of so much that is to come in American poetry, its verse form demands careful attention. First, there is no rhyme scheme or stanzaic structure, no fixed stress or syllable count. The stresses range between one ("Waiting") and four ("into the clean white sink"), the syllables between two ("Waiting," "crisped green") and eight ("all is in order for the night"). By definition, then, "Good Night" is written in free verse, however much Williams may have protested against the term.

What is the ideology reflected in Williams's choice of free verse? Commenting on "Good Night," Allen Ginsberg remarks:

> The mundaneness is interesting, to me, because it sees so clearly that it becomes crisp in meaning, still and shining. The water glass suddenly is a totemic object. It becomes a symbol of itself, of his investment in his attention in that object. . . . Because he sees it so clearly, he notices . . . what's particular about the object that could be written down in a word—he sees the object without association. That's characteristic of visionary moments. . . . You are not superimposing another idea or another image on the image that's already there. (36)

Direct treatment of the thing, the absence of imposed symbolism, the act of attention that perceives the radiance in even the most mundane of objects—these are qualities everyone has noted in Williams's poetry, but an account like Ginsberg's does not tell the whole story. As a genuinely democratic American poet, a physician in contact with the daily life of a lower-class ethnic community, Williams obviously focuses, as no poet had since Whitman, on the everyday, the seemingly trivial, the communal, and as such, the argument usually goes, he had to cast off the shackles of conventional metrical forms—forms he himself used in his earliest poetry—and invent a form that is "free," "natural," and capacious.

The problem with this argument is that Williams's poetry is not, in fact, natural and lifelike. Try, for example, to imagine an occasion when someone would say:

> In brilliant gas light I turn the kitchen spigot and watch the water
> plash into the clean white sink. On the grooved drain-board to one
> side is a glass filled with parsley, crisped green.

To whom would one say this and in what voice? Hugh Kenner is
surely right when he says, of the related poem, "The Red Wheelbarrow," "Not only is what the sentence says banal, if you heard someone say it you'd wince. But hammered on the typewriter into a
thing made, and this without displacing a single word except ty-
pographically, the . . . words exist in a different zone altogether"
(60).

"Hammered on the typewriter"—this, I think, is the key to
Williams's prosody: "A poem," as he puts it in the preface to *The
Wedge,* is "a small (or large) machine made of words" (*Essays,* 256).
Here Williams gives voice to a poetic that owes much to the avant-
garde artists, many of them expatriates, who came to New York
during the war. I have suggested elsewhere (Perloff 1983, 86) that
Picabia's "machine drawings" for *Camera Work* and *291*—for example, his witty homage to Stieglitz *(Ici C'est Ici Stieglitz / Foi et
Amour)*—are in many ways the visual counterparts of Williams's
poems, in that ordinary objects like cameras and spark plugs are
transformed into semiabstract, simplified geometric forms having
an erotic life of their own. Again, Williams's minimal poems like
"The Red Wheelbarrow" and the later "Between Walls" have much
in common with Duchamp's *Readymades:* in both cases it is a
matter of lifting the saying out of the zone of things said, of framing
the given object, glass of water or snow shovel, rubber sandals or
bird cage, in a new way.

Such "framing" or re-presenting has everything to do with the
technology of the early century: Williams is one of the first poets to
have composed directly on the typewriter (often in moments
snatched between patients); but the typewriter is only a small part
of the technology that includes the automobile (which figures in so
many of Williams's poems), the airplane, the telephone ("They call
me and I go"), the billboard, the newspaper headline. That technology was a threat to the environment—a frequent theme in
Williams—doesn't change the fact that the actual composition and
dissemination of the poetic text itself could now become tech-
nologized, a process that has gone much further in our own time as

a result of tape recordings, Xerox machines, computer printouts, video screens, and so on.

The immediate impact of technology on the Williams of 1916, in any case, was a new form of typography and lineation. In the case of "Good Night," it is lineation rather than the pattern of stresses that guides the reader's eyes so that objects stand out, one by one, as in a series of film shots: first the gas light, then the spigot, then the plash of water, and finally the "clean white sink" itself. The eye moves slowly so as to take in each monosyllable (all but four of the nineteen words in the first four lines, all but twelve of the sixty-seven words in the whole verse paragraph): *in, gas, light, turn, the, and, watch.* . . . The sixth line is suspended: it asks, What is it that is located "to one side"? The next line tells us: "A glass filled with parsley—." But what does the parsley look and feel like? Again a new line:

> crispéd gréen.

Next there is a wait as the water runs from the tap, and so "Waiting" gets a line to itself and a prominent line at that because it is moved over toward the jagged right margin of the poem. Notice that the poem would *sound* exactly the same if "Waiting" were aligned with "crisped" and "for" at the left margin; the effect, in other words, is entirely visual. And again, the ensuing lines are characterized by suspension: a "pair of rubber sandals" (line 12) do what? They "lie side by side" (line 13). But where?

> únder the wáll-táble . . .

As in Picabia's drawings, everyday objects are here granted a curious sexual power: the "pair of rubber sandals . . . / under the wall-table" anticipating the final line of the poem, "I am ready for bed." And yet the poet's separateness is stressed: he does not participate in the life of the young girls seen earlier that evening at the opera, the girls described in stanza 2 as "full of smells and / the rustling sounds of / cloth rubbing on cloth and / little slippers on carpet." Rather, like the "Parsley in a glass, / still and shining," he "yawn[s] deliciously" to himself, knowing that he will be alone in bed.

Indeed, there is nothing inherently free about this natural free-verse poem, which is less a vision of the mundane-turned-radiant than the creation of a field of force, set in motion by the poet's desire. Thus the sounds of the poem do not quite chime: "light" in line 1 receives what is almost a response from "spigot" in the next line, and when the full response comes in the "white" of line 4, the rhyme is internal, its harmony offset by the next word, "sink." Again, vowel repetition is something of a tease, visual chiming not always being matched by aural equivalence. The letter *i,* for example, appears ten times in the nineteen words of the first sentence, but the phoneme may be /i/ or /ay/ or even a /y/ glide as in the second syllable of "brilliant." Still, if one waits long enough, the "brilliant gas light" of the opening line is greeted by the rhyme of "night" in line 15. Each line, for that matter, waits for its fulfillment from the next, with "Waiting," coming, as it does, after "crisped green," exerting the central pull. When, at the end of the poem, the parsley image recurs:

> Parsley in a glass,
> still and shining,
> brings me back—

it is treated to characteristic Williams deflation: being "brought back" is one thing, but life goes on:

> I take a drink
> and yawn deliciously.
> I am ready for bed.

And of course that's what the title has told us to begin with. "It isn't what [the poet] *says* that counts as a work of art, it's what he makes, with such intensity of perception . . ." (*Essays,* 257). "Good Night" is, in the best sense, a small machine made of words.

V

Williams's poetry did not gain a wide readership until the last decade or so of his life. Since then, it has become increasingly popular even as, ironically enough, the drive that brought into being Williams's marvelous "suspension-systems" had lost much of its force. A second world war, a growing distrust of technology, as well as the public acceptance of free verse as, quite simply, *the* poetic form of the dominant culture, meant that defamiliarization had to come from new sources. In the later nineteenth century, the chief "renewing" source was, I have argued, prose—the prose of novelists like Stendhal and Flaubert—that Modernists from Rimbaud to Lowell called upon as a source of inspiration. A hundred years later, a similar turn toward prose has occurred, but the "prose" in question is less that of the novel (a form also put in question) than that of philosophy. By the early seventies, American students were eagerly citing Heidegger's definition of poetic speech:

> The more poetic a poet is—the freer (that is the more open and ready for the unforeseen) his saying—the greater is the purity with which he submits what he says to an ever more painstaking listening, and the further what he says is from the mere propositional statement that is dealt with solely in regard to its correctness or incorrectness. (216)

In equating the "poetic" with a mode of receptive listening and active speaking, rather than with any formal features, Heidegger paves the way for a notion of "poeticalness" that regards genre and, by extension, the question of meter and lineation, as irrelevancies. From the standpoint of poststructuralist theory, poetry is no longer any one thing (the lyric, the language of tropes, metered language, and so on) but rather that species of *writing* that foregrounds and insists upon the materiality of the signifier, the coincidence between enunciation and enounced.[7]

Such coincidence cannot be achieved, so the argument goes, by imposing on language an abstract pattern like the iambic pentameter. But since free verse has itself become conventionalized and subject to a number of abstract paradigms, the "rhythm of recurrence" has reared its head in new guises. Consider Beckett's short texts, known as "residua" (his own term), or "lyrics of fiction" (Ruby Cohn's), or "monologues," or, perhaps most commonly, "pieces."[8] Here is the opening page of *Still* written in 1974 for William Hayter, who illustrated it with a series of etchings (see figure) and printed the verbal-visual text in his celebrated Atelier 17 in Paris.

> Bright at last close of a dark day the sun shines out at last and goes down. Sitting quite still at valley window normally turn head now and see it the sun low in the southwest sinking. Even get up certain moods and go stand by western window quite still watching it sink and then the afterglow. Always quite still some reason some time past this hour at open window facing south in small upright wicker chair with armrests. Eyes stare out unseeing till first movement some time past close though unseeing still while still light. Quite still again then all quite quiet apparently till eyes open again while still light though less. Normally turn head now ninety degrees to watch sun which if already gone then fading afterglow. Even get up certain moods and go stand by western window till quite dark and even some evenings some reason long after. Eyes then open again while still light and close again in what if not quite a single movement almost. Quite still again then at open window facing south over the valley in this wicker chair though actually close inspection not still at all but trembling all over. Close inspection namely detail by detail all over to add up finally to this whole not still at all but trembling all over.[9]

This is approximately a third of the single seamless paragraph which is *Still,* a paragraph that culminates with the sentence, "Leave it so all quite still or try listening to the sounds all quite still head in hand listening for a sound." From "still" to "sound"—how does Beckett's text proceed and how shall we characterize it?

We may note, to begin with, that Beckett's syntactic units are not, properly speaking, "sentences" at all. Practically speaking, we associate the sentence with a model of wholeness and completeness. The typical sentence, so to speak, enacts a plot: "Pass the sugar, please!" or "We were in class when the headmaster came in, followed by a new boy, not wearing the school uniform, and a school servant carrying a large desk" *(Madame Bovary)*. The sentence, says Stephen Fredman commonsensically, "is a primary unit of writing whose purpose is to organize language and thought upon a page. . . . The period posits closure to a string of words; it asks us to regard the words between itself and the preceding period as a unit" (29–30). Thus the opening sentence of *Madame Bovary*, which I

Etching by William Hayter for Samuel Beckett's *Still*, 1974.
(Courtesy of Humanities Research Center, Austin, Texas)

quoted above, is followed by the second sentence, "Those who had been asleep woke up, and everyone rose as if just surprised at his work." Indeed, a unit.

But now look at the first two sentences of *Still*:

> Bright at last close of a dark day the sun shines out at last and goes down. Sitting quite still at valley window normally turn head now and see it the sun low in the southwest sinking.

When this is read aloud (and I have heard it read by the actor Alec McGowran), it sounds like this:

> Bright at last
> close of a dark day
> the sun shines out at last and goes down.
> Sitting quite still at valley window
> normally turn head now and see it
> the sun low in the southwest sinking.

The unit of rhythm here and throughout *Still* is a short phrase of irregular length and primitive syntax ("normally turn head now and see it"), a phrase heavily accented, discontinuous, and repetitive—a kind of shorthand by means of which the human consciousness tries to articulate what it perceives and remembers. Indeed, this version of what Henri Meschonnic calls the "third rhythm" is no closer to prose than to verse: "The prose of the poem moves in a direction that is, despite all appearances, the opposite of the prose poem. The prose of the poem . . . is the *mise à nu* of the subjective character of rhythm, the rapport between the rhythm of discourse and the speaking subject" (610–11).

This is not to say that the "third rhythm" is another name for the stream of consciousness. In the twenty-one-line unit before us, the word "still" appears eleven times in a complex series of permutations: "quite still" (three times), then "unseeing still while still light" (where the monosyllabic word can be adjective ["silent," "motionless"] or adverb ["yet"]), then "Quite still again," and so on. At the same time the secondary words gradually become nodal points, as when "Quite still again" modulates into "quite quiet apparently," or "Eyes that open again while still light" becomes "Quite still again then at open window."

But further, *Still* is, in Enoch Brater's words, "a verbal journey in disorienting repetition highlighting inversion, opposition, and indeterminacy" (8). That which is "still" is "not still at all" or "trembling all over." Or again, we meet the oppositions "see"/"unseeing," "rise"/"fall," "far"/"near," "western"/"eastern," "sunrise"/"sunset," "quite"/"not quite," and so on. Verbal slippage is likely to turn "quite" into "quiet," "end of rests" into "rest on ends," "quiet still" into "till quite." "Stillness," in other words, is anything but "still": everything in this text moves, shifts, changes before our very eyes.

But *Still* is by no means an exercise in abstraction. It is "about" a person sitting at a window, who watches the sun set. The figure has no gender designation, but there are references to eyes, a skull, head, cheekbone, nape, breast, forearms, arms, elbow, hands, thumb, index, fingers, trunk, knees, and legs. But there is no indication of how these "spare parts" relate to one another or to the body in the "small upright wicker chair with armrests" to which they presumably belong. As in Hayter's illustration, the figure's position is viewed mathematically rather than in human, let alone individual, terms. We know only that, in the course of the narrative, it is becoming darker (though not dark) and that the "right hand" is finally raised in a motion that seems to mimic the circle of the sun "till elbow meeting armrest brings this last movement to an end and all still once more."

But whose is the voice that tells us these things? The text gives us contradictory signals. "Bright at last close of a dark day the sun shines out at last and goes down": the voice that utters these words is not identifiable; it could be that of the figure in the wicker chair or that of a companion or again of an impersonal narrator. In the next sentence, "normally turn head now" suggests that the speaker is the person in the chair, but "Always quite still some reason" (sentence 3) implies the opposite in that the reason is not known. In sentence 4, the phrase "Eyes stare out unseeing till first movement" positions the observer outside the subject of the discourse, as does "quite quiet apparently" in the next sentence. But the angle of vision continues to shift: there is, in fact, no identifiable narrator, no transcendental ego who can bring these disparate references together for us.

In "Wandrer's Nachtlied," we find an "I" aware of itself and of its feelings, a coherent "I" in control of the situation. When the poet, that is to say, declares "Die Vogelein schweigen im Walde," the reader accepts the statement as valid, given the particular context of the speech. In Rimbaud's "Les Ponts," the relationship between "I" and "other" becomes more problematic: it is not clear, say, whether the minor chords that crisscross and flow away are *outside* the self or are part of its mental landscape. This disappearance of the distinction between subject and object is equally marked in Williams's "Good Night," in whose field of copresence, the "I" and the sprig of parsley in the glass become one.[10] But in Beckett's *Still,* the question of copresence gives way to a doubt as to the very existence of a unitary represented speaker. The inflections of the speaking voice, coming to us in short repetitive phrases, each permutating what has come before, give us no hint as to a controlling presence. To whom, for example, do we attribute the words, "Arms likwise broken right angles at the elbows"? To the narrator? The person in the chair? Or are they one and the same? Under such circumstances, the subject position, no longer granted to an identifiable or consistent speaker, can only be assumed by the reader.

In this context, we can see more clearly the function of the "third rhythm" in this and related texts. *Still* is a single paragraph because for Beckett there is no separation between different voices or different levels of discourse. Beckett's composition cannot avail itself of such imposed patterns as meter or stanzaic structure; even lineation may seem too restrictive a device, although the fact is that many poems that make use of the associative or third rhythm are lineated: the "prosaic" rhythms of John Ashbery, not essentially different from the rhythms of his prose work, *Three Poems,* are a case in point. Consider the following examples:

1. It was only much later that the qualities of the incandescent period became apparent, and by then it had been dead for many years. But in recalling itself it assumed its first real life. That time was for living without the reflection that gives things and objects a certain relief, or weight; one drank the rapture of unlived moments and it blinded one to how it looked from outside. . . .

2. All that we see is penetrated by it—
   The distant treetops with their steeple (so
   Innocent), the stair, the windows' fixed flashing—
   Pierced full of holes by the evil that is not evil,
   The romance that is not mysterious, the life that is not life,
   A present that is elsewhere.

The first passage comes from Ashbery's *Three Poems* (38); the second is the opening stanza of the title poem of *As We Know* (74). Both deal with the nameless "it" that haunts our experience, the privileged moment that we await even as we doubt that it exists. The first passage is in prose; the second in a purposely "prosaic" free verse, the rhythms almost coalescing into blank verse in line 2, only to be dispersed, by the time we reach line 5, into a kind of poulter's rhythm carried through sixteen syllables. Indeed, the "verse" of "As We Know" is surely closer to the "prose" of *Three Poems* than it is, say, to the verse of Williams's "Good Night," not to mention Goethe's "Wandrer's Nachtlied." To articulate a line like:

All that we sée is pénetráted bý ít —

with its clumsy shift, in the sixth syllable, from iamb to trochee and then back again, is to imply that a larger harmony is no longer a meaningful possibility. The same "point" is made in Charles Bernstein's "The Klupzy Girl":

> Poetry is like a swoon, with this difference:
> it brings you to your senses. Yet his
> parables are not singular. The smoke from
> the boat causes the men to joke. Not
> gymnastic: pyrotechnic.
> [47]

Not pretty, we might paraphrase this, ugly, with the line being a yardstick produced only to violate it.

It is one of the ironies of contemporary poetic discourse that the associative rhythm, the rhythm derived from speech, should become pervasive at the very moment when poets like Beckett and Ashbery, and especially the Language Poets like Bernstein, are positing what we might call the absence of the pronoun, at the moment when it is often impossible to decide whether the speaker is a "he" or an "I" or a "you," much less what that "I" or "you" might be like. Perhaps it is the poet's sense that, at a time when the spoken and written word are more pervasive than ever, when our visual fields are bombarded by billboards and manuals, and our aural fields by overheard snatches of conversation and catchy TV jingles, the individual voice can no longer be In Charge. Rather, the text

109

gives the impression that the story is telling itself, that it is available for communal use—a kind of score that we endow with meaning by "speaking it" ourselves.

Here an anecdote is apposite. In October 1969, when the Nobel Committee awarded Beckett that year's prize, the writer and his wife were vacationing in the tiny Tunisian village of Nabeul. Before they could be located, a frantic editor of a Norwegian situation was not much better in Paris, where many reporters could not even find Beckett's address. While this scramble for news was going on, heavy rainstorms in Tunisia cut off the ocean village from the desert mainland. In the French press, Beckett was accordingly dubbed "un inconnu célèbre" (Bair, 606–607).

"Un inconnu célèbre." The Unnamable is a far cry from the Goethe of 1780 who explains to Charlotte von Stein the precise thoughts and feelings that animate his poems, poems that will be read, in Weimar and beyond, as versions of his own life. Yet just as Goethean lyric gives expression to a particular view of natural process, so Beckett's *Still* employs a rigorous structure of sound repetitions and permutations that convey the tension between "still" and "trembling all over," between silence and the awaited sound, between the short *i* of "still" and the long *i* of "light," as in the construction "unseeing still while still light." Or consider the following chains found in the first five sentences alone:

> br*i*ght—sh*i*nes—qu*i*te—upr*i*ght—*ey*es—wh*i*le—l*i*ght
> la*st*—*st*ill—*st*and—*st*ill—pa*st*—armre*st*s—*st*are—pa*st*
> close—goes—go—low—afterglow—open—close
> s*itt*ing—st*i*ll—*i*t—w*i*ndow—st*i*ll—*i*t—st*i*ll—*i*n—w*i*ndow—
> w*i*cker—t*i*ll—st*i*ll—st*i*ll

This chiming continues throughout the text. Indeed, at the climactic moment when the hand of the unknown person is raised in the air, Beckett introduces what can be transcribed as two lines of blank verse:

> till midway tó the héad it hésitátes
> and hángs hãlf ópen trémbling in mĩd air.

But no sooner are we lulled by the familiar meter, than it is replaced by the choppy rhythms of:

> Hangs there
> as if half inclined to return
> that is
> sink back slowly . . .

and then by the sober scientific discourse of "thumb on outer edge of right socket index ditto left and middle on left cheekbone." Only when we come to the end of the text, do we realize that we have, all along, been "listening ["list—" is an anagram for "still"] for a sound"—a sound we can only imagine because none has been described in the text.

Beckett's principle of exclusion is thus rigorous: no colors, no dialogue, no specifiers, no identifiable sounds. Perhaps for that very reason, the final statement of desire comes across as deeply poignant:

> Leave it so
> all quite still
> or try listening to the sounds
> all quite still
> head in hand
> listening for a sound.

"The same sound," to paraphrase Stevens, "in the same bare place." Isn't Beckett's "song," after all, a late twentieth-century version of:

> Die Vögelein schweigen im Walde.
> Warte nur, balde
> Ruhest du auch?

Yes and no. Yes, in the sense that there are, of course, no new "subjects," only the old subjects rendered in new ways. But to call a poem a new "version" of an earlier one is also to admit that it has become something else. In the late twentieth century, to write, say, a straightforward "Ubi sunt" poem on the medieval model is hardly an available option, even as poets will continue to spin ironic and parodic fantasies on this time-honored topos.

By the same token, we must realize that the choice of verse form is not just a matter of individual preference, a personal decision to render a particular experience as a sonnet rather than a ballad, a prose poem rather than a free-verse lyric, and so on. For the pool of verse and prose alternatives available to the poet at any given time has already been determined, at least in part, by historical and ideological considerations. "A mythology," as Stevens put it, "reflects its region."

NOTES

1. Unpublished letter to Stanford University English Department, Stanford, California, March 1984.

2. See *Briefe,* Vol. 1, 314–15. Translation here and of the poetry is mine. Of the countless Goethe biographies, the English-speaking reader may find especially interesting George Henry Lewes, *The Life of Goethe,* 3d. ed. (London: Smith, Elder & Co., 1875).

3. *Werke,* Vol. 1, 59. Note that this is the second of two short lyrics by the same title. The earlier one (1776) has the opening line, "Der du von dem Himmel bist."

4. *Oeuvres,* ed. Bernard, 273. The translation used is Edward J. Ahearn's: see *Rimbaud,* 322, as well as the interesting commentary on 323.

5. The "Lettres du Voyant" are (1) letter to Georges Izambard, 13 May 1871; and (2) letter to Paul Démeny, 15 May 1871. They appear with facing English translations in Rimbaud, *Complete Works,* ed. Fowlie, 302–11.

6. The essay was submitted to *Poetry* in 1913, but Harriet Monroe returned it as incomprehensible. The text is cited in Weaver, 82–83.

7. See, on this point, Easthope, 13–18. Easthope provides here a convenient summary of Derridean theory as it applies to the question of the lyric.

8. See Cohn, 220–69, esp. 222 for an explanation of the term "lyric of fiction." There are excellent essays on the short "texts" or "pieces" in Brater (ed.), *Journal of Modern Literature.*

9. *Still* was first published in 1974, in a limited edition of 160 copies with original etchings by Stanley William Hayter (Milan: M'Arte Edizioni, 1974). It was translated as *Immobile* and published in Paris by Les Éditions de Minuit in 1976. The English version is included in *Fizzles* (New York: Grove Press, 1976), where it appears as "Fizzle 7," 47–51. All references in my text are to this edition.

For the publishing history, see Lake, 160–62. The etching reproduced here is from Lake, 160.

10. On the concept of "copresence" in Williams's work, see Miller, 285–359, esp. 287–92.

112

BIBLIOGRAPHY:
Works Cited

Ashbery, John. *As We Know.* New York: The Viking Press, 1979.
————. *Three Poems.* New York: The Viking Press, 1972.
Bair, Deirdre. *Samuel Beckett, A Biography.* New York: Harcourt Brace Jovanovich, 1978.
Beaujour, Michel. "Short Epiphanies: Two Contextual Approaches to the French Prose Poem." In *The Prose Poem in France: Theory and Practice.* Ed. Mary Ann Caws and Hermine Riffaterre. New York: Columbia University Press, 1983, 39–59.
Beckett, Samuel. *Fizzles.* New York: Grove Press, 1976.
Bernstein, Charles. *Islets/Irritations.* New York: Jordan Davies, 1983.
Brater, Enoch. "Still/Beckett: The Essential and the Incidental." In *Journal of Modern Literature: Samuel Beckett Special Number.* Ed. Enoch Brater. 6 (February 1977), 3–16.
Breunig, LeRoy C. "Why Frances?" In *The Prose Poem in France, Theory and Practice,* 3–20.
Cohn, Ruby. *Back to Beckett.* Princeton: Princeton University Press, 1973.
Easthope, Anthony. *Poetry as Discourse.* London and New York: Methuen, 1983.
Engels, Friedrich. *The Condition of the Working-Class in England,* cited in Edward J. Ahearn, *Rimbaud, Visions and Habitations.* Berkeley, Los Angeles, & London: University of California Press, 1983.
Fredman, Stephen. *Poet's Prose: The Crisis in American Verse.* Cambridge: Cambridge University Press, 1983.
Ginsberg, Allen. "Williams in a World of Objects." In *William Carlos Williams, Man and Poet.* Ed. Carroll F. Terrell. Orono, Maine: National Poetry Foundation, 1983.
Goethe, J. W. von. *Briefe.* Hamburger Ausgabe. 4 vols. Ed. Karl Robert Mandelkow. Hamburg: Christian Wegner, 1962. Vol. 1.
————. *Werke.* 6 vols. Wiesbaden: Insel, 1949–52. Vol. 1.
Hartman, Charles. *Free Verse: An Essay on Prosody.* Princeton: Princeton University Press, 1981.
Heidegger, Martin. *Poetry, Language, Thought.* Trans. Albert Hofstadter. New York: Harper & Row, 1971.
Knowson, James, and Joh Pilling. *Frescoes of the Skull: The Later Prose and Drama of Samuel Beckett.* New York: Grove Press, 1979.
Lanham, Richard A. *Analyzing Prose.* New York: Charles A. Scribners, 1983.
Lake, Carlton. *No Symbols Where None Intended. A Catalogue of Books, Manuscripts and Other Material Relating to Samuel Beckett in the Collections of the Humanities Research Center.* Austin, Texas: Humanities Research Center, 1984.

Meschonnic, Henri. *Critique du Rhythme: Anthropologie historique du langage.* Paris: Éditions Verdier, 1982.

Miller, J. Hillis. *Poets of Reality. Six Twentieth-Century Writers.* 1965; rpt. New York: Atheneum, 1969.

Perloff, Marjorie. *The Poetics of Indeterminacy: Rimbaud to Cage.* Princeton: Princeton University Press, 1981; Evanston, Illinois: Northwestern University Press, 1983.

————. "To Give a Design: Williams and the Visualization of Poetry." In *William Carlos Williams, Man and Poet,* 159–86.

Rimbaud, Arthur. *Complete Works, Selected Letters.* Ed. Wallace Fowlie. Chicago & London: University of Chicago Press, 1967.

————. *Oeuvres.* Ed. Suzanne Bernard. Paris: Garner, 1960.

Sonnenfeld, Albert. "L'Adieu supreme and Ultimate Composure: The Boundaries of the Prose Poem." In *The Prose Poem in France,* 198–214.

Weaver, Mike. *William Carlos Williams, The American Background.* Cambridge: Cambridge University Press, 1971.

Williams, William Carlos. "Author's Introduction to *The Wedge*" (1944). In *Selected Essays of William Carlos Williams.* New York: New Directions, 1954.

————. *The Collected Earlier Poems.* New York: New Directions, 1951.

114

David Ignatow

IN SEARCH
OF AN ABSOLUTE

This talk on the situation in poetry today will be, in essence, autobiographical. I believe, as do most of us, with certain exceptions, which I'll get to later, that poetry is personal in origin. Why not, then, trace the roots of my poetry so as to bestow an authenticity on this search for the absolute and, because most of us do agree that poetry is personal in origin, my tale and conclusion to it should, if not in detail, at least by implication, apply to the experience of nearly all of us. In brief, we do make up some sort of family among us, but what kind of family is the subject of this talk and my autobiographical account.

I will begin with the story of an experience I had in my mid-fifties, an experience that now finds itself confronted by a deeply troubled and divided present in poetry. There I sat in my mid-fifties in my car, waiting for a street corner traffic light to turn green. As I recall it now, I was mulling over a statement I had read several days earlier, which maintained that no scientific experiment can be purely objective, the factor of the observing scientist having to be included as a variable. As this statement hovered in my mind, I made an elated leap to connect it with the writing of poetry. The individual, as I already knew to my sorrow, is the significant factor in poetry too, but suddenly at the wheel of my car I felt myself completely free to write as I pleased, as if I had not been doing so from the start, but now I was released from a long-standing guilt about it.

Why this guilt, and where did it come from? There is the popular explanation for it: we poets do not contribute to the wealth, health, comfort, and longevity of the people and, often, not to our own either, and thus the personal dilemma, at least for most of us. This experience in my mid-fifties, however, did have its roots in the early days of my upbringing, which I will get to now to make that particular moment of my mid-fifties understandable. It began in the family. I was raised with two younger sisters, all of us, parents and children, bound in love and respect for each other. However, as I reconstruct it now, it was all predicated on the understanding that we gave respect and love to the family itself, meaning that one could not act outside the family without expecting to be looked on with some apprehension. Our every act had to be in the interest and welfare of us all. These family ties with one another by implication were indeed strong, to be violated only at the deepest traumatic cost to ourselves, as I was to know in short time.

I was my father's favorite, aglow in his loving approval of me. On my thirteenth birthday, that time of confirmation in the Jewish religion of one's arrival at adult responsibilities and duties, I asked for and received his permission with a smile and a nod to write my own acceptance speech. This sign of trust from my father clinched my then unspoken wish to become a writer, yet almost immediately after, with the onset of the Great Depression, we became bitterly alienated from each other. He demanded that I enter his business to work a twelve-hour shift, replacing another worker in order to bring home a salary to buy food for the family. I was acutely aware of the problems he confronted, but I was also experiencing, in my own outrage, a sense of his betrayal of me. On one level I knew my anger to be unreasonable, but on another I felt justified, not alone because of his past approval and support, but also because I believed he was betraying himself, which meant he was betraying me too. I found I had become deeply identified with him.

I was not without guilt at my determined stand against joining him in his business; I was angry too because of my feeling of guilt, which threatened to undermine and destroy my resolve not to submit to an exhausting, destructive twelve-hour shift. Bound in with this resolve was my effort to rescue and affirm that part of my father I yet believed in and loved, that part that was myself in him.

I soon found I was isolated within the family, its support withdrawn from me. Bitter as was my loss, even more anguishing was to witness the one person I had looked to for his authority on behalf of my ambition, that person hostile to that very life he had encouraged in me. Defiantly, I became my own authority and support.

And so to write began to mean to me to go against that one mainstay that has nurtured me in my ambition, my ambition having helped to undermine that mainstay, my guilt and anguish compounded and now as much directed toward myself as toward my father. A little before this time I had begun to read Walt Whitman. It was as if having found in him a correspondence to all I believed was the life I was then living within my family, or so I believed. In reaction to my break with my father and in a kind of excited depression, I made Whitman my surrogate father, his poems becoming my supportive family, yet with a sense of guilt still strong within me.

Witness again the sudden exhilaration at my release from guilt in my mid-fifties, which I recounted earlier, its affirming the individual freely for me. And yet there was to be a paradox, one I am about to relate that developed in later years and which impels this discussion toward its conclusion. However, to tell of this event will also help set the record straight as to my final relationship with my father, in itself the crux of this paradox. Years after my angry departure from home, he offered me the money with which to help publish my first book. He had then begun to prosper and even to take pride in me as a poet, but sadly, there was no way I could restore in myself his once overriding authority. Love me he did, but his advice, guidance, and moral support did not exist for me any longer. He was an ordinary man, and I no longer counted myself as any different either, considering the ordinary circumstances we now both faced of marriage, work, love, and fatherhood. I could see that both of us were subject to the same dilemmas of existence, which were without real solutions beyond what we could salvage through our own efforts and will. Ironically, it was an existence inner directed and, therefore, shaky, subject to the unpredictable and the unaccountable that assailed us from without as well as from within. I had to look beyond my father—and myself—for the truth.

In my belated acknowledgment that writing poetry was in essence the act of an autonomous person, free in himself, with the freedom to celebrate, I published an essay entitled, "The Necessity of the Personal," in which I praised the virtues and strengths of the poet as an individual, of encompassing significance for poetry, and for life itself. Here, I believed, I had found the absolute of which I had been in search ever since the break with my father and that now I saw to be an extension or development of the Whitman theme that I had for so long depended on, albeit ambivalently. Now its authority for me was grounded in the universality of the condition of the autonomous being. Wherever I turned I saw poets writing out of their own lives with a conviction and authority of their own that was both admirable and persuasive of the truth that I had only recently learned to embrace. And now I was among these poets, once more in a family, but this time of my own choosing and bent.

I wrote steadily and with confidence, free in myself at last to do so. What was it that awoke me to a reality other than this confident one, not very much later, which began a shift in my mood away from this supportive companionship that I had found in the writing of poetry? Why this change? What was its character? And why a troubling, renewed sense of guilt and anger on yet a new plane, one difficult to absorb and to transcend, since it resided in the very nature of my relationship to poetry and to my fellow poets. I ask myself these questions in order to find an explanation and, if possible, a remedy. I ask myself: If all of us, as I had believed, were united in the common goal of realizing ourselves through poetry, what causes a division among us? Who, if anyone, is responsible? Could it be that as individuals we must distinguish ourselves from each other by acts of hostility, indifference, and disdain?

I can understand this painful new development as in part a reaction to the excesses by some poets in their concentration on personal issues—so much that is trivial, inconsequential, or without form, taste, or reason for being other than to show itself as the poetry of the self. William Carlos Williams was caustic in his remarks on such sloppy work. So much poor writing may have signaled to certain American critics a breakdown in American poetry and as a result may have triggered the sharp reaction to which we are witness today. I am not about to name these critics or raise issues, since my point is to let these names and issues be reflected in the divisions among us, so that I may continue on the theme I have set for myself in this talk, to concentrate on the effect rather than on the causes, which we know. My reason for that decision will be clear enough as I progress in what I have to say. I am here to speak of myself as perhaps representative of those who feel threatened in their beliefs and practices and betrayed, as it seems, by exactly those critics I have just alluded to who claim their authority from Whitman. Of course, we would much prefer to accept a learned, sensitive authority and be at one with it in the endeavor to adapt Whitman to our contemporary needs, but what can we say when we find ourselves confronted by hostility, as if in our need to claim Whitman too, we were trespassing on private property?

This is not an emotional issue alone; I am also speaking of those paradoxes and ironies to which I earlier referred. I honor those same critics for their belated appreciation of Whitman, he whom I and many others have been reading and writing to and about for nearly fifty years while he was yet being ignored, often ridiculed, by those very institutions and their academicians who now have raised him to an eminence among us. But is there still not the possibility that we will find Whitman in the basement once again in some not too distant future? It's as if he has been made a means with which to exclude from recognition those same poets, such as Robert Bly, Oppen, James Wright, Gary Snyder, and Robert Creeley, to name only a few who derive from Whitman. Is this not already a disguised form of hostility toward Whitman?

So now, for those like myself, our guilt attendant on our rejection of those criticial voices that we would have preferred to call our own, we carry on, once more having to realize we are our own authority and support; that there are no fathers among us; that we must make do with ourselves; that the child is father to the man.

Unquestionably, we need comments, observations, and critiques but certainly not so as to divide the poets from each other with self-important judgments, as though separating sheep from goats. We do not need shepherds of that breed, especially not those who claim to elevate criticism to an aesthetic position and mode equal to, if not superior to, poetry itself. What more do we need to demonstrate the disarray among poets today than such a claim that sets poets against critics and poets against poets, as the critics preside in judgment among us as in lordly domain. Where is Whitman in this?

I am in agreement that there must be change, at the same time that I am reminded that change carries within itself the cause for such change, so that, as it absorbs the past, it must also struggle against it to exist as change. Thus change cannot deny or reject the past, without losing its own character as change. We do not as yet kill off our parents and grandparents, except perhaps by forgetting they exist, only to remind ourselves of them as we ourselves begin to age.

However, let me go directly into a subject more closely related to this talk, for example, that of the more recently stated theory of indeterminacy as drawn from the work of past poets and with reference to the more recent work of younger poets. I am speaking in particular of *The Poetics of Indeterminacy,* by Marjorie Perloff. Reading it, I am reminded that it was precisely a reaction to certainties, assurances, and blandishments that triggered the revolution among early twentieth-century poets, such as Eliot and Pound, who brought with them the then explosive power of their doubts, ambiguities, and rejections. And when I read about Deconstructionism, it reminds me of the Marxist campaign of the early thirties and mid-forties that sought to bludgeon the so-called bourgeois poets into conforming with Marxist theory and practice by denouncing those poets as submissive to the demands and needs of capitalism and imperialism. In other words, the Marxists sought to strip these poets of their own uniquely personal commitments and contributions. In turn, the poets, once stripped of their individuality, were to become instruments for accomplishing the Marxist revolution. Now we have the theory, to put it as simply as possible, that no writer exists uniquely in himself or herself but again is the voice tuned to the voice of his or her culture, and this is given to us in the dress of intellectual probity, scholarship, and deeply keen self- and societal analysis. Do we need a repetition of the earlier Marxist campaign in its latest academic venture?

As for indeterminacy, we should welcome it as a restatement of Pound's dictum, "Make It New." In making it new, we find our language perforce indeterminate, especially as to how and what to say that can set itself in contrast to the tried and worn. A tone of resistance to the old and tried becomes the clue to the new, as the new works to emerge in full strength and meaning. This is what I want to save, this effort at renewal. This is what is under attack, the voice that does not conform to literary criteria given from on high.

In brief, I am making a plea for a certain tolerance for what is emerging, but with a plea for respect too for what has made possible that which is emerging. There are no longer absolute criteria for judgment, not even in oneself. That is one of the surprising and troubling conclusions I have come to, and so in a way I agree with Deconstructionism, for the individual is in doubt today, exactly as there are no set judgments as to what is and what is not true. That pertains to the nature of poetry too. It is simply as protean as is life itself, but one survives and writes with all that is a spur to writing, as if in defiance, as if to distinguish oneself from the chaos. That is where absolute judgment may be made—the poet discovering for himself or herself a form or order that is yet free to change into still another shape and sound. And so I welcome in myself those poets and critics who are at work seeking to express the emerging new, its indeterminacy in relation to the old and the tensions arising from the introduction of the indeterminate, a situation we have seen and experienced in recent past literary eras and which continues in character with our times.

In conclusion, if there can be a conclusion to a discussion such as this, where there are strong aesthetic and philosophical differences and even heated debates among us, we must not forget that without each other we lack significance in ourselves. We need one another if only to become distinguished in ourselves from each other in our right and reason. This is an absolute I cling to, and it gives me much pleasure. It is family once again, and I am deeply happy to be here.

I have written a two-and-one-half-page addendum to this talk, as it happened, on the spur of the moment, again dealing with the subject, the absolute but, I believe, on yet another level, one I felt compelled to write. It is, again, personal, but perhaps even closer in its way to summing up my view. It may rightfully be termed an addendum, an afterthought, something to round out and complete a nearly private experience on the subject of the absolute. It begins as follows: It's never possible for me to give any one fixed account of what I'm trying to do as a poet, it varies so with the circumstances in which I find myself. At one moment I may be thinking of writing the definitive account of the spirit since Christ; at another time I will want to incorporate in my poems every theory Freud developed; at still another time I am involved in my daily routine life, with aside for love or pleasure or domestic tranquillity, and yet I can't totally forswear these plunges into the absolute, which I am susceptible to.

The absolute is my deepest preoccupation, which, naturally, I, like everyone else, must fail at and in my path through life must trust that this preoccupation will bring me to some revelation that will stay with me until eternity beyond the grave. I am serious. I want, as poet, to speak the whole truth and nothing but the truth, so help whoever or whatever is there to whom or to which I may swear my faith. Let it or who listen or not, I will make my allegiance clear and unequivocal. I want an absolute revelation but also want my daily existence, so how do I mediate between them? Is mediation possible. This conflict too lies beneath the surface of my wish for the absolute and, as I can guess, undermines, dilutes, circumscribes, and disintegrates it, the sad, sad part of this ambivalent existence.

I am ready for death, and is that the final absolute revelation? So be it. I know of no other certain event that could bring its own truth with it, and if this is what I am looking for, then a welcome to it. I write of death often, and it may be that I have not been aware that the revelation has been with me for all this while, ever since I can remember, as far back as my childhood when I stood leaning against the gate of a cemetery and looked out into the sky and spoke to it, as if it were listening, as if it were the being to whom I should address myself in wonder. I was answered from within by the emergence of a poem.

Since then, death has been a stimulus to my work. Is that not a revelation, seeing myself in the perspective of death, which speaks to me clearly of my life. I turn to my life and write about it with the exactness that love demands. Love, of course, because it is love that the imminence of death stirs in me for life, and when I am finally quit of life I will, again I hope, have written only with love of the ugly, the critical, the angry and sarcastic, equally with the tender to persons and to life itself. Death is this two-faced Gorgon, for death is my theme, but life is my subject, and I smile on everyone.

And so here I have just given a firm account of what I am doing as a poet, I who am so full of contradictions, but the leisure is mine in having discovered an absolute that, I know, I will forget or pass through in time and other circumstances than this in which I am now writing. Yet I should tell myself over and over that there are no absolutes, if this is the situation where I keep finding absolutes in every alley and crossroads of my life. I should say that each absolute is for its time, and let it go at that. I should be content with that, and yet, though I have told myself this repeatedly, I cannot rest with that thought. I keep searching, restless, afraid that I am missing something so obvious, and staring me in the face, that which could give me my sense of immortality. For it's immortality I want when I seek after the absolute, to discover and grasp it between my hands, to win it over into my body, to make my body an absolute too, immortal.

Am I afraid to face and acknowledge that which is being told me throughout my changeful life and thought—that there are no absolutes and that alone is the final one on which to rest my search? How celebrate, enjoy, and live in the pleasure of that discovery? By acknowledging my own limits, but somehow through this changefulness in me to be identified with that which is forever. I must bow my head and live as long as life matters.

Denise Levertov

HORSES WITH WINGS

Pegasus, a horse with wings: he flashes into sight of the inner eye with a silvery grace no poet ever possessed. And he is not a poet, not a poem. But to reflect upon him may tell us something new about both or, more likely, will tell us something old but not recently remembered. For attributes, totemic associates, symbolic images not only possess their own identities but express something essential of the person or class of persons to which they are attached. And Pegasus is persistently linked to the idea of poetic inspiration.

Hawthorne's nineteenth-century vision exquisitely saw him thus:

> Nearer and nearer came the aerial wonder, flying in great circles, as you might have seen a dove when about to alight. Downward came Pegasus, in those wide, sweeping circles, which grew narrower, and narrower still, as he gradually approached the earth. The higher the view of him, the more beautiful he was, and the more marvellous the sweep of his silvery wings. At last, with so light a pressure as hardly to bend the grass about the fountain, or imprint a hoof-tramp in the sand of its margin, he alighted, and, stooping his wild head,

124

began to drink. He drew in the water, with long and pleasant sighs, and tranquil pauses of enjoyment . . .

Then,

Being long after sunset, it was now twilight on the mountain-top, and dusky evening over all the country round about. But Pegasus flew so high that he overtook the departed day, and was bathed in the upper radiance of the sun. Ascending higher and higher, he looked like a bright speck . . .

But scholarship reminds us that he was not all compact of grace and charm. His antecedents are unpromising—dark and violent—for one whose legend has come down to us as principally benevolent.

What analogies in the activity of poem-making or the nature of poets and poetry may be illumined by his myth? What do his own origins tell us?

His Parentage

The father: Poseidon, god of the sea, is above all a representative of the undifferentiated energy, a power unaware of itself, amoral, a source of life but also of terror. The individual who, admiring poetry, language, Nature, attempts to make verses but is not impelled by some trace at least of that power produces only mediocrity. Just as Poseidon is associated with tempestuous seas rather than with glassy calm, so poems rise up in the poet from intensity of experience, even though they may evoke things calm, delicate, or still, and even though composition, more often than not, takes place when emotion is re-collected, its fragmented elements regathered by the imagination at a later, and *externally* tranquil, time.

Poseidon causes earthquakes, though it might seem that ocean, however stormy, is a remote source for inland cataclysms. Just so may poetry cause personal and social effects distant from it in time or place, setting in motion a chain of events beyond the poet's will or knowledge, although perhaps consonant with his or her hopes. It is in this propensity that Poseidon the earthshaker calls to mind Shelley's "legislators" who in our time are figured forth in a Brecht, a Pablo Neruda, a Yannis Ritsos, or a Nazim Hikmet, but also in poets whose work affects the values and vision of their time less explicitly.

125

Poseidon as an embodiment of fecundity bespeaks the ramifications of such distant effects, wave upon wave into the distant horizon; and here his benign aspect appears, for in rocking, shaking, and opening out the static, passive, and finally receptive earth and making springs both hot and cold to jet from its caves, he causes it to bring forth nourishing plants. Thus does poetry rock and shake and open the mind and senses, moistening their aridity and enabling humans to bring forth their spiritual fruits.

The mother: Medusa. We may say Poseidon, god of the unconscious depths, is a powerful but morally neutral, dual, or ambiguous force; but what are we to make of Medusa? Is there any good to be known of her? Is there any trace of her in graceful Pegasus?

First we must note that Pegasus has an equine heritage on both sides of his family. The primordial force of water—at once nourishing and destructive, and symbolic of impetuous desire—is associated very anciently with the horse of night and shadows, galloping out of the entrails of earth and the abyss of ocean. Similarly, Medusa's legends most anciently seem to place her as a manifestation of the Earth Mother's terrible and devouring aspects, which take on dragon forms and various other animal guises, including that of a mare. Demeter herself was often depicted as horse-headed, was not unrelated to the Furies, and bore (to none other than Poseidon) the horse Arion, two of whose feet were human and who could speak like a man. Medusa, then—although it is also said that she was for a time, before Poseidon ravished her, a beautiful maiden—embodies the nightmare, the *cauchemar.*

Her equine connections are with the same unconscious animal force and fertility as these of Poseidon, who, if he took her in his equine form, as most accounts assert, came sweeping into Athene's temple with white mane flowing, a tidal wave with thundering hooves, his sperm the milky jade color you may see as the breakers turn at the shoreline. The great oceanic horse is beautiful; but Medusa's horse aspect is part of her malignity.

This monstrous mother, whose hands were bronze, whose wings were brass, whose teeth were fangs or tusks, and whose hair was a writhing mass of snakes, was the only mortal among triplet sisters. Her serpentine hair is said to have been given her by Athene, furious at the destruction of her temple; but since all her siblings and half-siblings were monsters, it seems that her malign nature existed potentially even before her appearance became hideous. Her significance has been perceived as incarnating perverted impulses: a *refusal* of harmony, a *willful* wickedness, rather than an incapacity for goodness. The word *Gorgon* is related to *gargle, gurgle,* and *gargoyle;* Medusa has been called "a shriek personified." All who gazed upon her were instantly petrified—paralyzed by the full, unveiled, unmediated vision of evil. The fact that Perseus managed to get close enough to sever her neck without himself being turned to stone, by the ruse of focusing on her mirror image—that mirror being indeed his shield—seems to suggest the way in which art provides a mode of perceiving evil and terror without being immobilized but, on the contrary, enabled to come to grips with them. Frobenius saw in the Gorgon a symbol of the fusion of opposites; however, what has been perceived as Medusa's refusal of internal harmony results in a stasis of conflict, not a positive synthesis. The components of her presence are utterly disparate and remain so. Her face, even though depicted as having elements of beauty, is contorted in a frightful snarl, as if she horrifies even herself. Contemplation of such "fusion," or rather, such simultaneity of warring elements, can kill—that is, it can defeat or explode the conscious rational mind, for it reveals a state beyond linear reach. But the experience of poetry provides, like the mirror of Perseus, a means for human consciousness to transcend the linear and by fitful glimpses, at least, to attain a vision of ultimate harmony, as we shall see.

Erich Neumann, with a Jungian perspective, describes Perseus's mirror strategy as the *raising into consciousness* of an image that paralyzes only as long as it remains unconscious; and he makes a point of the pun of *reflection* inherent in the story. I would by no means dispute this; but his account is concerned with the universal psychological principles carried in the myth; whereas, for poets, and thus within the work of art, the myth's particular significance is not the attainment of consciousness as such but the transformation and activating of conscious and unconscious experiences brought about by the imagination. And it is notable that when Neumann turns from Perseus and his mirror to Pegasus, he identifies the latter as the released "spiritual *libido* of the Gorgon," (my italics) who "combines the spirituality of the bird with the horse character of the Gorgon." (Here it is of interest to note that according to one account, it was as a bird that Poseidon came to the then fair Medusa, in that flowery meadow within the precincts of Athene's calm temple, and not as a wild horse. A seabird, it would have been, with its hungry cry and fishhook beak, fierce-eyed, as apt to dive under the tossing surface as to glide and hover on the salt breezes; symbolic, as bird, of spirit, but yet a wild spirit.)

His Nature and Associations

Pegasus issues from the blood of Medusa (and specifically from her neck, that area of transition between two territories, mental and physical). Medusa, though able to embody opposites (the dual nature of the Earth Mother, fertile yet destructive; or, in later manifestations, her youthful beauty and subsequent ugliness) was not capable of so mingling them as to transform and transcend their conflict, for all her energy is expressed in willful spite; but from the conjunction within her of Poseidon's undifferentiated and ever-flowing energy and her own fixed intensity is born—or wrested out of her by a slash of the sickle—a new form of "fusion of opposites," one that is more truly a fusion: Pegasus. The earthy physical horse is all complete—not, as in the centaur, the hippocampus, or the hippogriff, half horse and half man or fish or griffin, and not, as in his half-brother Arion, a horse with two human feet and the power of speech. Nor does Pegasus undergo periodic metamorphosis into a bird. He is at all times a horse (and a sexually potent one, for though no mate or offspring of his is ever mentioned, he is referred to as a stallion). He is a perfect horse; but a horse possessed of the superlative enhancement of wings. The development of horse symbolism from chthonic darkness and malign associations to the glorious team that draws the chariot of the sun is recapitulated in the development of the Pegasus legends, the earliest of which accord him no wings, and in his story itself, which depicts spiritual energy rising from such murky sources. In him contrasts are reconciled, and not by the disappearance of their characteristics but by their new and harmonious combination.

Poets—not, let it be emphasized, in their personal human aspect (or not in any greater degree than for any other individuals in whom the imagination is alive), but as poets, in the activity of

128

poem-making—possess like Pegasus some inherent power of exaltation. But it is equally important to recognize that Pegasus was not constantly airborne. It was by striking his sharp hoof hard upon the rocky earth that Pegasus released the fountain of Hippocrene, the fountain of poetic inspiration henceforth sacred to the Muses. (Some say, too, that it was not until the moment that Medusa's blood, spurting from her neck, *touched earth* that he became manifest.) Poet and poem must strike hard and sink deep into the material to tap spiritual springs or give new birth to "the winged fountain."

In poetry we may observe traits of the parents as well as of Pegasus himself. There are poems vast, restless, almost formless, yet powerful, which evoke the character of Poseidon and the ocean's tidal rhythms. There are Medusan poems of rage and hatred, sharp-clawed with satire, writhing with serpentine humor, and flashing forth venomous tongues of denunciation or despair.

And then there are those, far more numerous, which in various proportions combine, like Pegasus himself, earth and air; and it is these, not those in which the traits of Poseidon or Medusa dominate, which are most representatively poems. They may walk, trot, or gallop, but they have the inherent power to soar aloft. Some poets hold this power in reserve, keeping Pegasus on a tight rein; others avail themselves of it with more or less frequency. Such flights are not to be equaled with abstraction, as may too easily be done if one assumes that the earthy horse represents the concrete and the wings the abstract. Pegasus as horse does indeed present the sensual, the sensuous, the concretely specific, but that physicality is itself related to the unconscious; that is, not only to the instinctive but to the intuitive. And his wings, which do not deform but increase and enhance his equine characteristics of speed and strength of motion, express not the abstractions of linear intellection but the transcendent and transformative power of imagination itself.

But it would be no service to the understanding of poetry's essential nature and the poet's vocation to smooth over its stern or daimonic aspects. Pegasus, sired by a ruthless god, born in violence of an abhorrent monstrosity, is himself a daimon, a force, an energy. He is not, as Heine put it, a virtuous utilitarian hack; nor is he a children's pet. Bellerophon only tames him with the help of a magical golden bridle, the gift of Athene. It is a beneficent act to help destroy the devastating Chimaera, whose three heads—of a goat, a snake, and a lion—embody licentiousness, insidious venom, and ruthless dominance; and the story reveals in parable that inspiration, not courage and strategy alone, overcomes these evils. Yet, not himself destructive, Pegasus, by lending to Bellerophon his indispensable swiftness and power to rise aloft, has become accessory to the performance of a killing. As a flying cloud, he may carry life-giving showers but can also bring the devastation of flash floods. And after Bellerophon's hero-deed is done, it is the speed and levitational power of his steed that tempt him to hubris. Extreme speed is a way of referring to a kind of excessive eloquence, the words tumbling out too fast for coherence, and too many for each to be just and indispensable. A poet flying high and swiftly becomes a kind of bird, whose speech is not intelligible to humankind; or a breath of the storm wind, which breaks what it sweeps over. Pegasus, anciently known as accursed as well as blessed, in latter days can perhaps be seen in this aspect as the steed of poets willfully abstruse or brutally verbose. Finally, Bellerophon attempts to fly upon him to Olympus—and then Pegasus throws him. Whether or not Zeus sent a gadfly to sting him into this action, or whether he himself resented Bellerophon's presumption, the glorious familiar becomes instrumental in the hero's fall from grace, both by being that which (innocently) tempts and that which, misused, rejects further cooperation. Thereafter he himself is translated to the Olympian stables and becomes the bearer of thunder and lightning "at the behest of prudent Zeus"—of those tremendous words from an apparent nowhere ("out of the sky," as we say), whether sounding within the mind or out in the bustling world, which come sometimes to strike us with terror or remorse and in a flash to illuminate an obscure history or reveal an abyss at our feet.

Eos, the dawn, sometimes rides Pegasus, bringing a saffron shimmer of first light. This daybreak appearance may bring to mind the astonishing poetry occasionally uttered (and occasionally written down) by young children, and also the poetic efflorescence that often takes place in adolescence. But like that of early morning sunshine, these promises are not always fulfilled. The poet of extraordinary gifts who early produces major work and dies very young is, or has become, a rarity; and the earliest work of those who live longer is even more rarely of more than historical interest. It is the pristine value of initial inspirations that Pegasus more aptly signifies when regarded as the horse of dawn. No matter what metamorphoses poem or stanza or image within them may have to pass through to become all that it can, its source and first appearance should not be despised.

Mantegna depicted Pegasus with Hermes. I have not found a source for this association, but since the painting shows the gods foregathered, one may suppose that after the downfall of Bellerophon, Zeus having summoned him to the Olympian heights, Pegasus and wing-footed Hermes would naturally be drawn to one another. Hermes is the god of fresh wind, who clears the skies; of travelers; of cunning wiles; of eloquence; guardian of flocks; messenger and psychopomp—a fit companion for one with the attributes of Pegasus. If Pegasus struck forth the fountain of inspiration, it was Hermes who invented the lyre. Indeed, the two share so much that one may take that list and apply much of it to the winged horse—swift as the wind, clearly a potential benefactor of travelers, provider of the springs of eloquence. And though we don't find in Pegasus specific parallels for Hermes's cunning and trickery nor for his shepherd role, affinities with them are easily discernible in poets and poetry.

Jane Harrison, in *Themis*, speaks in passing of Pegasus "receiving" Dionysos at Eleutherae; being given, that is, in a powerful and unmistakable flash of recognition, the perception of a divinity. If it is indeed our Pegasus she refers to, I would interpret this event as emblematic of the way in which creative power has no upper limit; a sublime potential remains even when a poetry has seemed to fly to the extremes of its own possibility.

His Siblings

The offspring of Poseidon are many. There are a few who seem, however, to have a special relation to Pegasus. First of these is Chrysaor, his unidentical twin, formed like a man of great size and splendor of bearing, who stepped out of Medusa's spilt blood bearing a huge golden sword. Subsequently he united with "great Ocean's daughter," Callirhoe, whose name means Beautiful

Stream, and fathered the monster Geryon whom Heracles later killed. Then we hear no more of him, as if he had sunk beneath the waves he wedded, carried by that river out into deep ocean. In him we may see figured the mind that never comes to consciousness. Born of the unconscious and the nightmare, it struggles as far as the beauty of one stream, plunges in, and is borne away, leaving behind only an aberrant production soon to vanish in its turn; just as an individual may produce one unfinished, unshaped poem. The figure of Chrysaor also suggests wasted talent: mighty in appearance and with that attribute, the golden sword, he yet does no deeds and has no story.

Arion, with human speech and a trace of human form—two of his four feet—was one of the many half-brothers; his mother was Demeter, who had taken on the form of a mare when Poseidon, as a stallion, pursued her. Arion was dark and powerful and was ridden by Heracles and by Adrastus (survivor of the "Seven against Thebes"). Here is language without poetry, at the service of action; a plain prose. In contrast, Pegasus himself, not endowed with speech, yet acts as divining rod for the poetic fountain.

The third sibling relevant to my theme is Bellerophon. For though supposedly the son of Glaucus, Hesiod reveals that in fact Poseidon, by the wife of Glaucus, fathered Bellerophon, and that it was he who provided Pegasus to help Bellerophon in his adventure. Bellerophon's ostensible father, Glaucus, was trampled and killed by his own horses, whom Aphrodite had driven mad in revenge for some offense; and it is the ghost of Glaucus that horses are seeing when some inexplicable terror makes them stall and rear. But Bellerophon himself is a notable horseman. Though there is no identification of him as a poet, his close association with Pegasus, with springs and flying, as well as the inspired ingenuity with which he avails himself of his magical familiar in the strategy for slaying the Chimaera, suggest that he may stand for one. Or rather, if we look upon him and Pegasus together as forming a whole (as horse and rider do when, both superb, they are perfectly attuned to one another), then Bellerophon, to whom that bridle was given in dream by Athene, goddess of vigilant and industrious intelligence, stands for the craft and skill necessary to the full activity of inspiration and creative imagination. Each needs the other for the fulfillment of his powers. Hawthorne, speaking as always in parables, tells that Bellerophon, after he first tamed him, offered Pegasus his freedom. Pegasus took flight, circled the skies, and once more spiraled down—returning voluntarily. And once again, when the Chimaera's bones and ashes lie strewn across the plain, the rider frees the steed and is refused. Once craft and imagination have endured together the struggle to slay a monster or create a poem, imagination does not just fly off never to return. Pegasus was never really *tamed,* not *broken* like a common horse; it is only through the magic of special, goddess-given dream-intelligence that Bellerophon is able to exercise his regular equestrian skills upon him. But he does freely choose to remain, as a comrade. It is only when humility is lost and arrogant technique assumes it can assault heaven itself that the rider falls and the winged horse soars beyond reach.

Conclusion

In reviewing what Pegasus has to tell us about the poet, we find, then, these correspondences:

The poet inherits a protean and unconscious power, fertile, amoral, capable of shaking mountains or shaking dry seeds to life.

✦

The poet also inherits heterogeneities strange as Medusa's, whose distorted human face looked out from among such an anomalous collection of bodily traits—snakes and claws, wings and scales. These Gorgonian features correspond to the quaking magma of emotion, which, presented in poems of autobiographical confession or furious opinion, smothers response and turns to stone the minds over which it flows. The poet's inherent contradictions vary, in kind and in proportion, with the individual; but the archetypal poet, being also a representative Human Being, "Man (or Woman) the Analogist," contains the potential for many intensities, for all the passions and all the appetites; and—on a more differentiated level—for satire and sentiment, thundering prophecy and delicate nuance, comedy and the sublime. The poet has to be both a dreamy visionary and a meticulous and energetic worker and is often tormented by those conflicting needs.

◆

The poet (always, I must reemphasize, in the work of poetry, and not in his or her mundane individuality) reconciles these disparities and incongruities. Here we see Pegasus as a metaphor for the poem rather than for the poet. We must take his emergence from Gorgon and sea god as a given; the poem, correspondingly emerging from the poet, an autonomous third term, results from an alchemy scarcely less mysterious. Like Pegasus, the poet (and the poem too) is animal. Fully a horse, Pegasus is not particularly intellectual. His intelligence is intuitive. But a fine horse is alert in every rippling muscle; its ears, its nostrils reflect complex awareness. And it is as consistent, as harmonious throughout its being as Medusa was inharmonious. Even the excrement of a horse takes the form of neat spheres, like brown tennis balls, full of grain for sparrows and pigeons. The poet as animal is human and must accept and explore all that he or she incorporates—the gift of the senses, the gifts of memory and language and intellectual discernment, and too the burden or curse entailed in each of these gifts or blessings; but above all the poet must treasure the gift of intuition which transcends the limitations of deductive reasoning.

To say that the poem, as well as the poet, is animal means that it has its own flesh and blood and is not a rarified and insubstantial thing. It is compact of sounds, guttural or sibilant, round or thin, lilting or abrupt, in all their play of pitch or rhythm, durations and varied pace, their dance in and with silence. Even its marriage to the Euclidean beauty of syntax is a passionate and very physical love affair, and often it pulls the gravity and abstract elegance of grammar into that dance to whirl like a Maenad.

◆

Pegasus has wings added unto his equine completeness. And the poet has, beyond even the penetrative gift of intuition, the power of imagination. The bridle of skill and craft may give Bellerophon power to direct the flight of the horse; but no skill, no effort, can produce wings where there are none. The imagination is the horse's wings, form of grace, unmerited, unattainable, amazing, and freely given. It is with awe that any who receive it must respond.

134

Charles Bernstein

BLOOD ON THE CUTTING ROOM FLOOR

Imagine that words have a life of their own, radio-controlled by an automatic pilot called history. Imagine, that is, that it is not we, as Humpty Dumpty liked to think, that control our words but our words that control us. Control? Well, let's say, say more than we ever intend to say, do more than we know what to do with.

Imagine, that is, that writing is an artificial intelligence—*intelligence* in the sense of having a power over mind, *artificial* in the sense of transpersonal and nonhuman (it neither breathes nor bleeds, nor ever has, though its origins issue from flesh and blood).

To understand language as artificial intelligence is to conceptualize writing as a kind of psychic surgery—knitting together pieces of deanimated flesh until, like the monster in Mary Shelley's *Frankenstein,* they come alive. Has there ever been a more lucid (or lurid) description of the relation of writer to text than this from Shelley:

> My imagination, unbidden, possessed and guided me, gifting the successive images that arose in my mind with a vividness far beyond the usual bounds of reverie. I saw—with shut eyes, but

acute mental vision—I saw the pale student of unhallowed arts kneeling beside the thing he had put together. I saw the hideous phantasm of a man stretched out, and then, on the working of some powerful engine, show signs of life, and stir with an uneasy, half-vital motion. Frightful must it be; for supremely frightful would be the effect of any human endeavour to mock the stupendous mechanism of the Creator of the world. His success would terrify the artist; he would rush away from his odious handiwork, horror-stricken. He would hope that, left to itself, the slight spark of life which he had communicated would fade; that this thing which had received such imperfect animation would subside into dead matter, and he might sleep in the belief that the silence of the grave would quench forever the transient existence of the hideous corpse which he had looked upon as the cradle of life. He sleeps; but he is awakened; he opens his eyes; behold, the horrid thing stands at his bedside, opening his curtains and looking on him with yellow, watery, but speculative eyes.

As Karl Kraus has observed, "The closer the look one takes at a word, the greater the distance from which it looks back." Or as Shelley goes on:

> I thought that if I could bestow animation upon lifeless matter I might, in the process of time (although I now find it impossible) renew where death had apparently devoted the body to corruption.

I propose Dr. Frankenstein's creation as a central image for a poem because, in the blasé sophistication of the humdrum, there is all-too-great a willingness to domesticate that which is beyond our control and in so doing cede that measure of responsibility we can assert. This may begin to suggest the inadequacy of a word like *imagination* to convey what is going on in a poem, or the kind of poem I'm interested in, since it's all too adequate to describe most poetry.

Nor am I suggesting that language is a given entity apart from the world. Rather I am speaking of that language which comes to be in the world as the condition of a specific place, a specific negotiation by a writer that does not appropriate words but invests them. Not that the words inhabit us (only) (or as much as) world inhabits us through these words. Always the hard part—whether it be in a poem or essay—is to leave the mechanics (language operates so, can do this and this) and enter into the engendering. Language is not self-determining (that is, the always wrong-headed call of a perspective based on the ideas of the arbitrariness of signs), nor is it determined by forces wholly external to it. Rather, language is a living necessity making place and time in the only world in which any of us lives for any lifetime. We are confronted by language as much as confront with it; its shapes arise from the way we handle that which occurs.

The description of a poem's making as a kind of psychic surgery emphasizes that poetry is a *technology* that makes, not exactly, as William Carlos William had it, "a . . . machine made of words," but more like a *flesh* made of words. If *flesh* seems too organic a metaphor, it is not intended to oppose a *social* construction with a *biological* one but to point to how *self* is as much a social construction as a poem. The practical implication of these observations is both to debunk the association of technology primarily with scientific rationality and to deepen the conception of what fuses a poem composed of discrete pieces into a whole greater than the sum of its parts.

Although the root of *technology* is *techne* (the Greek word for practical knowledge, craft, or art), in our culture art has lost its legitimacy as knowledge-producing. The exclusive association of "scientific method" with knowledge production is reductive and represents a dominance of the ideology of science over other knowledge-producing investigations, which are generally agglomerated together as *aesthetic*. Art proposes and pursues *methods* of acquiring knowledge that are alternative to scientific models.

In terms of writing and technology, two major topics might be considered: the technology of writing and reading and the effect of technology on writing and reading. The most important modern technological development for writing and reading has been the combination of inexpensive printing and photocopying with increasingly efficient typewriters/word processors. These developments—a kind of second Gutenberg revolution—have made available to writers the means of producing their work independently, without going through capital-intensive, centralized publishers. At the same time, they potentially make available to readers access to a wider range of contemporary writing than ever before. Specifically, the minimal cost of book production enables "literary" and other writing a relative freedom from constraints imposed when the largest possible audience is sought (constraints that may inhibit the choice of syntax and style as well as subject). Nonetheless, the potential benefits of this technology have not been fully realized due to distribution problems, attitudes toward publishing originating in relation to older printing technologies, and the continuing limitations of literacy levels and reading education.

Even more fundamental than understanding new technologies for the reproduction of writing is understanding the nature of writing as such. Alphabets, for example, remain perhaps the most formidable technologies human culture has produced. Readers can usefully be regarded as operating highly sophisticated technology. Yet little attention is paid to understanding the effects of alphabets and other reading and writing technologies. The technology of writing has many more dimensions than are "read" by most users; the technology is not fully "accessed." Poetry has an important, if often vacated, role in supplementing minimal reading values and in this sense can be understood as among the most useful tools for making alphabet technology available.

A cautionary note is necessary here. Compared to the alphabet or even inexpensive reproduction technology, the word processor threatens to become more a tool of industrial Taylorism than a means of increasing access to the many semantic strata embedded in writing. The current plethora of word processor ideology is the latest attempt to domesticate writing—not in order to inhabit it (which was, for instance, the project of Thoreau) but to trivialize it. The word processor has about as much chance of instructing us about the nature of writing as the threshing machine had to instruct us about the nature of soil. The analogy is specific: the relation of soil to vegetation is comparable to the relation of writing to human consciousness. The pen is mightier than the word processor in that, in comparison to what the pen makes available in respect to fully accessing the potential of alphabet technology, the word processor offers a microscopic efficiency and a number of severe handicaps.

The relatively uncritical acceptance of the word processor is another chapter in the ascent of efficiency over and against other human values. The indelibility of ink, with its intimations of an extension of the blood through the fingertips and the related gesture of making a mark, places writing in a different dimension than that of the etherealized, all-too-correctible space letters occupy in a cathode ray tube or liquid crystal display. Since the alphabet is a visual and tactile technology, the specific types of visual media used potentially affect writing and reading as much as the differences among drawing, lithography, and etching affect the meaning of an image.

Certainly, the ability to make changes in a text more easily is a valuable efficiency and may make writing less intimidating for some people. But this efficiency tends to obliterate the positive value of "mistakes," which are a purely negative factor in the commercial and industrial and "educational" contexts in which most writing is processed—an attitude about correctness that makes writing intimidating in the first place. Spelling searches may save time; they also will produce ever greater spelling standardization than at present and will tend to eliminate all that can be gleaned from wading through a dictionary distracted by alternative word choices, or just distracted, "weighlayed" before returning to the "text" proper. Grammar searches are likely to enforce centralized styles of composition, further eroding both conscious and unconscious participation by users in determining language forms. Of course, machines do not cause these problems; word processors may permit a far greater degree of decentralization of spelling, grammar, and style, making independent publishing and writing easier to accomplish. At the same time, word processor *ideology* reinforces the idealization of "clean copy"—a defleshed, bureaucratic, and interchangeable writing.

No doubt some writers will use word processors to counter just the negative tendencies sketched here. But the potentially liberating aspects of a technology need to be considered in the light of how that technology is employed in society overall. Industrial word processors (the operators, that is; the same word stands for both the machine and its users), with no choice over the writing they process, face an additional, even more ominous, set of problems. Because word processors make possible a desocialization of the workplace leading toward cottage industry piecework, organized labor action is severely limited. Atomized workers at geographically distant terminals compete for who will take the lowest wages, while constant monitoring of characters typed per hour prevents slowdowns or plugouts. The potential for control is unprecedented—and this control regulates a physical rigidity of posture for the worker that is far more restricted than that of a typist or assembly-line worker.

Just as planes and cars did not replace walking, and alphabets did not replace orality, word processors will not replace older writing technologies. For every real gain a technology provides, there is a real loss. Rather than "replace by improvements" the more accurate image is "supplement with new modalities." Only when it is understood how and why technologies are harnessed for social control and exploitation can it begin to be possible to change these uses and put the technologies in the service of positive social transformations.

Machines will never replace writers, anymore than, as the story goes, they replaced cowboys; machines won't take that much abuse.

Yet, for the most part, it is not writing technologies but writing practitioners that block realization of reading values and stunt the developing of writing values. The invocation of normative writing styles, as intrinsically related to emotion or truth, can be understood as an attempt to control what can be thought and expressed by regulating the flow and configuration of language. Contrary to what had been suggested, for example in Louis Simpson's presentation yesterday, the so-called "plain style" is not the abused stepchild of official verse culture in America. Rather, it is the *dominant* verse rhetoric of academic creative writing programs in this country: a dominance institutionally supported by prizes and awards and critical support in official media and a dominance predicated on the *exclusion* of other modes of writing—contemporary and historical—whether they be described as difficult or gay or primitive or third world or black or abstract or feminist. The claim of and for a plain style is involved with an homogenization of the concept of voice and person, implicitly advocating a voice that is white, male, middle class, and heterosexual—whether practiced by men or women, blacks or whites.

It is important to note, given the tenor of discussion at this symposium, that professional poets as much as, or more than, professional critics may be hostile to alternative developments

140

within poetry—most eager to heap abuse and, within their limited power, exclude. To some extent, this is a product of the myopia that affects those deeply rooted in their own perceptions, and the context of those perceptions. Fairness is not necessarily a positive aesthetic value. But where judgment is prized, the danger of arrogance looms large, and where arrogant judgment looms, authoritarianism is sure to follow. We see this in the self-serving presumption of a "Poet" claiming, over and against the "Critic," the rights of Self and Authority. It is not just that no one mode of writing can assert a privilege over any other, but also that such formulations represent such a high degree of generalization and abstraction that any real—*useful*—distinction between criticism and poetry can no longer be made. Too often, such cries, as it were, in the wilderness, are strategic academic sorties to curb dissent so as to leave the field clear for the poet's own critical position. (Anti-intellectualism is a form of critical opinion, weirdly at home in a sphere of intellectual labor such as poetry.)

Poetry is potentially the most powerful technology to realize the multidimensionality of reading values—to sound the sonic, measure the lexicon, and refuse a standardization and regimentation that deafens us to the living past in language and diverts us from enacting living presents—decentered and plural—*for* language.

But these living presents may be more than can be accounted for; rather than being devourers of words, we may find ourselves devoured by them. The latter scenario is the legacy of the willful refusal to recognize the power *in* words; that power cannot be overturned or mastered, but it can be heard and channeled. When you put bits and pieces of language together you get more than the sum of the parts, the process resembling Dr. Frankenstein's stitching together pieces of flesh and engendering not dead matter, not an abstractly arid and random collation of parts, but a simulacrum of human being and a being in its own right. This is the story of the poem, its internal narration, as the kidneys and liver and heart narrate the body's story. We are, then, systematically de*lude*d—led from play—by reductive understandings of such techniques as collage or juxtaposition or parataxis. The problem with *juxtaposition* is the emphasis on a possibly arbitrary relation between two elements, placed side by side, which tends to undercut the overall system of relationships—the total prosody—that makes a poem whole. That is, every part of a poem relates to every other part—the parts are fused, coalesced, grafted together. *Collage* and *parataxis,* while accurate descriptions, may minimize recognition of the degree of overall musical and thematic construction. In this context, Denise Levertov's term, "organic form," was an attractive alternative to free verse. The problem, however, is that it may suggest a unity of naturally harmonious parts—again a biological as opposed to cultural unity that misses the interpenetration of these aspects in creating the *social flesh* that is the poem. As Sergei Eisenstein writes in *The Film Sense* (translated and edited by Jay Leyda; New York: Harcourt, Brace, Jovanovich, 1975), "the image planned by the author has become flesh of the flesh of the spectator's risen image" (34). But Eisensteinian montage is also a limiting case since it suggests the primacy of a thematic "image" ("single, unifying, and definitive" [70]) determining—presumably in advance—the choice of elements to be juxtaposed. Insofar as this image is understood as "single, recognizable, and whole" (16), it precludes thematically and ideationally nonidentical material. ("Each representation is, in the image sense, individual, dissimilar, and yet identical thematically" [34].) This would necessitate making a distinction between the "common denotation" of sharply conflicting elements, which is the essence of Eisensteinian montage, and some other, less iconographically representable, whole. Irreconcilable material, that is, may produce an unforeseeable (indeed unseeable) fusion that is not an image in the Eisensteinian sense.

Dysraphism may be a useful term in this context. Medically, it would mean a congenital misseaming of embryonic parts—*raph* means seam, a rhapsodist being one who stitches parts together, that is, a reciter of epic poetry. So different parts from the middle, end, and beginning—it's a 4-D image—are fused together to become one entity.

These considerations hold open the possibility of a maximum *differentiation* of parts—style, vocabulary, syntax. You start with the integrity and autonomy of parts and find the whole in them. What made Dr. Frankenstein's creature a monster was just the reverse—starting with a preconceived whole and tailoring the parts to fit.

Reconsideration of the possibilities of the part-to-whole relation will allow further alternative prosodic techniques to the common

142

and positivistic rhetorical techniques of "ego" unity and rationalistic expository unity. At the broadest level, the part-to-whole relation means the relation of one text to another, one poem to another, and one book to another; the idea of the interweaving of all of the work of a single author and beyond that of the related interweaving of the works of different authors. This is common enough as a reading practice, as when one skips through a number of books at the same time. As a writing practice, there is the collaboration of writers on a single work as well as the appropriation by a writer of other texts. In these and other ways, the end points of a given poem or a given author are radiated outward. On another level, the part-to-whole relation concerns syllable to word, word to line and word to phrase, phrase to line, line to stanza, line to poem, stanza to poem, poem to book, and so on. Within this conceptualization, the territorial integrity of the poem begins to break down under a shifting focus that suggests a number of places in which the membranous line that may be called closure or a poem's end can be invoked. What is the smallest or largest discrete unit of a text? Where does mine stop and yours start? Every caesura, whether the line break or the last page of the book, opens up to a possibility of continuing (rereading the book, going on to another) or *stopping*. For the practicing poet and practicing reader, the concern does not so much have to be with an increased definition of prescribed boundaries as with how these provisional limits— horizons—are invoked or provoked: allegorically as the continuities and fissures of a life (Lyn Hejinian's *My Life,* Robert Creeley's *Pieces*), structurally as the component parts of meaning-generation (Ron Silliman's work), narratively as the progression of story (Laura (Riding) Jackson's *Progress of Stories*), historically and geographically as the creation of a place (Charles Olson's *The Maximus Poems*), and so on.

The poetics of part to whole cannot help but expose motivations for, and principles of, unity and the mechanisms by which they are approached. Louis Zukofsky's *"A"* manages to do this with the metaphor of a life's work. Its carefully composed articulation of distinct movements, as in a symphony, permits maximum differentiation section to section without recourse to a single thematic or syntactic underpinning to create unification. *"A"* seems exemplary of a genuine negative capability for fusing a poem together: significant for each of its endings and completions; serial, in the Spicerian sense, more than thematic.

Consider a work composed of a number of autonomously distinct pieces, which nonetheless functions as a whole by articulating the relations among the parts: that is, has an overall configuration whose music is composed of differences. But what are the possibilities for a whole that is not constructed along narrative or overtly thematic/historical lines? I've pointed to some problems with an overly explicit or regulatory constituting framework—whether called coherence, closure, or unity, ruling out possibilities for heteroclites, anomaly, oddness. One alternative image to the uniplanar surface of "ego" or "ratio"nally organized writing is of a möbius textuality, aspiring not toward the arbitrariness and accumulation of juxtaposition but rather the fusion of social flesh. That is, the succession of displacements involved in a möbius rather than otherwise rhetorically unified poem are not centrifugal but centripetal, do not displace from the site of the poem but enact an emplacement *as* the poem.

Of course, any movement, any duration involves displacement, which can be more or less disguised. The poem can acknowledge its duration as an emplacement, as *metaphor,* insofar as metaphor means to transfer. So we get to duration in a poem by a series of substitutions or replacements that don't *stand for* or in *place of* but themselves embody that moment of time. Duration, then, becomes not a series of constantly postponed absences but the site of the con*fusing.*

So the poem enters the world, and each of us beside it, facing it. It keeps beat not to an imposed metrics but to the marks of its own joints and the joints of the reader's projection. The poem sounds as music the marks of its continual newness in being made; and the only mark of its past, of its having been made, is the blood on the cutting room floor.

Gerald Stern

WHAT IS
THIS POET?

I always have a hard time answering questions like "What is a poet?" (What is a child? What is a carrot? What is justice?). I am tempted to give a Gertrude Stein answer, which is an evasion and a metaphor and a statement as well about the very difficulty of doing such a thing. Such a poor thing. What is a poet, then, is what a poet is about. But to begin with it is what poetry is about. Although no two poets are about the same thing. And neither is poetry. I suspect a poet began early in life being a poet. And he learned to listen like a poet and even talk like a poet. Although not all poets began early in life. That is, to listen and talk. I remember I was very young when I first learned to listen, but I was quite old, I remember, when I learned to talk and listen to my own satisfaction. Not to mention Kenneth Burke's or Louis Simpson's. To the best of my knowledge I had a vision one day while walking up some stone steps on the inside of the Cathedral of Learning. This is in Pittsburgh. To the best of my knowledge I was going up and not down and I stopped at a stained-glass window and felt dizzy. I wore bow ties then and dou- ble-breasted suits, but I carried in my pocket an orange notebook where I carefully wrote out one sonnet after another. I wrote them

145

down. I was an addict of Untermeyer then and given to memorizing poems. My dizziness was a discovery. I was to be abandoned because I listened and talked like that. I was cut loose from my tribe. Even though I wore bow ties and played right halfback for a while on the Pitt football team. I felt this thing thoroughly, though I tried not to explain it to myself. Up to that point I had never seen a poet. Though I heard about him in Untermeyer. All this is very important because it is important. It is important not for the poet but for those who like to read poems and listen to them and who like to know what a poem is and who like to know what bothers them in what a poem is. For some poets this is important too. But for some more than others. It has become important to me this fall.

I am tempted to carry on like this for twenty-two pages. It is tempting, although Stein says somewhere in her lectures that temptations are not very tempting. She says that even though they are. I noticed I moved quickly into the biographical. It is a way out these days, but it is also an important way in, and it always has been so for the poet. Indeed, how could he, and she, begin anywhere but with the question, "What is *this* poet?"

I believe every poet, when he tries to understand why he is a poet and why he is the kind of poet that he is, returns to a certain place, a certain time, and a certain set of circumstances. Even if he is blind and sentimental about that place, or even if he is a little resentful and self-pitying, he nonetheless identifies with it and remembers that it was there that he was not only nurtured but armed with values and even given his voice. He might break free of those values once or even twice later on, but it would be in terms of that first place, and even on its conditions, that he would do so. I don't mean that if he was at Harvard in the late 1930s or at Columbia or Iowa in the early 1950s or Provincetown in the late 1970s that that was the decisive influence on him. I mean that there is a tremendous year, or two years, in his life when the events are more luminous and more symbolic than they ever were before or will be again. I mean that time operates differently then and that the mind and the spirit create a crustacean order out of the softness it had once lain in.

It is interesting that when we think of those luminous times and places, those awakenings, we tend to think of group awakenings, at least when we talk about artists: poets and painters. There seems always to be a movement, a collective action, or a buddy system, whether we are at Oxford or in Montparnasse or in the Village. I remember, to give an obvious example, how the "new" English poets—Auden, Spender, MacNeice, C. Day Lewis—were linked together for a few years in the late thirties and early forties as if they all were divided from the same egg. One talked loosely of their political prejudices, their use of a Modernist vocabulary, their creation of a new sensibility. Looking back now, or even looking closely then, we can, and could, easily see the radical differences among them. It may just have been the power of Auden's personality, or his genius, that temporarily united them, or it may have been the result of some crude and useful publicity. But they were published, at least at first, together and were taught together, as a group. So it was with Beats and Black Mountaineers and Sad Academics; and so it was with the Apocalyptics; and so it is with Language Poets and Gymnasts. I am moving slightly away from the subject. I mean to emphasize not literary movements as such but small theaters of learning and action, whether or not they generate or reflect literary movements. And I want to emphasize that those "theaters" are, at best, places for normally isolated poets to exhange ideas and tears with each other, and I want to emphasize most of all that the poet, as least his most critical part, is not formed there but altogether somewhere else and that some poets—many poets—have never been involved in such theater, that they learned what they had to learn, and learned to talk and listen, and borrowed or forged or concocted for themselves voices and dramas and subjects and controversies and obsessions—styles you might say—by themselves, and sometimes all by themselves, with only the dead and distant writers to witness and to encourage.

I was writing poems, and reading books, in a kind of lovely and peaceful isolation in the late forties, 1948, 1949, in Pittsburgh, and I had come to my "place" without training or support or any kind of preparation or conditioning. Not even an uncle or a kind teacher, all motherly or brotherly. My undergraduate training was in philosophy and political science. I took one English course during my four years at the University of Pittsburgh. I won't speak of my high school years. They were despicable, as far as learning was concerned. I played pool and ran the mile. At home there was *Life* magazine and *The Jewish Criterion*. There was a copy of *Alice in*

Wonderland—it had belonged to my dead sister—hidden on a closet shelf and I myself had two books. One was called *Lost with Lieutenant Pike*—it was the sad story of Zebulon Pike and his aborted attempt to climb what later would be called Pike's Peak; and the other was a large book, folio size, containing narratives and colored pictures of the great explorers, Da Gama, Cortez, Columbus. There also was a bible, in English, and several leather-bound prayer books in Hebrew. I was given to reading, though, and it must have been at a fairly early age because I remember being scolded several times for reading in class instead of paying attention. There was very little stillness in my culture and it was one of the things I had to learn to create. I remember being in the woods when I was seventeen or eighteen—I was a camp counselor—and reading Scott out of a little leather book with my right elbow in the grass. The book had a lovely purple cloth marker. In the fall of 1947, just out of college, I was reading Whitman and Sandburg and Jeffers and Auden and Dickinson and Masters and Yeats, mostly in anthologies. And I was reading Shakespeare and Marlowe and Spenser and Chaucer and Keats and Wordsworth and Swinburne. I was getting my English education. And I was reading nineteenth- and twentieth-century novels. I had gotten hold of lists of "great books" and I was ransacking the library and the few bookstores in Pittsburgh. I read in odd places. There were certain park benches I loved, certain restaurants. At the Carnegie Library I read in the genealogy room, an old scarred table, some high leather chairs, and some locked-up glass cabinets. Nobody else came there. I was in the 52–20 Club. I got twenty dollars a week for fifty-two weeks, as part of my World War II GI Bill. It was a system designed to reabsorb veterans into the economy, but I used it to buy some free time. Twenty bucks a week was not all that bad. I had spent a good portion of my army time in the stockade. I read the New Testament while I was there, for the first time, and learned to wield a huge sledgehammer about twelve hours a day in relative comfort. It was while I was in the stockade, sleeping under a bare illuminated light bulb, that I decided once and for all to become a "writer"—whatever that meant. It was my second vision. Among other things it meant I would not go to law school, as I was half-destined to do, or get a Ph.D. in political science. It also meant I was going to leave the world and know the muse only, as Emerson said, but I didn't altogether know that yet. I will have to spare you the details of my incarceration and save them for my own *Enormous Room.* Only that I had a special court-martial, that the trial lasted for two days, that I could have received up to thirty months on my charges, and that I was found not guilty on all counts. Of course I did spend a few months inside waiting for my trial to begin, but I forgave almost everybody, since I was young—twenty-one—and I had a lot of time ahead of me, and since I am anyhow very forgiving. I have no idea why I turned to poetry then. It certainly wasn't because I had been educated through poetry and that when my emotions demanded something I would turn to that naturally. I think that, for me, poetry was a kind of last recourse this side of sanity, and that it was the way—I discovered—to respond to injustice and cruelty and meaninglessness and stupidity. I tried, and I sometimes still do try, reason and logic as a response. The precise language of argument. But poetry is more precise, as it is evasive. That is what I discovered. I think my sister's death and my parents' response to it was one of the things that eventually turned me to poetry; and I think the endless abuse I took as a Jew in violent, hateful Pittsburgh also turned me to poetry; and I think that mad America drove me into it, as Auden says Ireland did to Yeats. Also maybe the love of language, the passion for form, and awe in the face of the extreme ugliness and extreme beauty of that city.

I'm not sure where I would have gone and what would have become of me had I continued all alone. I certainly wasn't lonely and I didn't at all feel deprived, but I did meet two others, Jack Gilbert and Richard Hazley, who were writing at that time in Pittsburgh—probably the only two others—and the three of us quickly became a little group, and we suddenly had the great joy of exchanging books and testing ideas and doing a little posturing. We supported each other and were perhaps a little guarded of each other. Maybe we loved each other. As I recall I was the only one who was doing any serious writing yet. Jack intended to become a novelist, though he did put "poet" (instead of "student") on his passport when we all transferred our *locus* from Pittsburgh to Paris, France, a year or so later. Our critical position was "the poet in a hostile world." We had contempt for the bourgeoisie, we dressed outrageously, we dreamed of Europe, we were poor. We were living in a kind of darkness, but it never occurred to us to pity

ourselves. In fact we thought we were lucky. There were no readings then in Pittsburgh, and no workshops, and little poetry. The
universities at that time didn't have poets teaching or residing
there—or hardly at all—and there were no M.F.A. programs and
readings and circuits and layers of awards and prizes and presses
upon presses and poetry in the schools or on the lawns or in the
privies. I guess Iowa already had its program going but it never
occurred to any of us to go *there*. Aside from anything else it would
have been a terrible betrayal to reduce poetry to craft. It was too
holy for that. It had become our religion.

We were reading Pound and Eliot and Yeats and Cummings and
MacLeish and Hart Crane and Robinson Jeffers, of the moderns. Not
much Stevens or Williams yet. I was reading Auden too. And Rilke
and Rimbaud and Yeats's last poems. We memorized and recited to
each other dozens of poems. Oddly enough, we spent very little
time showing our own poems to each other, and if we did, we did
not labor over the details. I think Pound was the central figure.
Mostly *Personae* and *ABC*. A few of the *Cantos*. The Bollingen
controversy was raging then but there was no issue of where our
sympathy lay—with the artist and against the Philistines. I had been
obsessed with politics and believed in socialism and, of course,
hated fascism, but a poet was under siege. We certainly were in no
position then to examine Pound's absurd and cruel ideas, let alone
his bathos and silliness. He was, for us, a generator of soul. It was
in this context, with this background, that we confronted the
new academicism when it came our way. We were horrified, and
amused a little, when we read the new poems. We had no idea at the
time that poets would deliberately betray the holy. Yet, since we
were rather dumb critically and lived in a kind of isolation, we
didn't know quite what to do except to rip up their books and rage a
little. And we could berate them with the same voice that we be-
rated the general foolish conservatism of the late forties and early
fifties, hiding its brutality and arrogance behind manners and fake
decency and niceness. We saw an easy connection between the two.
Maybe we were blessed, living in the dark ages among those three
rivers, for the black cloud of poetic conservatism moved very
slowly over the Alleghenies; and even as we reached back for more
solid nourishment from an earlier period, we were, without knowing it, anticipating a later time. If we had only known it, if we hadn't

been so modest and stupid and terrified, we would have realized our strengths, not our weaknesses. I don't know how to sum up our collective vision or even my own aesthetic then. I have a sneaking suspicion that when we said "Pound" we were really saying something else. Certainly I moved quickly to incorporate the Jewish prophetic tradition and Blake and German expressionism and the Russian. And Milton and Shakespeare and Coleridge. And Hazley and Gilbert, though a little more loyal to Pound, also moved away a little. But I mean something else. Perhaps it wasn't Pound we were inspired by—though we adored his poems—but a heroic or even mythic idea. Perhaps, as Trilling says of the Keats reflected in his letters, it was the heroic mode we were after—we wanted to idealize the heroic and live heroic lives, whatever that meant to us, and clearly Pound was a hero. Perhaps we were searching for something even deeper or more intense or absorbing. Perhaps we were searching for Orpheus, we poor poets. Perhaps the search for power and divine form, as realized through beautiful singing, is always a search for Orpheus, as Rilke suggests, and in one way or another a poet is he who becomes a liberator—as he creates his song. My God! If this is true, it's no wonder that we had such contempt for the worker ants, we kings. We were not just provincial bohemians leading indulgent lives; we were on a great mission, and we were saving the world, even if it refused to be saved, or scoffed, or, worst of all, didn't listen. We were subduing wild beasts, and moving trees, and visiting hell and prophesying; and we were redeeming ourselves from oblivion, and death. From time. And we were reviving Emerson's and Shelley's conception of the poet as the center of civilized life and of poetry as the ideal vocation. We were possessed by a powerful spirit, however clearly we understood it, and we were expressing ancient ideas and feelings, though we had no name for it.

I have gone through great changes in my life, and I have had bitterness and false hope and recently some success and praise, and I have changed subject matter and shifted my posture and altered my outlook a little and modified my rhythms and changed jobs; and I have been weary and angry and frustrated and anxious; but I have never abandoned that dream. I don't know how. It's almost as if I don't have a choice. I'm not complaining; and I have no regrets, as the little sparrow says. True, I am able to lead a less

151

ascetic existence and I am even able to enjoy money and posses-
sions a little, and I own property and pay insurance and my children have gone to college and I am looking forward one day to
being a grandfather, but always there is a demand, or if not a
demand a longing, or if not a longing a sweetness I must taste over
and over and over again. I had an unusual life as a poet. I wrote in
isolation and lived in a kind of confusion for a couple of decades,
even though I was a social being and was articulate and boisterous.
I seemed never to have understood, though I understood everything. I was never satisfied with what I was doing. As I look back on
the early part of my career—of my life—I am surprised, even
amazed, at how stubborn and foolish I was; how unwise. Only
slowly am I forgiving myself. I mention all this not to be self-
indulgent and not out of self-importance but only because, for this
occasion, I am discussing a certain journey—my own—and how it
illustrates the nature of a poet, as we are trying to understand it, and
how it illustrates the nature of poetry.

I had my third vision when I was about forty and teaching at a
state college in western Pennsylvania. I had just all but abandoned a
long poem that I had been working on for almost seven years and I
was suddenly empty and lost and altogether alone. I wandered
through the alleys and in the woods talking to myself. I was sleep-
less. I had trouble meeting my classes or talking to my friends and
family. From my present perspective I see what happened to me as
part of a personal enlightenment, albeit a very peculiar one, and I
was about to be freed—as a poet—from years of encumbrance.
But then all I saw was ruin and bankruptcy. I had been a practicing
poet for two decades and I had nothing to show. But after a short
while—maybe six months, maybe a year—I stopped struggling or
even competing. I didn't care what year the poets were born who
were publishing in the magazines and I became more silent and
less boisterous. And I started to write those poems, one after another, that in a few years I would collect in *Rejoicings*. And there has
been no letup since then. It is interesting that my crisis, as I describe it, occurred in my fortieth year, a real *crise de quarante,* and I
am sure that there was a great psychological implication—I could
even talk about it—but I want to spare us the boredom of my
particulars. As far as those new poems were concerned, they didn't
seem that different from what I was doing ten or even twenty years

earlier. Maybe what happened was that I shifted a little or caught the light in a different way or focused more clearly. Maybe it's just that I was destined to be a poet of the second half of life and that I needed the first half to pass as content, or subject matter. Maybe I learned finally to accept my, and nature's, limitations. Maybe I was able to accept my own happiness.

I think a lot about Whitman, and sometimes Emerson and Shelley. I am amazed by Whitman's knowledge and by the way he states the problem. I sometimes think he had a secret text—I am tempted to say *the* secret text—and that his poems, particularly *Song of Myself,* were an allusion to that text and a metaphoric rendering of it, even a series of riddles. The whole truth he kept to himself and released a little bit at a time. But then he lost or burned the text, good democrat that he was, a democrat and yet a priest, one of the very few. Surely he read carefully what Emerson had to say about the poet, and surely he was the poet Emerson was dreaming about, or almost, and surely this has been said too many times. Emerson was certainly not a poet we read in the late forties and early fifties, neither his essays *nor* his poems. He was windy and obscure and abstract and pompous and preacherly and optimistic and ungrounded. But he attacked the effete literary establishment of New England, and he was, if sometimes tight and cowardly and proper, also gauche and wild, and above all else he viewed the role of the poet as central in the remaking, indeed in the very making, of the American vision. In *Nature,* for example, he spoke specifically of the need for an intermediary or archangel who would be to the nation what Christ was to the first Christians. He was very specific about it. The poet, acting from his own character, acts for us all. He is the representative man. He is Christ. Homer.

If we could have found a way of converting Emerson, or translating him—putting him to use—we would have probably emphasized his concentration on ecstasy and spontaneity and intuition and on the holiness and power of language. Or we would have emphasized his concentration on the visionary moment and his search for a paradise within to overcome the loss of Eden, real or imagined. All these things. And the poet as liberating god, and the sense of poetry as religion, and the attack on ossified language, and the elevation of what he called the celestial—what we would call the unconscious—and the paean to nature's original ecstasy, and the view of the poet as prophet and healer, and the vision of all life as symbolic. If we could have found a way of converting him. As it was, we were able to use some of Emerson, although decoded and transformed. After all, we had just gone through World War II and the death camps and the dropping of the bomb. And we had an overwhelming sense of having lost power and control, and even the most childish and trusting of us were obsessed with the idea of evil. Essentially we had to find a way of holding on a little to the dream and yet live in that terrifying and exhausting world. For me it was a double loss, for I had to abandon the socialist and humanist ideal I had still clung to as a wistful boy, years after the Stalin purge; and somehow, as I abandoned that, or at least began to look at it more realistically, I all but abandoned its Jewish version, compounded as it was with the greater loss, in Poland and Germany. I was overcome with mourning—and nostalgia—strange bedfellows for my newfound aestheticism. Swinburne and Debs; Pound and Pico della Mirandola, arm in arm. Most of all I was resisting, though blindly, and with confused critical acumen, the petty academicism and the small poetry that was then all but taking over. I was doing it with my celestial self, lungs bursting.

As far as Shelley was concerned, it was, like Emerson, his sense of the poet as prophet and visionary and lawgiver, and his sense of poetry as an act of inspiration and purification that moved us, though we seldom talked about him at that time since we were a little dumbly obedient to Eliot's view of Shelley's thought. And Arnold's. It was hard to resist those deadly critics, one with a view of Shelley as an adolescent, the other with the view of him as an innocent angel. I think I was more indebted to Shelley than I wanted to admit. As much as anything else, it wasn't the detailed argument of the *Defence* that interested or moved me; it was the sense of urgency and seriousness in his poetry and in his life. And though I may have derived more pleasure from reading "The Flea" or the "Valediction" than from *Prometheus* or *Adonais*, it was the spirit of Shelley that I bore with me when I sat down with my sharpened pencils, my clean tablets, and my statue of David. Certainly I never felt, at least consciously, that despotism, ignorance, superstition, and evil sprang from the "extinction of the poetic principle," or that poetry was the source of "whatever of beautiful or generous or true that can have place in an evil time," in short,

154

that poetry could save us, but it did save me, even if by other principles than those elucidated by Shelley, although I am not quite ready yet for my own *Defence*.

I think of the poets of the eighties and seventies and wonder what unforeseen use they made or are making of Shelley and Emerson. I ask the absurd questions. Do they think poetry is divine? Is it at once the center and circumference of Knowledge? Does it turn all things to loveliness? Is it the record of the best and happiest moments of the best and happiest minds? Is the poet more delicately organized, more sensible to pain and pleasure? Is he the true founder of religion, the one who utters the powerful secret? Is he the one without impediments? Does he break our chains? Is he the true land-lord, sea-lord, air-lord?

These are absurd questions—in the glaring light of day—for any poets, but they are more absurd for the poets born, say, after 1935. And I think this is so because those poets seem to have chosen a less dramatic, shall I say less Orphic, view of themselves. (Although this could change again.) I think this is true; and I think they did so for a number of reasons, if indeed I can use the word "choose" to describe the turn they took. I think one of the reasons was a sense of helplessness, even hopelessness, brought on partly by the bomb and its aftermath, including permanent global terror and tension, and partly by the terrifying intrusion and control of the body politic—government, school, television, draft, IRS—in their lives. The dance of the sixties does not disprove this. The poets of protest, then, Bly, Ginsberg, Levertov, for example, were born in the 1920s. All of them. There were younger black and women poets, yes, who were politically conscious, but their attention was turned to specific problems, and the poetry was an offshoot of the problem. Hardly what Orpheus had in mind. The other reason—for the decline of the Orphic—was, in one way or another, the new mode of education and training of the poets, the university and the workshop. Or the professional expectations of the poets, working in a college or university, a school, with all the hazards of misfortune that could inspire and generate. Perhaps what has happened to the poets I am discussing is that they have lost the great memory. I think that's what happened, and I think it will take them a little time to regain it. Or maybe it was our generation that started to lose the memory, the faith in the celestial, and maybe we were able to live

155

off the rot for awhile, most bitterly and beautifully, and there are only bones left for the others. Although neither the university nor Bohemia nor the bourgeois spirit can tape the mouth of Orpheus shut for too long, nor drown his song. Not even thought manipulation or the enshrinement of ignorance, America's present contribution to spirit. I think there are marvelous poets in America now, and some who were born in 1935 and some in 1945 and some in 1955. I am talking about a state of shock, and a general condition. The history of literature is always characterized by noise and then silence. If this is a period of extraordinary isolated poems and moving, generous poets, it is also a period of "silence." Those poets themselves may, of course, be relieved—even delighted—by the circumstances, or they may look with horror at Shelley and Emerson—even Whitman. Or they may insist that Orpheus will play his pipes in a different way, even change his name. I myself am variously excited, or bored and irritated, by the poetry I see. That part is no different than it was thirty years ago.

In the meantime I am remembering that Shelley wrote *A Defence of Poetry* in response to Thomas Love Peacock's satiric essay *The Four Ages of Poetry*. And I remember, with amusement, that peacocks have become a problem again, and that all around they are waiting to spring or preen or scream, whatever it is that peacocks do. Sometimes, in pure peacockry, they lecture us on the demise of poetry; sometimes they fan us a little with their brilliant feathers. My brutal and wise self says never trust a bird with an eye in the middle of his ass or one who drags his beauty in the dust. But I am careful of all birds, those owls that blink once a month; those brave turkeys of the wilderness; those parrots; those bleeding canaries; those shitting pigeons; even those eagles. I myself am a bird with only a few impediments. I have large wings and a heavy body. And my voice is simple and clear. Like all the others, I abandon myself to the wind; like all others, I eat without stopping. I am full of impatience and good vision and anguish and sorrow and cunning. And I love the weeds. As always.

Kenneth Burke

POETRY AS SYMBOLIC ACTION

When planning this talk with the unwieldy title "Poets, Poems, Poetry, Poetics" (with the tentative notion that I might also sneak in *"ars poetica"* when focusing upon the characterizing of one particular poet's style and substance), I intended to begin by building around a poet's observations on a poem of his own: Poe's essay, "The Philosophy of Composition," purporting to be an account of how he went about the writing of "The Raven."[1] By reference to the *principles* involved in the production, he would try to show, he said, "that the work proceeded, step by step, to its completion with the precision and rigid consequences of a mathematical problem." My full discussion of this matter had been published in the Fiftieth Anniversary number of *Poetry: A Magazine of Verse* (October 1961), under the editorship of Henry Rago, but I had a (I now think mistakenly) abbreviated version of it in my essay, "Poetics in Particular, Language in General," in the 1968 edition of my volume *Language as Symbolic Action: Essays on Life, Literature, and Method.*

Methodologically, Poe's error is in confusing the logically prior and temporally prior (as the word *principium* in Latin means both

logical "principle" and "beginning" in time; and in Greek the corresponding word *arche* has the same duplicity of meanings). But
once we dispose of that erroneous usage in Poe's essay, it seemed to
me, he does suggest an arrangement such that there would be
different but related and complementary jobs for poet and critic to
perform.

In my abbreviated discussion of Poe's discussion of the principles embodied in the writing of "The Raven" I summed up the
issue thus:[2]

> The poet's job is simply to write his poems as best he knows how.
> He may actually do some theorizing of a sort. At the very least, he is
> likely to have some rules of thumb that he goes by; and often he will
> be quite vocal as to the kind of poem he does *not* want to write. But
> he needs make no mention of any such notions, and can treat them
> in as flimsy or haphazard a fashion as he likes. They're not his
> business. Yet they *are* the critic's business. And to the extent that the
> critic carries out such a task, he contributes simultaneously to the
> vitality of criticism as an autonomous activity with its own principles,
> and to the glory of poetry by showing that the poems are "prin-
> cipled" (insofar as the critic's formulations bring out the modes
> of judgment implicit in the decisions which the poet's work ex-
> emplifies, regardless of whether the poet explicitly told himself that
> he was makng such decisions).
>
> In sum, the poet as poet makes a poem; and his ways of making
> the poem are practices which implicitly involve principles, or pre-
> cepts. The critic, in matching the poetry with a poetics, seeks to
> make these implicit principles explicit. But he may not be wholly
> equal to the task—whereupon other critics may arise who offer
> solutions somewhat different from his.

A couple of years ago, I happened to see an excellent article (in
The New York Times Book Review) by Richard Wilbur on Poe's
critical works. But since he didn't mention Poe's "The Philosophy of
Composition," I wrote him about my notions. I'm glad I did because it brought me the lively rejoinder which I quote from. He
says in connection with my article that it is:[3]

> . . . so far as I can now remember, the only essay to take Poe's
> article seriously. I agree with you that there are principles implicit in
> any act of poetic composition, that the critic may discover them and

assert their logical (if not temporal) priority. This is true, I think, even of a poet like Frost, who insists so on the passivity of the poet before the oncoming poem. Frost may feel that the poem just happens to him, in a series of surprises, and arrives at last at a statement fore-felt but not foreknown. Nevertheless, the poem turns out to be a Frost poem, all full of implicit decisions about technique and dealing, in a fresh way mostly, with one of the several themes which make him write. And it would be an illuminating critical exercise, having read the Frost poem, to try not merely to describe it but to prescribe it.

I've always mistrusted "The Philosophy of Composition" for the reason which you give, that Poe tricks himself, or tries to trick the reader, into believing that "The Raven" was made according to a fully conscious "genetic" series of procedures. As a constructor of detective tales, in which the writer reasons backward from the solution, Poe would have been likelier than another to work in such a manner, yet I cannot believe that he did. One ground of my unbelief is Poe's insistence, almost everywhere else, that imaginative genius operates in an intuitive and infallible flash. Dupin solves "The Purloined Letter" in its essentials *before* the police have acquainted him with the details of the case. Kepler, as Poe repeatedly tells us, "dreamed" his astronomical solutions, and then worked out the demonstrations at his leisure. Poe continually tells us, of Dupin, that such imaginative genius as his comprehends all other kinds of genius— that the brilliant poet, for example, cannot fail to be also a brilliant mathematician and reasoner. "The Philosophy of Composition" strikes me—in part—as an effort to make the reader believe that a poem has been written by a sub-genius, that rational prodigy whom the poet's genius subsumes.

I suppose one could infer some of Poe's "principles" from "The Raven," but there is the difficulty that the poem is unlike almost all of his other poems in respect of narrative fullness and in respect of dramatic changes of mood. I avoided discussing "The Philosophy of Composition" in my *Times* essay because I had just 1500–2000 words, and it would have taken too long to establish that article's kind and degree of truth.

I intend to discuss further in another connection the matter of the two "priorities," logical firsts and temporal firsts. And in both of my versions I discuss the fact that the poet is not necessarily the person best qualified to define the principles that his own work embodies. (A notable section of Coleridge's *Biographia Literaria* is a quarrel with Wordsworth's formulation for his own verse, as stated in his preface to *Lyrical Ballads,* as much of a manifesto in the realm of literature as the Marxist *Communist Manifesto* was to be in the realm of politics.) Also, on the subject of Poe's ardent "conclusion" that the ideal lyric should aim at *Beauty,* an "intense elevation of the *soul,*" with an effect best got by a "tone" of "sadness," since Melancholy is "the most legitimate of the poetic tones," and "Never losing sight of the object *supremeness,* or perfection," having asked himself, "Of all melancholy topics what, according to the *universal* understanding of mankind, is the *most* melancholy?" to which rhetorical question "*Death* was the obvious reply." That leads to his grand finale, "this most melancholy of topics" is "most poetical":

> When it most closely allies itself to *Beauty:* the death, then, of a beautiful woman is, unquestionably the most poetical topic in the world—and equally is it beyond doubt that the lips best suited for such a topic are those of a bereaved lover.

That passage turns me in three directions. First, there's that point about "*supremeness,* or perfection" as the poet's "object." Of course, poetic diction is synonymous with saying the right thing; the poet is not satisfied with his lines until he decides that they are *just right.* And though Poe's pompous way of saying as much may be resented, I take it as beyond all question that, although at different moments in history criteria of stylistic propriety may vary, even a poet who may be in his personal relations quite a scoundrel will, if he is truly a poet, feel squeamish about the way he says things, though if he is a real pro he can sometimes be persuaded that a modified expression would be preferable.

Consider how "perfectly" right Poe was, in going from a parrot to a raven for the "quothing" of his "Nevermores." And in this connection I recall that Stephen Foster, looking at a map of the southern states, first tried "Way down upon the Pedee River" before hitting upon the vocables that did supremely well by his somewhat related topic, nostalgia. He was, like me, a citizen of Pittsburgh, which, when I was young, was still at the height of the era marked by the three great technological freedoms, the freedom to waste, the freedom to pollute, the freedom not to give a damn. Technology's self-criticism, environmentalism, was but in a state of emergence; I recall the hellish flames of the steel mills blazing all night, while there were always mirages in the sky over Pennsylvania, when they were visible, of oil wells just brought into production though not yet capped. And in the town itself, my father told me, there were wells which at night, when not being used by the mills, were allowed to discharge into the air—whereupon the first nightlit ball fields were inaugurated, as the big boys would toss a lighted torch into the stream of escaping gas to use the light for their play, and another mirage would be reflected in the sky above Pennsylvania, the home of Pennzoil, cans of which are still for sale in garages, at least in my area of the nation.

But reverting to the theme of Foster's nostalgia, which as a "topic" is not far from the same slant as Poe's melancholy, I'd like to indicate how, by sympathy (*not* "empathy," a replacement that irritates me considerably, though there is a legitimate place for this neological translation of the German term, *Einfühling*) my *critical* responses led me to a poetically versified response thus:

Lines Found in a Bottle

"Dear Friends, and Gentle Hearts"
—words found on Stephen Foster,
who died dead drunk

Dear friends, and gentle hearts
Dear hearts, and gentle friends
Far away way down done gone
Dear strangers all my life
Dear strangers all to one another
Swanee me you'll find now movin' on.[4]

My reasons for introducing this turn will be made clear later.

Meanwhile, note that there is a fundamental twist involved in our concern with Poe *as a poet.* In Chapter XIX of Aristotle's *Poetics,* he touches upon an issue which now turns up in, of all places, *psychoanalytical* theories of poetic genius. In that chapter (no, this is in Chapter XVII, but it involves considerations which are, as I shall show, integrally tied in with the later chapter), regarding the "agitated blusters and the angry man rages" (Loeb Classical Library translation) which the tragic poet must convincingly present, we are told that "poetry needs either a sympathetic nature or a madman, the former being impressionable and the latter inspired." (In a footnote the translator, W. Hamilton Fyfe, adds: "Genius to madness here allied" is meant here.) The "necrophile" theme is so recurrent in Poe's works that his critics, most of whom would belittle the tract as little more than a myth designed to disguise his personal incompetencies, though some might acknowledge the topic in its own right as a radical aspect of his particular *ars poetica* (bordering on even such operatic flourishes as the *Liebestod* windup in Wagner's *Tristan und Isolde*).

But however you may feel about the issue as we have discussed it so far, there is another point which should certainly be considered. Turning now to Chapter XIX in Aristotle's *Poetics,* note his observations on "Diction" and "Thought" *(diánoia)*. In Aristotle the basic structure of his *Rhetoric* (as what he calls in this chapter an "architectonic") is built about "topics" *(topoi,* literally "places"). The work is designed to list the various topics that can be used to affect (produce emotional effects upon) and persuade an audience.

My first book of literary criticism (I had already published a book of stories with declamatory passages that finally became outright poems, which I thought of as being like arias in an opera) started out with an attempt to define "literary form" and ended by going from poetry as a means of *self-expression* to poetry as a means of *communication* (an address to an *audience*). This is no place to discuss all the ins and outs of that subject, particularly since the section of the *Poetics* which deals specifically with the problem of *catharsis* is lost, though there is a section in the *Politics* which gives us the rudiments of tragedy as medicine for the audience and says that he will develop the subject more fully in the *Poetics*. In Chapter XIX of the text now extant, Aristotle, on the subject of Diction and Thought, specifically refers to *Rhetoric* which, like Poe's essay, discusses the reliance upon *topics* to produce "effects" upon the audience. With regard to death as a topic (or theme) that produces the response of tragic dignification we need but recall the emotional effect upon our whole nation produced by the seven tragic victims in the fireball of the NASA spacecraft *Challenger,* and we can realize how radically Chapter XIX of the *Poetics* ties in with the Rhetorical matter of topics that Poe lays such stress upon. All told, instead of snooting that essay, I'd suggest that, if only as an experiment, critics try applying it *mutatis mutandis* to poetry in quite different grooves, or "thought-styles."

For instance, however far the verse of William Carlos Williams was from the style of "The Raven," and however impatient he might be with Poe's "Composition" number, it is remarkable how well his concerns when planning to write his *Paterson* epic match criteria Poe was talking about. His letters written during the period when he was working on the poem tell of his involvement in *his* judgments of what he should do with *his* problems of diction in the way of "*supremeness*, or perfection" in deciding upon the "stance" of his verses. And even a kind of "double provenience" figured in his search, as with the possible notion that Poe's formula for the most beautiful topic to use as a *poet* was grounded in a purely personal affliction, his *necrophile* affliction. But as I interpret Williams's theory of "contact," his dual capacity as poet and physician, though it also involved morbidity, well, as I stated the case in my commemorative article, "William Carlos Williams, 1883–1963":[5]

> Trained to crises of sickness and parturition that often need came at odd hours. An ebullient man, sorely vexed in his last years, and now at rest. But he had this exceptional good luck: that his appeal as a person survives in his work. To read his books is to find him warmly there, everywhere you turn.
>
> In some respects, the physician and the poet might be viewed as opposites, as they certainly were at least in the sense that time spent on his patients was necessarily time denied to the writing of poetry. But that's a superficial view. In essence this man was an imaginative physician and a nosological poet. His great humaneness was equally present in both roles, which contributed essentially to the development of each other.[6]

And my article throughout turns up with variations on that theme. There were so many respects in which Williams, while writing *Paterson*, was paralleling Poe's pronouncements about the principles of composition (and so *very* differently!). I had intended to discuss all that. Also, since in both cases we were in the orbit of death as a topic, I had hoped to introduce a poem by a devout believer in Williams's verse, and like Williams, professionally in contact with persons confronting the immediate reality of diseases and dying. Thus, I insert a superb poem by John Stone (from his book, *In All This Rain*), along with some comments of mine:[7]

Death

I have seen come on
slowly as rust
sand

or suddenly as when

someone leaving
a room
finds the doorknob
come loose in his hand

First, in one or another of its many aspects as a topic, Death always has been and always will be (until we're all dead) a Timely Topic. And the variations on the theme are endless.

Some works get their effects by amplification—this one is a marvel of succinctness. Its first stanza of ten words is matched by a second stanza of twelve words, with a line of four words to mark the turn from one to the other. And the ends of the two stanzas are marked by the monosyllabic rhyme, "sand-hand."

The briefer a lyric is, the more jealously every syllable counts, and here every one counts to perfection. In a sense every word but one ("suddenly") is a monosyllable. For "slowly" and "leaving" are but variations of "slow" and "leave," the adverbial "ly" and participial "ing" having the quality of similar one-ness, while both "someone" and "doorknob" are pairs of one-syllable words printed as two-syllable.

I take it that this aspect of the diction helps accentuate the sense of downright *finality* in the poem, which *totally immediate* in its sense of presence, not just a *death* but a *dying;* nay more, right here in front of us and imaginatively *within us,* a *sudden* dying.

This suddenness makes it in effect a *violent* poem, as violent as though it were about someone being *murdered.* And *there's* the astonishing twist: nothing could be less violent than something coming loose.

For "slow" death, imagery of dessicated *things,* rust and sand. For *this* death, a *narrative.*

Stone is a devoted understudy of William Carlos Williams. But this quietly startling lyric is so "naturally perfect" in its trimness, its *directness,* I can't think of a single such piece by Williams that superseded it. And it's not "derivative." It's a spontaneous utterance in the same literary groove that Williams worked in. Doubtless part of its intrinsic "spontaneity" (such that it "rolls out just right") derives from the fact that, also being professionally a medical doctor, Stone like Williams here re-enacts his "contact" with reality as *dialectically* pointed up by the dramatically, or histrionically, hence *a fortiori* lyrically absolute yes-no contrast of life/death alternatives whereby the poet's *medium* appeals to readers' imagination through a wordage that induces them, as it were, to experience the quasi-happenings so *immediately.*

Among anthologies of such poetry there are many that claim to include all the "best" published in the field—and if Stone's poem isn't among their selections, they are to be forgiven only in case their editors didn't know of it. As I see it, its ironic way of *flowering* qualifies it as an *anthology*-piece beyond all question.

About the edges of death as a topic are age and decrepitude. For this reader, at least, the image of the doorknob draws secondarily on concerns about decrepitude; for death is a kindness that modern medicology has ingeniously many ways of denying us, even sometimes compelling oldsters to live on, as hardly more than a vegetable, until their funds are so exhausted that they will have bequeathed nothing to their children.

And wow! do I forever reach for the likes of doorknobs, beginning with the handle of my cane. And once, opening a door backwards on a ramp to a storehouse in our garden, I lost my grip, fell backwards on the ramp, stretched out backwards on the ground, the back of my head hitting exactly four inches from a cement block that happened to be lying on the lawn.

My observations concerning Williams and *Paterson* underwent quite a change en route. I began solely with the vicissitudes of the attitude towards Poe's rationale as regards his writing of "The Raven." I introduced a further development of that matter. I referred to a section in J. W. Mackail's volume, *The Meaning of Virgil for Our World of Today.* Here the author accentuates the nature of the *Aeneid* by saying not what the poem *is* but what it *ought to be* (as though the poem were, like Williams's *Paterson,* in the planning stage during which he refers to the problem impulsively and compulsively in his correspondence at that time). Mackail's quite appealing device here is to write as though, in response to the cultural situation of Virgil's times, he were putting in an order for precisely the kind of poem that the *Aeneid* actually is. And I pick a few details that most quickly illustrate the method:

> The work must be a national poem. . . . It must establish and vindicate the vital interconnection of Rome and Italy. . . . It must link up Rome and the new nation to the Greek civilization. . . . It must bring well into the foreground of the picture the historic conflict between Rome and Carthage. . . . It must celebrate the feats of heroes. . . . It must find expression for the romantic spirit, in its two principal fields of love and adventure. . . . It must exalt the new regime.

I don't recall what I wrote to Williams when referring to Mackail. But it did strike me that Williams was in effect telling himself what he should do, as regards both topics and style, and in keeping with his principle-of-principles, CONTACT. And his corresponding attempt to think and write "in the American grain" would be, in his way, the writing of a "national" poem, at least as compared with his rival contemporaries, Pound and Eliot, cultural émigrés. The conditions of patronage were such in Virgil's day that a poem designed to "exalt the new regime" (thus beginning "Arms and the man I sing") was quite "in order" if not written "to order," as a medium of *dignification* (in contrast with Ovid's ingratiating *sportiveness,* which was decidedly out of order, to his considerable misfortune). But we can take it that Virgil's epic was written by a poet who was as spontaneously turned in the direction of the military dominion bequeathed by Rome (whose god was Mars, the god of war, and guided the empire to a victorious *pax Romana,* surely not the direction that Williams was spontaneously trying to bequeath himself for *Paterson,* his epic of so totally different a sort). The Mackail presentation suggested some analogies to Williams's situation, in trying to decide what he should put in his order for—but he apparently saw only the *differences.* I don't recall his ever mentioning to me how he took the matter. But he did once send me a single page which repeated seven times in handwriting Poe's line, "Order is heaven's first law." The first time everything was in perfect order.

Each time things got more mussy, and the seventh time it was but an illegible eruption.

By taking "Paterson" as his topic Williams got total contact, uniting his ways as poet, his views as a doctor, his circumstances as citizen and taxpayer, with the scene, the region, in which all such activities were grounded. And all this added up to what you might get if you took the *Baedeker* as a form that might be adapted to purely artistic purposes. You buy a *Baedeker,* for instance, to some town noted as the locale of certain artworks. The *Baedeker* gives details about the history of these works, also info as to exactly where they are. You are also told about hotels, motels, restaurants, prices, notable characters, surrounding bits of landscape. To what extent could we see in Williams's literary *Baedeker* imaginative equivalents of such factual matters? Also, in this adaptation of the form to literary purposes, you get such purely literary principles as "no ideas but in things" and "a city is a person."

In an earlier stage when travel books were "factual" implements, Swift adapted the form to totally literary purposes by using it as a vehicle of satire. Williams, in a post-Wordsworthian cultural situation, would adapt a "factual" form to artistic purposes in keeping with a contact principle, which would be *his* way of using the imagination to help us see what is right there in front of our eyes and we couldn't see it. *Paterson* thereby becomes an Ideal, Total *Baedeker,* being all in one the Art Exhibit, the conditions of the place where you go to see it, and the Poetic Person whose imagination makes the poet's locale personable as an art exhibit.

Out of the whole situation I proposed to settle for that division of labor whereby we could but ask that the *poet* wrote what seemed just right, and the *critic's* job was to formulate the principles involved. Aristotle's *Poetics* was in that relation to the poets and their poetry. For although there are places where his book is like a manual, a "how to" tract, everything he says about the writing of tragedy is explicitly based on the *analysis of what poets have already done.* So I intended to work with that alignment.

Although I am not a full-time poet, I do view my poetry as a basic part of my sixty-plus years devoted to the professional stating of my attitudes. I have already published *Book of Moments: Poems 1915–1954,* which was later included in my *Collected Poems: 1915–1967.* And as soon as time permits I hope to prepare for publication my later efforts, for which I have the tentative title, "Attitudinizings Verse-wise, While Fending for One's Selph: And in a Style Somewhat Artificially Colloquial." The title is not wholly accurate, since many of the items are as orthodox in their phrasing as I could possibly make them; but several are as shaggy in their way as my plans called for. The polarization between certain poets and critics at the "What Is a Poet?" symposium made me realize how my ambivalent situation in the poet-critic issue had been manifested in some of my verse itself.

First, when Henry Rago was editor of *Poetry: A Magazine of Verse,* he was kind to both my criticism and my verse, even to the extent of asking whether I cared to suggest a reviewer for my book of verse. (The reviewer I suggested agreed to do the job. He signed it with his usual pseudonym, W. C. Blum, the Dr. J. S. Watson, Jr., who introduced Rimbaud's *Season in Hell* in *The Dial,* of which he and Scofield Thayer were joint owners, which is to say joint moneylosers. And oof! How different Rimbaud from Rambo, a moneymaker to the extent of obscenity, thanks at least in part to approving words from our President.)

Rago had announced that during the summer issues *Poetry* would accept and publish only work by new contributors. But precisely at the beginning of that period E. E. Cummings suddenly died.[8] My world, like his, was interwoven with the comings and goings of *The Dial,* but his much more so. I was startled by the news—and spontaneously decided to pick up a book of his and write a kind of commemoration by turning from each page to the next, citing from or referring to each such page in turn, in a way whereby my words became a kind of appreciatively impressionistic context. I sent the piece off to Rago immediately, saying that although the considering and publishing of it would be delayed, if he did take it I hoped that he could publish it as soon as possible to get the added appeal of its "timely" value. To my total surprise, Rago wrote back saying that he had changed the rules of acceptance during the summer and would publish it in the next issue.

Not until much later did I, as a critic who was also a highly responsive reader of Cummings's verse, realize that I had made him in effect a "collaborator" in a poem of mine own. So I enrolled myself thereby as a poet of sorts, by simply using my *critical* aptitudes in a way that fitted in with the ways of song. (Marianne

168

Moore may have given me a hunch in that direction, since she was able to make even dull excerpts sparkle by her use of them in her poetic contexts.) And my job was easier, though not essentially different, by my way of collaborating with Cummings and thereby making him a collaborator in my poetic tribute to him. But I got entangled in the problem of quoting enough without quoting too much to substantiate my attitude. So quotes from my poem "To the Memory of e.e. cummings" (which incidentally turned the obviously paronomastic possibilities of a previous statement I made into "cummings and goings on"), and trying to settle on the topic of his "unfew unold things indeed with un," his "unnery":

> until the untilled land
> beyond the last crossing over into
> the non-undeadness of an
> obituary.[9]

Next consider the "singing" of critical analysis in my "Poetic Exercise on the Subject of Disgruntlement" (*Collected Poems*, 253–62). Having taken many notes on the subject of the pollution implied in rites of purgation, on going over a batch of them I saw the songfulness implicit in the very tenor of them. But the critical slant that guided their selection also had, as a kind of "side effect," a sense of the motivational quality intrinsic to them all. It's hard to convey the effect by brief quotation because the effect is got by the piling up of such details (the rhetorical form called "amplification"). But the quality of the lot might at least be indicated by this selection:

> Victim, martyr, guilt, wereguilt,
> Debt, redemption (that is, ransom from captivity),
> Blood-feud, blood-guilt, sin-offering, blood-offering.
>
> By "sin-eater" is meant "a man who (according to a
>   former practice in England)
> For a small gratuity ate a piece of bread
>   laid on the chest of a dead person,
> To take the sins of the dead person upon himself."
>
> Brutus: "We shall be called purgers, not murderers."[10]

Then, as Greek tragedy itself ended with a Satyr-play, I added another movement on the sportive side, like reversing the order of Milton's movements in his pair, "L'Allegro" and "Il Pensoroso."

But once I got into the act in my double role as both poet and critic I could add developments of my own to the "double provenience" aspect of the subject (the question as to whether the "principles of composition" in Poe's writing of "The Raven" reflected simply his behavior as a *poet* or also were symptomatic of "necrophile" propensities). My definition of us as "Bodies That Learn Language" involved me in such speculations as my chapters "The Thinking of the Body" and "*Somnia ad Urinandum*" in my *Language as Symbolic Action* volume. And these pieces of mine which, in my role as a critic who both remembered the experience of writing and later seeing them (psycho-)analytically from without (cf. the discussion of my sonnet "Atlantis" on pp. 328–29).

But the most far-reaching speculations of that sort concern my "declamatory" novel (antinovel?), *Towards a Better Life*—and I fell behind in my schedule because I got involved in trying to summarize what was going on there. It is an "I-story," the fictive writer of which is cracking up. In the last chapter he is so far gone that the story ends in a set of disconnected fragments. It was almost as though the very story itself were cracking up. "Gossip-wise" I got involved in a kind of poet-critic relationship whereby this critic, in writing an imaginary I-story about a guy who was cracking up, had got so deeply immersed in his topic that the distresses of the author's fictive character began, as it were, rubbing off on the real character of the author himself, decidedly a variation on the theme we have touched on at the start of this article with regard to the possible "double provenience" of the death-and-beauty theme in Poe's essay.

But my analysis kept increasing, since I had already taken many notes on the subject of *Towards a Better Life* along the lines of my hit-and-run material for an essay, "When You Use Words, Words Use You." And after lingering with that topic so long that I overstepped my deadline, I had to drop those confessions entirely, since I had gone far enough to need still more time. The ironic twist of the whole business is that whereas the author had written a story that scared him, by further critical analysis he could tell himself why implicitly in the *end of the line* for the fictive character there were the harbingers of a Next Phase for the author himself.

170

NOTES

(The following notes have all been added by the editor, Hank Lazer.)

1. This essay, completed by Burke in late March 1986, begins by referring back to the talk which he gave on October 20, 1984, at The Eleventh Alabama Symposium on English and American Literature: What Is a Poet? Burke's original talk covered a wide range of materials, from thoughts on Williams's *Paterson* to some of Burke's recent thinking on myth and dreams. Much of the talk consisted of Burke's frustrated fumbling through the many papers and books he brought with him up to the lectern, and the resulting lecture, when transcribed, was not one which Burke wished to publish. Attempts to edit and patch up "Poets, Poems, Poetry, Poetics" were not successful.

Even so, engaging topics emerged from portions of that lecture: the relationship of prescription and/or intention to the writing of poetry, and the relationship between "poetic" and "critical" activity. Burke and I continued to stay in touch by phone and letter. Working from a combination of his original lecture, some selections from (his own) *Language as Symbolic Action,* and a list of questions which I sent him (some of which focused on general considerations of the relationship between poetry and criticism, others of which, based on my own growing admiration for Burke's poetry, asked about the relationship in his *own* writing between poetry and critical writing), he began another essay.

In late March 1986, Burke sent me the essay which appears in this volume, and he asked me to edit it. My first impression was that the essay still needed a great deal of work. After all, so much of it was couched in hypothetical language (I would . . . , I intended . . . , I might . . . , etc.), and the essay had several sections which said things like "Hank: Insert here the two paragraphs you mention on p. 33 of my LSA volume . . ." and "omit as you prefer any of the stuff I have included." Least promising of all was the running head for the thirteen manuscript pages: "Burke's Letter." So I called him—he was staying at his son's house in British Columbia—and told him I would reread the essay and we would talk over possible changes by phone the next week.

With this third or fourth reading of the essay, I finally saw what Burke had done. It was something he has always been doing in his essays: he enacts (or dramatizes) the subjects he writes about. And then I saw just how subtly and complexly finished the essay was. Thus, an essay on principles, prescriptions, and intentions (and the entangled logical and temporal priorities of all three) would of course play with those very issues through its own tone and instructions. After my many questions to him about problems of genre distinction, he had given me an unclassifiable, decidedly

171

hybrid piece of writing: part retrospect (of the original October 20, 1984, lecture), part collage (incorporating some pieces of his earlier writings on these subjects, Burke's analysis of a poem by John Stone, a letter to Burke from Richard Wilbur, and portions from Burke's own poetry), part literary and personal autobiography, a radical revision of his earlier talk, and a meditation on death and dying—all recast as a new talk or essay and sent as a letter.

As editor, I used principles of indentation and margins to indicate where Burke shifts back and forth between "new" and "old" writing. In fact, finally, my editing job became rather slight, except for the initial task of understanding some of the complex intentions and enactments of "Poetry as Symbolic Action."

2. The two paragraphs which follow are from Burke's "Poetics in Particular; Language in General," in *Language as Symbolic Action: Essays on Life, Literature, and Method* (Berkeley: University of California Press, 1966), p. 33.

3. The three paragraphs which follow are from a letter to Kenneth Burke from Richard Wilbur, September 20, 1984.

4. Kenneth Burke, *Collected Poems: 1915–1967* (Berkeley: University of California Press, 1968), p. 191.

5. The entire essay on Williams can be found in *Language as Symbolic Action,* pp. 282–91. These two paragraphs are from p. 282.

6. An equally insightful assessment by Burke of Williams as poet and doctor is mentioned in Paul Mariani's *William Carlos Williams: A New World Naked* (New York: McGraw Hill, 1981):

> Burke would remember an incident during this stay in Tampa when he and Williams had strolled slowly down the beach together. It had suddenly made him more aware of what Williams had meant by insisting so long on contact with the things of one's world. "A neighbor's dog decided to accompany us, but was limping," Burke wrote:
>
>> I leaned down, aimlessly hoping to help the dog (which became suddenly frightened, and nearly bit me). Then Williams took the paw in his left hand (the right was now less agile) and started probing for the source of the trouble. It was a gesture at once expert and imaginative, something in which to have perfect confidence, as both the cur and I saw in a flash. Feeling between the toes lightly, quickly, and above all *surely,* he spotted a burr, removed it without the slightest cringe on the dog's part—and the three of us were again on our way along the beach.

Tactus eruditus: the knowing touch. For Burke that incident summed up Williams' kind of poetry: a sheer "physicality imposed upon his poetry by the nature of his work as a physician." (754)

7. Burke indicated to me that this discussion of John Stone's poem (which I have here indented) first appeared "on the Bulletin Board of the Emory [University] division with which I was associated in my role there for five winter terms as what I called 'Verbalizer un Residence' (though not so classed in the solemnities of Institutionalese)."

8. E. E. Cummings died in 1963.

9. Burke quotes the last stanza from "To the Memory of e. e. cummings." The complete poem can be found in Burke's *Collected Poems*, pp. 147–53.

10. *Collected Poems*, p. 254.

PHOTOGRAPHS

The photographs are by Gay Chow.

1 : Participants in the Eleventh Alabama Symposium: What Is a Poet?, held October 18–20, 1984, at The University of Alabama. Left to right: Charles Bernstein, Helen Vendler, Gregory Jay, Marjorie Perloff, Charles Altieri, Gerald Stern, David Ignatow, Louis Simpson, Hank Lazer, Denise Levertov, and Kenneth Burke.

2 : Audience

3

4

5

6

10 : Panel discussion. (From left)
Louis Simpson, Helen Vendler,
and Charles Bernstein.

11 : Panel discussion. (From left)
Hank Lazer, Denise Levertov,
Charles Altieri, David Ignatow,
Marjorie Perloff, Gerald Stern,
Gregory Jay, Helen Vendler, and
Charles Bernstein.

12 : Hank Lazer and Kenneth Burke

13 : Kenneth Burke

14: Marquee at the Bama Theater in
Tuscaloosa for poetry reading.

PANEL DISCUSSION

PANEL DISCUSSION

LAZER: . . . What we have here is our concluding panel discussion, which as Shelley puts it, involves the "unacknowledged legislators of the world." Also, I'm reminded of a revision of that phrase by the poet George Oppen, who refers to poets as the "legislators of the unacknowledged world." I would like to thank the nine participants in the symposium for attending this event and for sharing their views with us and, for the next couple of hours, to continue to share their views about poetry and what is a poet. And I'd like to thank you for coming here to listen. When I began to put this panel together, it should be fairly obvious by now that part of the interest was to create some diversity and controversy. The issue of what is a poet, as Coleridge let us know, is also involved with what is poetry, and these joint issues are issues that the nine people on this panel feel very strongly about and are devoting their lives to dealing with. So it was to be expected that we would have differences of opinion.

Someone asked me, "What kind of principle did you have in mind in putting this together?" For a while I thought the only answer I could give was, "None, except to allow this diversity to take place." But I guess there is one short proverb that in a way may

185

speak to what we're attempting to do here, and that is William Blake's proverb, "In opposition is true friendship." I think that part of what we have here is a kind of dialectical argument that will be taking place. Part of the conviction and desire behind this particular symposium is that the articulation of different viewpoints is in and of itself worthy of our attention.

I tried to address this issue—particularly the relationship between poetry and criticism—in an essay, "Critical Theory and Contemporary American Poetry" (recently published in *The Missouri Review*), which some of the participants have seen. David Ignatow, in looking at that particular essay, said to me, "What are you trying to do? Do you think the lion and the lamb are going to lie down with one another?" And I said, "No, I don't think that really is what's going to happen, but what we can have happen is a presentation of principles, a presentation of viewpoints, and have that discussion take place." And that is part of our purpose today.

JAY: I'd like to try and frame a sort of overall response to the conference by taking up Hank's point about opposition and friendship and trying to suggest a point for common argument and for balancing some of the competing claims. The phrase that I want to ask about is a phrase made notorious by Heidegger and others, which is the phrase "poetic thinking," but I want to frame it by returning for a moment to Helen Vendler's keynote address and to her book on Keats, if I could be so presumptuous as to summarize what I learned from reading that. The argument that she made about "The Ode to Autumn" and, indeed, about the odes of Keats, had to do with the relationship between sensation and thinking, between feeling and intellect, between analysis and emotion. It seems to me that often in the heat of polemic we tend to talk in binary oppositions, in dualities—as if one could *choose* between thought and sensation, one could *choose* between intellect and emotion. One thing I found fascinating about her argument regarding Keats was the way in which she dealt with the odes as a progressive self-reflection on Keats's part of the balancing relationships and the claims made by both thought and feeling on the writing of poetry. And I think her argument was, at least as I understood it, that a turning point came in "The Ode on a Grecian Urn" and in, finally, "The Ode to Autumn," in which the relationship between poetic feeling and poetic thought coalesced in a kind of rigorous poetic thinking. The key argument she made was that Keats constituted himself not only first as a speaker of poetry, as an emoter of poetry, but also as an audience for that poetry—that he doubled himself in a certain way—that he was his own best critic, finally, and that there was a fundamental critical operation that takes place in the writing of all great poetry. So I guess that leaves me with a series of questions I'd like to throw out to the panel about the common ground of poetic thinking that I think joins both the writers and the readers of poetry, since the writers of poetry are involved in poetic thinking (both about their own poetry and the poetry of others), and the readers of poetry, it seems to me, think with the poems that they read.

So my questions are a series around this idea of poetic thinking to which you can respond any way you want. They really boil down to: How does the thinking that goes on in poetry differ, if it does, from the thinking the poem invites the reader to do? Where can we or should we draw the line between poetic and critical thinking? What's poetry thinking about today, now, in the contemporary scene? Is it just to characterize contemporary poetry as an indulgence in sensation or sentiment without thought? Is it just to characterize contemporary criticism as a kind of heartless, intellectual distancing from the felt reality of common life? Doesn't the poet seek to achieve a distance from his own emotions, and isn't the critic writing in passionate response to the feelings that poetry engages her or him in?

[Laughter, mumbling, then silence]

ALTIERI: I can't stand the silence; I had no desire to speak first, but, well, I hardly did. No, I really can't stand the silence. Let me rephrase that in a way; I think you get at something. It would seem to me that when you talk about poetic thinking, you isolate a *generic* quality of thinking. It seems to me much better always to keep a noun whenever you use the notion of thinking, that is, it seems to me a better way to put it to say, "thinking about an X," with the certain kind of intensity that provides for a reader a sense of the reader's own humanity, in one form or another, which, in some sense, aligns this act and that state with states which have been carried by, in some sense, the traditional history of poetry. I mean it just doesn't get us any further except it separates any notion of a special sensibility within the poetic to keep the notion of the *object*

187

crucial. Actually, there is a reason now I wanted to say this: I feel completely embarrassed in many ways by the notion of trying to impose some sense of standards on so diverse a group. I'll come back to that—I didn't want to talk about this much; I just wanted to get this started. But it seems to me that when you have this diverse a group what's interesting about it, to go back to the family metaphor, is you recognize the range of different forms of intensity that people seek, different kinds of contexts into which they go, and it seems to me that what Blake meant by that statement was that we define one another's limits. And I think that we have to keep *that* as a crucial look. There are a range of functions poetry serves, and there's a range of critics and poets defining one another's limits by how they address that. To me the crucial analogy is the fact that in music we expect a wide variety of practitioner levels and a wide variety of participation. And it seems to me that the world of poetry has a great deal to learn from the world of music.

VENDLER: I wanted to say something about Gerald Stern's charming account of his own youth the other day. I was thinking as I listened to him about growing up in the city without a poetic context and eventually reading, in the lonely way by himself in the genealogy room of the library and writing and finding friends and eventually having those excited talks about the poets you were reading and not much knowing about the poets you were reading, as he said, not knowing, perhaps, about Pound's ideas, but being thrilled by having read some early Pound and then "lighting out," so to speak, for the other territory, Paris, and finding a larger world. I think that's probably my story, maybe Charlie's story, maybe Marjorie's story too. I was struck by how impossible it was to understand—and maybe every story—you don't know when you're a young person where your enthusiasms are going to lead you. It seems to me that probably poets and critics alike start off as kids in libraries, very much isolated and knowing that the rest of the kids are not reading Baudelaire, and there you are all by yourself. And you don't know when you're fifteen whether this will lead you to be a poet or whether it will lead you to be a critic or whether it will lead you to be a teacher or whether it will lead you to be a journalist or what it will do—you're just one of those people that has followed this track. And then the friends you make at that time may turn out, some of them, to be novelists and not be poets, or to be critics and not be poets, or you might end up a poet, or you might be a critic and one of your friends will be a poet. But I think that the *genetic similarities* among us are very strong, and it should be remembered that the subsequent differences, nonetheless, rest on a base of grand genetic similarity.

STERN: I would like to respond, if I may, to that. May I?

LAZER: Yeah, let me just interject for a second and give it back to you, Gerry. Along the lines of what Helen was saying here, the other metaphor that may operate is from one of your poems, Gerry, and that is the notion of the red coal. It seems to me the particular critics we have here, as well as the poets here, are passionately involved with poetry as your red coal metaphor describes that activity of writing, that demonic possession of writing, it seems to me Marjorie, Charlie, Helen, Kenneth Burke's work, is also an impassioned involvement in that sphere of poetry. . . .

STERN: I think that's true, and when Helen made her comments I was thinking of Wordsworth's *Prelude*, which, after all, is just such an autobiographical rendering of the poet's spiritual life, of *a* poet's spiritual life. I suspect that if a critic—and we got stuck with these words, I was listening to Kenneth Burke this morning agonizing over the symbol—and we get stuck in a semantic marsh—critics, scholar, professor—for which I apologize. For the language, not for my own gestures, which were somewhat misinterpreted by me and others. If a critic—I use that word now with eighty thousand quotations around it—would then proceed to write the story of her own life, say in Boston, say in an isolated little Catholic college, and so on, a wonderful and specific humane story, and write that down, if she chose to do it in poetic form, it could be an extraordinary poem. I'm not being facetious here or arrogant in any way. The thing is that poets arrogate to themselves, if you will, life. It's kind of unfair, for they pay for it in other ways. In perhaps an extreme act of narcissism, because somebody said that somebody called me a narcissist yesterday, and I'm very sensitive to that, that they think of their own lives or their own emotions or own experiences as overwhelmingly important—which each of ours is to each of us. But in a sense, perhaps what they're doing—they're doing a lot of things, but one of the things they're doing—is, in order to pay for this, they put it in form. They detach themselves from it. They organize it musically. They submit it to magazines; they submit it to

189

critics; they submit it to their loves. There's a lot of things going on.

I couldn't agree with what Helen says more. I'm not suggesting that poets are superior to other people. I don't even think that Emerson believed that; maybe Shelley believed that. I don't even think that Emerson believed that. But I'm happy, Helen, seriously, that you brought that up. I want to express sisterhood, brotherhood, as human beings, but then *distinctions* in our professional roles . . .

LEVERTOV: This seems to relate to my sense of the poet's function—a primary function, let's say at least, of the poet—which is to articulate his or her own inner or outer experience, outer always together with inner, sometimes inner with less outer. And so, by articulating his or her inner and outer experience, to act as the voice of those who don't have the ability to do so. Not that a poet sets out to express what he or she *thinks* is the experience of others, but by, with the utmost honesty, fidelity to experience of whatever kind, including aesthetic, that he or she has, the poet becomes that voice for others. Not deliberately, but this is the result of that kind of fidelity to his or her *own* experience, *because* we are "members one of another." We are not that different from each other. The poets simply are people who have a very special relationship to language, which enables them to articulate feelings and experiences and thoughts, and the osmosis of those things, which are shared by everyone. And the fact that a demand from the mass of people in our country at our time scarcely exists—that does not have anything essential to do with the nature of the poet. The function of the poet remains there, accessible to that demand when the demand arises; and the demand, of course, does arise all the time from individuals, although, for sociological reasons, not all the time from large groups of persons.

IGNATOW: I think Denise has correctly stated the situation, the nature of the situation of the American poet. And that actually contrasts with the nature and situation of the critic, as I understand critics. Critics then turn and examine the lives of the poets, rather than examine their own lives in relation to the poets. They don't have the capacity, or their training doesn't allow them to first look into themselves openly for us to examine, as at the same time they examine the poet's life and work. So the distinction is very clear in my mind that the critic, at least as it's practiced today, criticism is

190

merely a study of (objectively as possible) the work of the poet without in any way giving an idea of where all of this is coming from except through theory. We want to know the psychology of the critic, just as the poet only gives his psychology through his work. But we never really know the psychology of the critic or the life of the critic, the biography which gives him or her the context in which to study the life of the poet and the work of the poet. There is that distinction.

PERLOFF: I'd like to go back to something Helen said. I'm teaching right now the basic literary theory course—Plato, Aristotle, Horace, mostly—so I've been very caught up with my students in discussions of Chapter Four of *The Poetics:* the pleasure of recognition. And after all, no matter what our views are, and I think everybody at this table would agree, when you ask, what is the origin of poetry, what do people like about poetry, it certainly begins with children, and it begins for all of us in what Aristotle calls the "pleasure of recognition"—that we say, "Oh, I've had that feeling, but the poet puts it so much better"; or, "I've had this experience, but look at how wonderfully it's put." In all kinds of ways. The difficulty, though, comes in what are the experiences that we find meaningful and interesting, and that's where you're going to have a great deal of difference of opinion, even if we can all say that "genetically," as Helen put it, we're on the same wavelength.

For me, to get back to what Denise said a minute ago—I guess I'll play the optimist in this circle—Helen said to me before, "You're always the optimist." I don't think it's so true that it all depends how you define a poet; I think Laurie Anderson is a wonderful poet. I define her as a poet, and you go to a Laurie Anderson, not just show, but they had a big exhibit at UCLA this year of her videotapes, her poems, her photographs—I assure you, it was mobbed; people responded to it beautifully, because they're having the pleasure of recognition. I do believe that, and I believe there are other people with whom they really have that pleasure of recognition. It does *change* from time to time; but I don't believe that we now have a hostile audience that only watches television or that the poets are not appreciated because people are only at the ball game. I don't believe that. So, I think you just have to try and get a sense of what it is people *are* doing; clearly the visual sense, because of television, because of film, has become much more important. That's just the way it is. That isn't necessarily very bad, and there's still a lot of room for poetry.

IGNATOW: I would like to have my question answered by any one of the critics present: whether it's true what I have said that the emphasis in critics' work is upon the study of the poet, so that we have no idea from where the critic is coming.

BERNSTEIN: I'd like to answer that question, if I could. And this was in the original question. I have a difficulty with generalized terms like "the poet," "the critic." For many years I would only refer to myself as a writer, which is what I would prefer to think of myself as being because of this kind of generalization of "the Poet" with a capital P. I find this a very problematic term, and I find it leads to a great deal of confusion. I think that most poets and most critics are bogged down in unreflected, rhetorical ideologies and that, therefore, to me, their work is not useful and interesting, although it's possible that it's useful and interesting in specific contexts for certain other people, if that can be shown, possibly. I think that, in that sense, it's true that a great deal of American poetry written in the last twenty years is absorbed with questions of emotion and autobiography in a way that makes that work not useful and interesting to *me*, because it assumes those things as a rhetorical mode, and therefore has nothing to do with emotion, but is a kind of conceptual art. Emotion stated simply as a fact, as a *fait accompli*, is a kind of analytic conceptualism. On the other hand, a very intense analytic experience, say Willard Quine, whose work I have little sympathy with, I find to be an intensely emotional quest for certainty. I can't really read it except as an intense emotional blockage on his part and an expression of his need to eliminate ambiguities, and that is the way I read that work.

So those categories seem extremely problematic because people then get stuck into certain kinds of rhetorical strategies, and they praise those strategies as if the strategies themselves and the rhetorics themselves were what we are after. And I would say that in respect to the issue of philosophical prose or critical prose, critics who *do* do what David has asked, I would think the classic case, my favorite work by Roland Barthes, is *Roland Barthes par Roland Barthes,* which does exactly the kind of inventory of Barthes's personal history combined with his philosophical ideas, and that, I think, is a work—though I have not read it in French, only in

192

English translation—but insofar as I had access to that work because of that limitation—seems to me as compelling and interesting as any work of poetry from France or England that I've read over that same period. And at the same time we have sitting at the table with us a person, Kenneth Burke, who we just heard speak, who again, I think, completely combines constant reflection on the nature of his thought, the multidisciplinary (I mean multidisciplinary in every sense) as the introduction pointed out, philosophical, sociological, psychological, autobiographical, and those comminglings in his work, his openness—also the work of Stanley Cavell that specifically examines the nature of the kind of openness that I'm talking about would give another instance of somebody who deals with this question in an interesting way for me. So I think the problem is too generalized; there are always going to be exceptions, and then one's going to always say that the normal practice of any given form of writing is going to be problematic to most people.

IGNATOW: Let me ask you this: If poetry is not emotional, then what is it?

BERNSTEIN: I think poetry is related to the nature of the human and that the human is a complex interrelationship of all the words that we have in our language—from *to* to *of* to *emotion* to *motion* to *light* to *air* to *green* to *blue* to whatever else—and that to restrict a word like *poetry* and to equate it to another word like *emotion,* which are *not* the same words, seems to me reductive.

IGNATOW: Maybe we ought to define what we mean by emotion. What do you think of Dante's *Inferno* and *Purgatory* and *Paradiso*—is that emotional or not?

BERNSTEIN: Primarily . . .

IGNATOW: Do you think that grew out of an emotional need?

BERNSTEIN: Actually, I think somebody else should speak now. . . .

ALTIERI: I think that critics also ought to be given the grace of the notion of music; that is, there are lots of functions and lots of levels. But I want to take the tack of trying to distinguish first- and third-person functions within this idea, to some extent in the spirit of Gerry Stern's remark and to some extent, as you can see, in relation to this. I don't think anybody wants to deny the notion of emotion, but the question is: If you start trying to make equations, then you

193

may limit the notion of emotion. This isn't any way of spreading it out; it seems to me we have—let's call it *investments* rather than emotion, I think that's in the spirit of what Charles is talking about. And we have certain kinds of first-person, certain kinds of third-person investments. And it seems to me you can distinguish the *operations* of poet and critic, though *not* the person. Another reason for talking about functions and investments: We can see that any given writer is both poet and critic.

It seems to me that David is right in recognizing something about academic criticism now, which I find really terrifying in a lot of ways, is that the competition for jobs, the competition to win the mastery of or to win the attention of the masters, produces a difficulty of keeping distinct first- and third-person functions, so a lot of the best young academics I think now seem to me entirely third-person creatures.

JAY: What does that mean, Charlie?

ALTIERI: What that, what that means is that the set of predicates that they use for values in their intellectual life are the set of predicates that they learn in the classroom out of frameworks of literary and social theory; that is, the dialectic between first-person life and the operations that one learns in graduate school seems to me, to a substantial degree, eroded by the kind of pressures that are now on academics.

JAY: That's not true.

ALTIERI: Well, let's suspend that . . .

BURKE: Can I tell you what I think? . . .

LAZER: Yes, go ahead, Kenneth.

ALTIERI: I sort of made my distinction, but go ahead.

BURKE: I work on a general pattern of this sort: First, look at the thing so you didn't even know who wrote it—look at it just like that. Then, so's you know the other role of poems—read it, look at his poem in relation to all the other poems he did that give—put little—notions back and forth to one another. Then, suppose you had all his biography, you know his notebooks, you know this and that—as a citizen and taxpayer you read him; his act as part of his whole life that way. But you have a way of dealing with the thing in itself, and then also dealing with it just as a matter of human beings in general. I think you have a—those are roughly, they overlap, but they get, there's a little pattern—I work from them that way.

194

ALTIERI: Let me just finish my distinction. I've . . .

JAY: Then I want to disagree with that distinction.

ALTIERI: . . . distinctions, and I want to get them out. It's my form of thinking, . . . it seems to me, would you?

LAZER: Briefly, Charles.

ALTIERI: My form of thinking is not brief, but . . . It seems to me that if you take what poets do, is that in some sense they have to cultivate and resource the authority—not, let me say, traditional poets—okay, because I think Charles reverses this in a very interesting kind of way. They have to take the source and the authority of their productions, both of those points largely in first-person terms, and what happens in traditional poets is the third-person function, the critical function tends, as I think Gerry just said, to be *formal* to a large degree rather than discursive. Donald Davie once said to me that the poet, at least in his eyes, the poet cannot know that clearly what he or she is about, because then it becomes in some sense pleading. It becomes argument. I think whether or not you want to take that particular formulation . . . It seems to me the critic, on the other hand, the traditional critic, has to take as its sort of source and authority, third-person terms. That is, the language by which I as a critic take a poem, I feel the obligation to be in some sense a public language. The problem is I'm in an academy where the public language is rather highly refined and often irrelevant, and I take the authority of what I'm doing to be the capacity by which I attach my own work back to some history of third-person terms. And in some sense then the nondiscursive dimension in what I do, what correlates to the formal dimension in the poet, is the dimension of *passion,* which to me has to always come sort of in in the interstices of those third persons, because my whole, the root of representatives that I feel that I stand for concept in a way that poets stand for life . . . And I think that both could stand for passion.

JAY: I think that that's a really reductive, it's a really reductive way of representing both poetry and criticism, Charlie. And I really think throughout this whole conference you've backpedaled on positions you've taken in public, and I think you don't agree with David. I *don't* agree with David about the function of criticism, and I *don't* agree with the equation of poetry with emotion, rather, either historically or on contemporary terms.

ALTIERI: I didn't say *emotion;* I said *first-person investments.*

195

JAY: I think that the achievement of authority in poetry comes precisely when the personal life is left behind for the achievement of something that transcends it. I think that the critic is always interested in the achievements that transcend personal experience . . .

ALTIERI: Well, what is . . . A poet can't say . . .

JAY: Will you let me talk? Will you let me talk, Charlie?

LAZER: . . . He'll let you talk.

STERN: I would like to say something about Charles, if I may.

LAZER: Go ahead, Gerry.

STERN: He's not . . . Are you done?

JAY: No. All I wanted to say, what I wanted to say, Gerry, is, and I really don't think that's a true representation of younger critics like me who come to third-person discourse incredibly passionately engaged by both their selves and their emotions and the issues . . .

STERN: I agree.

JAY: . . . that those involve; we read the texts of theorists because they involve our common lives, the issues; they compel our hearts and our minds and they speak to us poetically, whether or not they're lineated or not.

STERN: Okay.

JAY: And poets themselves, of course, claim their authority not because they publish poetry, they publish lineation, but because they earn our respect through the work that they do.

STERN: Absolutely. And the fact is that there can be first-person, if you will, that seems to be (there seems to be a hierarchy here). There can be first-person and third-person criticisms; there can also be first-person and third-person poetry. And it may spring from the same location or locus that Charles mentioned, or it may not. But the point is, there's a peculiar thing going on here, so far in the panel. There's kind of a straining—in a way, straining after gnats—we all want to be identified as poets, *both* critics and poets. There seems to be an *idea* here—let me put it this way—there is a superiority of poet over critic. There is after all . . .

BERNSTEIN: But only *some* people are putting that superiority forward. Now who *are* those people putting that forward? And *why* exactly are they doing it? What are their motivations?

STERN: *You're not,* Charlie. You're putting the *other* point forward—that *critics* are superior to poetry.

196

BERNSTEIN: I'm not . . . *I'm* putting that forward?

STERN: It seems to me.

LAZER: Charles put forward the notion of *writers,* Gerry.

JAY: Yeah, Charles's point is still my point too—which is that we're all writers. We're different *kinds* of writers, but we're all . . .

STERN: I understand. I'm trying to make a distinction, though. I'm really trying to make a real simple distinction . . .

LAZER: Are *you* putting forward that hierarchy?

STERN: No, I'm not. I'm putting forth a *distinction,* only a distinction. I want to be understood, not that poets are superior to critics, nor critics superior to poets—but that they are *different* from each other. And they are different from each other in certain respects, in the way they, and there may be, and in the future this distinction may break down. And there are overwhelming, there are very interesting instances where critics are, if you will, poets, and poets are critics. One could think of Nietzsche on the one hand, one could think of Heidegger, and one could think of certain poets who perform chiefly critical activities. But I think so far we are agonizing over the distinction of what is a poet and what is a critic. Why don't we just accept that there are differences? That there are different functional differences?

PERLOFF: Well, the fact is, again, if you go back into history, the greatest critics have also been the poets. Sidney, . . .

STERN: Yes, with exception of Hazlitt.

PERLOFF: "An Apology for Poetry" is probably the great critical document of the sixteenth century.

STERN: Right.

PERLOFF: Samuel Johnson, Coleridge, who was—Coleridge has been quoted all day today . . .

STERN: T. S. Eliot, Matthew Arnold . . .

PERLOFF: Eliot, Pound—who was a greater critic than Pound?

BERNSTEIN: Creeley, Zukofsky, Stein . . .

PERLOFF: Yeah, plenty of others, so I don't see this distinction . . .

[Mumbling, almost everyone talking at once]

LAZER: Denise has something to say too . . .

LEVERTOV: I'd like to suggest this way in talking about the differences between poets and critics. I think we can assume that whatever else, poets produce some work which is primary in the sense that critics react or respond to that which the poets do, or in the

197

other arts, the composer, the painter, etc., etc. Okay, so the critics ideally, to my mind, are ones whose response to the work of art demands of them articulation, and it demands an articulation which they have the generous impulse to share with others, both because they have some confidence in the interest of their own response, which is not arrogant. It's not arrogant because it is an expression of their being, the way that the poet's poem is an expression of his or her being. And it is also generous and not arrogant in being a way they hope, consciously or unconsciously, will make that work of art to which they have responded equally accessible to others. And that if others have already had access to it and have responded to it, they want, through articulation of their own response, to perhaps open up a further area or another layer of possible response to it. The activity of criticism ideally is in its very nature an expression of a longing for reciprocity. They would like to receive responses of others in the same measure that they give *their* response. And so the activity of criticism does not have to be always in those terms a positive one—the response may be a negative one, and for didactic, pedagogic reasons of principle, because they think there's something really pernicious about a certain work, and they want to explicate that. But that's not the *primary* function; the primary function is to share, I think, *positive* response, to define it, to *re*fine it and make, around this primary object, a reciprocal discourse occur.

LAZER: Marjorie, do you want to respond?

PERLOFF: I'd like to say just a very brief thing about that. Many of you quoted Pound's *ABC of Reading*. Gerry Stern quoted it yesterday as the seminal book. We all know that Pound in a certain sense was a total crank—he threw Milton out; he threw out all of English literature from Chaucer to . . . how far down the line? Four centuries or so, and yet we think he's a great critic. When Johnson dismissed "Lycidas," was that being . . .

STERN: Or Shakespeare.

PERLOFF: Was that an appreciative response to the primary source? No, and yet we think of Johnson as a great critic. I don't think that is the function of the critic.

STERN: Well, wait, while we're still on this subject (aren't we?)— Johnson also dismissed Shakespeare, if you remember.

[Mumbling; many people speaking at once]

STERN: Well, just say, he rewrote him, he rewrote him . . .

ALTIERI: But we wept at what he left out . . .

LAZER: Let me, as bastard, claim a minute or two in here.

STERN: Well, let, I won't, before you become a bastard, let me just say . . .

LAZER: Maybe some others want to . . .

STERN: I think Marjorie helped us in our thinking a lot by indicating that—Charles, darling—I think Marjorie helped us a lot by indicating that there have been writers in the language who have been both poets and critics. I'm not being mean or facetious—I really appreciate that. But I think one of the ways we can understand the question that has come up to us so far, I think, is to examine the works that they did as, if you will, critics, as opposed to or apposed to poets. Say Pound in his *Cantos*. In the *Cantos* he is obviously, I know, being critical, and he is a critic, etc. Oppose that to the *ABC*. Or Keats's letters as opposed to the odes. We can go on and on. I just think there's a difference, I think one of the ways we could make progress here is to examine—and I'm responding mainly to what Charles said before—is to examine if there is a difference in *function,* as Charles said, or difference even in *thinking,* a difference in *behavior.* Maybe there isn't in how individual poets perform as critics . . .

JAY: I do think that there's a difference.

LAZER: Do you want to respond to that?

SIMPSON: Yeah, I would like to say something.

JAY: Let Louis talk . . .

[Loud clapping]

SIMPSON: I think that this distinction between poets and critics as it's going around here is not good. I've never met a poet who was not a critic. It is impossible to be a poet without being a critic as you write. And most of the good critics have much of the poetic feeling in them. You've mentioned Schlegel; you've mentioned Coleridge, of course. The differences come when we attack schools of criticism or attitudes of criticism. That is valid argument. I don't think anybody here, any poet of this panel, would deny the absolutely useful function of good criticism. But I personally as a poet today find certain tendencies in criticism which I consider bad. They may have had a grain of truth in them, but as far as what I consider the making of poetry to be, they are very harmful. For example, the treating of a poem as expository prose, which has to be explained in terms of expository prose, ignoring its dramatic unity or its effect upon the feelings of the reader as a read or heard thing, to me is bad criticism. And there's a lot of that around. There are more serious questions being raised, such as, I think, Charles's basic point, and I think Marjorie shares it to some point—the attempt to remove from the poet himself or herself some sort of controlling truth. This is a point on which we will not agree. And to think that culture produces poems—this is a very fighting point on which we will not agree.

LAZER: Let me refocus things for a second. Let me pose a different question, and a long question, dealing with this exact issue we've been talking about for a while, dealing with the function of criticism. But I would rather redirect our attention to the function of the poet for a moment and raise two quotations from earlier addresses. Helen Vendler in her lecture Thursday evening asserted that the use of the poet in human terms remains constant, even through the vicissitudes of cultural change. And Marjorie Perloff's lecture began with an epigraph from Ezra Pound, "No good poetry is ever written in a manner twenty years old," which suggests to me that style is, in fact, not separable from poetry's function, which seemed to me a major part of Marjorie's address. Setting those two quotes next to one another, that seem to me rather opposed quotes, I would like to ask two questions of all the panelists: Does the *function* of poetry change? Helen seemed to be asserting it does not; Marjorie seemed to be asserting that clearly it does. The follow-up question would be: What is poetry's function today?

PERLOFF: . . . What do you mean by the function of poetry?

LAZER: Does the *style* of it change?

PERLOFF: That's self-evident . . .

[Many people talking at once]

BERNSTEIN: [sarcastically] No, the style is always, it's always the same. Always been the same, and it's the same everywhere. Since the paleolithic. Evidently before the paleolithic there was a different style, but at the paleolithic it all became the poets writing poetry.

LAZER: What do you perceive the function of poetry to be, Charles?

BERNSTEIN: I think that there are many functions to poetry which shift and change in different contexts and that's the difficulty. I certainly agree with, see, the reason I certainly think that there's a difference between poetry and criticism, which I think is not *essential* in the nature of writing and therefore not eternal, but a situation that has to do with audiences, distribution, jobs, professional networks, things like that, which I think we tend to underrate. It seems interesting to me that professional academic poets are making this particular issue apparent in this context; whereas in fact, it seems to me, my quarrel is not, is also with critics who reflect a viewpoint different than the one that I have and reject and, or, not even reject, but perhaps make inaudible that work which I consider to be important. But I think it's unfair not to realize that it's actually poets who are the policemen of official verse culture in the United States. And so from the perspective of a poet outside the academy and from the perspective of many people that I know who are not associated with academies, cannot get teaching jobs . . .

STERN: I don't think you're right, Charles. Who? What poets are the policemen? Would you like to name some poets who are the policemen?

BERNSTEIN: Yeah, I'll give you a group, I'll give you a group.

STERN: *Names* . . . of the policemen.

BERNSTEIN: I'll give you a group. You want me to? No, I'm not going to, I'm going to give you *institutional* groups. I'm going to say those poets, those poets who . . .

[All sorts of shouting voices]

STERN: I've got the names of thirty-seven hard, fast Communists in the State Department. . . . McCarthy never named one . . .

BERSTEIN: No, I'm going to give you an institutional definition of that.

LAZER: The question deals with *functions* of poetry. Is being a policeman what you concede to be a major function of the poet? Is that a major function of the poet?

BERNSTEIN: Is that a function of poets in our society? Absolutely.

LAZER: Okay, what are some other functions?

BERNSTEIN: That's not a function I prize.

LAZER: What are the functions that you prize? What is the function of *your* poet, Charles? What other functions do you prize?

STERN: Would you tell me who the policemen are, please, Charles? Would you give me a list of names?

BERNSTEIN: Yeah, I'm talking about those poets who are involved in the award networks, the creative writing programs, and the major media reviews.

STERN: Okay, who are they? Who are these poets?

JAY: This is a, this I think has become . . .

LEVERTOV: Absurd . . .

JAY: . . . will degenerate the sense of accusations that won't be productive for dialogue.

STERN: So, I'm going to tell you something . . . That's a policeman's activity right there, and I'm not agreeing with you. He may choose not to name names. But if he suggests there are names, you can't just let it go at that. I'm saying that that's a kind of McCarthyism, and I'm reminding Charles . . .

BERNSTEIN: I'll give you an historical . . .

STERN: Please, Charles, let me finish my statement. That there was McCarthyism in America in the forties and fifties, and my talk yesterday was really partially much addressed to that issue. And I don't like McCarthyism under whatever guise it appears. If you say there are, if you say there are policemen performing certain functions, name them; if not, don't say it.

BERNSTEIN: All right, let me give you an instance. William Car— . . .

[Many voices]

LAZER: Wait a minute, let Charles finish. . . .

[Inaudible]

BERNSTEIN: I think that what I'm saying is that there's a coalition among, I mean we, everybody is allowed, the other members of the panel who are poets are allowed to make these comments, "The critics are doing all these things." Well, all I'm saying is that there are plenty of poets who are doing the same thing, who are excluding other people. We all exclude each other; we're all partisan. I would give you as the central instance the person that William Carlos Williams called the great disaster for our letters, T. S. Eliot, a poet whom I admire as a poet, but I think did operate in that officializing role. Now, that seems to me the central instance.

IGNATOW: You're right there.

BERNSTEIN: Thank you. If you think I'm right in that one instance, that's, I'm trying to talk about that one quality; I don't think Eliot was a bad poet, and I don't think he was a bad critic.

IGNATOW: There is evidence that T. S. Eliot did what he could to keep William Carlos Williams in a small niche.

202

LEVERTOV: What does that have to do with the function of a poet?

SIMPSON: Yes, but right now . . .

PERLOFF: I don't see it . . .

LAZER: Louis, why don't you speak to that issue, please.

SIMPSON: I like what Denise just said. I could give you the name right now of the most influential person in American poetry, and it's not a poet; it's Harold Bloom.

BERNSTEIN: I think that that's true too. I agree with that. And I think that his role is totally negative in policing, even though I admire aspects of his work.

SIMPSON: I would like to get back to Denise. What she just said. I would like to get to the subject of what is a poet or what is a critic, but something more . . .

ALTIERI: I want to try a philosophical definition of this. May I?

LAZER: Louis, did you want to address that issue, that is, what functions do you see for a poet?

SIMPSON: Well, my function I said yesterday was, I'm a worker; critics work very hard, I know. But what I mean is my function is a *primary* one, as Denise said; I'm up against the coal face, chunking out this coal. Then I bring it to the surface; then management takes over. [Laughter] Now between labor and management, there's going to be a certain amount of really valid ongoing disagreement, and they are *not* the same function; they are different. And if I were a professional critic, my function would be quite different from the one I have. Now when I get a little upset is when I see management—or let's drop that metaphor—when I see critics elevating Language poetry (to put my cards on the table) to a very high level, language, it seems to me, starts to get out of touch with the coal face, and something very strange happens to poetry. You cannot become that abstract about it. And it starts to destroy contemporary poety.

[Various voices]

BURKE: Can I say something now? I've been quiet all this time; let me get a little bit in here. Sitting here quiet as the devil. [Clapping] This is a sad, satiric poem ["He was a Sincere, etc."]:

He was a sincere but friendly Presbyterian—and so

If he was talking to a Presbyterian,
He was for Presbyterianism.

If he was talking to a Lutheran,
He was for Protestantism.

If he was talking to a Catholic,
He was for Christianity.

If he was talking to a Jew,
He was for God.

If he was talking to a theosophist,
He was for religion.

If he was talking to an agnostic,
He was for scientific caution.

If he was talking to an atheist,
He was for mankind.

And if he was talking to a socialist, communist, labor
     leader, missiles expert or businessman,
He was for
     PROGRESS.

[Clapping, laughter, sighs]

IGNATOW: If we can't get beyond this, I think we'd better stop.

PERLOFF: I'll try to answer Louis, since I think that thing on the Language Poets was probably directed against me.

SIMPSON: No, not necessarily.

PERLOFF: The interesting thing is that when you were trying to set up a distinction between what Helen had said and what I said on the function of poetry, where I don't think there really would be a distinction at all. I think that we would both feel that we believe poetry is an imaginative transformation of reality, that it refines our insights, that it is beautiful language—whether it is of perilous seas and fairylands forlorn, or whether it is . . . well, there are so many, you know, I can take any lines from any great poems or rather take the whole poem, and they might mean the same thing to us. The problem then comes with how you deal with the contemporary, which is where we, for instance, differ and where lots of us around the table differ. And that is very hard to analyze because there the first person comes in, and this is where I disagree with Charlie. It

204

has to do a lot with our own experience. If I try to ask myself, Why do I think, for instance, that Charles Bernstein's poem that he read the other day, or "Dysraphism," which is a poem I have written about a little bit in the piece I did on Language poems, why are those very interesting poems to me? It's because I think they do mirror my experience and the way my life goes on, and I'll just tell you one little anecdote about that. I had interviewed Charles in his house on Amsterdam Avenue, and when I was back in L.A. I played that tape driving on the Santa Monica freeway. And I heard an ambulance, and I pulled over on the left, or right, I guess, should be the right, shouldn't it? [Laughter] I always pull over on the left—that's my problem. [More laughter] Anyway, I pulled over on the right, and nobody else was going over. And I stopped and nobody else was stopping, and suddenly I realized that the ambulance was on the tape, and it was on Amsterdam Avenue, and it took me back to that moment three months earlier when I had interviewed him. And I thought that kind of simultaneity is something which to me is tremendously interesting because I think that's what experience is like today. This has nothing to do with my feelings about Keats, whom I adore; Wordsworth, whom I adore; other poets who work in different ways. I think what the Language Poets—I shouldn't say them as a group—let's say Charles; there are others I don't like—like all groups, some are better, some are worse—I find them interesting because I think they are a young group trying in their own way to capture precisely the experience of what it's like to be alive today.

VENDLER: I think that one of the things that came to me, came to be evident to me, as the conference went on and we heard from different people in different ways, and even today, is that there should be a distinction drawn between criticism and reviewing. If people were really hot and bothered about criticism, they might be talking about Schleiermacher, you know. But it's not what we hear that they are so incensed about Schleiermacher's views or they're terribly cross about what Dr. Johnson said about *Twelfth Night*. I mean, it's not the issues of criticism that are causing ill feeling. It's the practice of reviewing and the terrible problem that people are reacting to their contemporaries, and the contemporaries are feeling either attacked sometimes, ignored sometimes, excluded sometimes, put in a niche sometimes, prevented from publishing sometimes, not given the prize sometimes. And then the natural thing for all of us, if we're refused tenure, is not that we didn't deserve tenure, but that, you know somehow, they didn't like our political opinions, or they didn't agree with our theoretical position or whatever. It can never be, I wasn't good enough to get tenure. It's always, The tenure committee is old fogies; or the tenure committee has never really understood what I'm up to; or the tenure committee thinks I vote wrong; or whatever. I mean this is what we all do when somebody doesn't fall in love with us. We never say, I'm really not very lovable; you always say, This person has false values; this person only wants beautiful blondes; whatever it may be. And I mean it's a perfectly natural explanation function that you create a construct which explains that you have been ignored or passed over for the prize or not reviewed or reviewed badly or isolated in your niche or whatever it is. I don't think this actual reaction to reviewing can ever disappear, because it won't disappear from love matches, and it won't disappear from tenure; and it won't disappear from human nature. But I do think that that temporary abrasiveness between whatever you want to call it— prize committees and reviewers and the poets that they're judging or giving prizes to—shouldn't be confused with the differences between poetry and criticism. And that's why if you move entirely away from the personal, those personal encounters and personal judgments, and try to consider when we're all safely dead, and, you know, the whole question of personal feeling has been dropped. Milton cannot feel bad that Dr. Johnson didn't think well of his poem "Lycidas." I mean you have to remove it . . .

STERN: He's furious.

[Laughter]

VENDLER: He's furious, yes. You have to remove it from that particular level and think about criticism, not reviewing, *criticism,* which I would prefer to think about people writing about dead poets and leave the issue of live poets out of it; and think about poetry, and think about dead poets and leave live poets out of it, because the issue becomes very confused when you bring in the matter of contemporary reviewing and prize awarding.

SIMPSON: That sounds very good, except it sounds like the absolute perfect defense of things being as they are. The status quo. If the establishment ever spoke, it would say exactly, I'm sorry, what you just said.

206

VENDLER: Not a defense of the status quo, because the very function of criticism often is to change the status quo. One of my aims in life is to change the fact—I still haven't succeeded, so I'm still trying—that people can get up and say that Stevens has no relation to the common life. If I can ever succeed as a critic, no one will be able to keep that status quo going. My aim in life is to change the status quo.

LAZER: Go ahead, Denise.

LEVERTOV: I'll try to be very brief. I'm getting increasingly appalled by the way in which this discussion—not in the latter remarks that you made, Helen, but in general—our discussion keeps getting more and more provincial, parochial, and we keep not talking about fundamental issues. And we also keep ignoring, for example, the fact that in this country at this time, there is a whole body of literature, very exciting literature, developing and beginning to flourish wildly and wonderfully by black poets, and by Chicano poets. All this is totally ignored and, perhaps even more important (well, not *even* perhaps but *obviously* more important)—we are talking away here, talking about prizes and naming names and all sorts of . . . or *not* naming names, and all this is absolutely parochial irrelevancy and ignores the fact that as a species, we are standing on the very brink of extinction, that we live in a time of unprecedented crisis. Why are we not talking at all about if, and how, and in what way poetry is or can be relevant to that issue? Can it, by awakening the awareness and imagination of people, effect some change, help us to make that essential choice that we've still got some chance to make before we do ourselves and everything else in? I mean—talk about fiddling while Rome burns! [Clapping]

IGNATOW: Well, that's precisely the problem with our present criticism as I've read it. It deals with the minutiae of the work of the poets, and it takes the work of the poet out of social and political contexts. And when you read it, you read, I feel as if I'm reading in a vacuum. This is one of my problems with the very best critical work I've been reading. And I'm referring to Helen Vendler, who I consider one of our finest critics; nevertheless, she does not represent the poet within a particular milieu of his time and place and does not wish to at this point, as I understand, as I see, does not wish to study Chicanos or study the problems of Reagan in connection with poetry and the whole atmosphere which is created by a person like

Reagan. Where is all this in poetry? Why isn't this discussed? Matthew Arnold discussed this in his time. Why aren't critics doing this sort of thing now?

LAZER: Let me ask Charlie to respond, because his most recent book is intensely involved with cultural and social questions, exactly as you're asking for, David.

ALTIERI: Thank you . . . It seems to me that the first question is metaphysical, and that is that mediocrity is everywhere, including in ourselves, including what we're reflecting at various times. Here, and it seems to me that in some sense everything we do has to both recognize that and resist that. And it's in that light that it seems to me one can try to distinguish—again traditional and typical are not the exclusive and all the qualifications you can add—critics' and poets' function and also again in all the differences, you've got to see the limits. On the level of the critics' function, it seems to me if you take the comments by Marjorie and Helen, which are in a way close and in a way opposite, it seems to me that the critics are the repositors in some way for a kind of collective responsibility for two kinds of history. That is, the history of measuring greatness in some way, of keeping the scope alive, and that seems to be Helen's primary orientation, and the notion of keeping the pressure of a collective present history on, again it seems to me, poets who have to focus and concentrate and cannot have the orientation towards collective balance scope that, in some sense, the critical mind has to seek. So that, and part of the problem of criticism is balancing those two ways of keeping history alive, because they're contradictory to one another.

JAY: I'd like to try and historicize this question. I mean, Gerry asked a long time ago that we talk more particularly about the distinction, right? Now obviously there's two things you can say. I mean on the one hand you can try to talk about it in a kind of historical context, I mean, what are the *essential* differences between people doing various kinds of writing? But I think much more particular, we can talk about how has, in the twentieth century, right, the pressure of the kinds of lives that we've lived—both in the United States or in Western Europe or in Vietnam—how have the pressures of those lives changed the forms of writing, whether poetic writing or critical writing? Now to speak from my own kind of writing and to a certain extent, I think, to speak for both Charles and a little bit for Kenneth Burke, there's been a tremendous pressure to see that for, throughout our culture, writing which we call poetical has been language poetry in a very fundamental way. And that the representation of reality in a kind of clear and lucid way is in some context a naive idea. We have to explore the technology of representation, the way we use symbol systems, and that when writers become self-conscious about the forms of literature, the forms of criticism, the forms of writing, as they explore symbol systems, they are *not* leaving the real world or the common life; on the other hand, they are going intensely *into* the very modes by which common life and reality are in fact being *produced*. We *produce* the world; we *don't* come upon it as a found thing; we come upon it as a created thing, and some of those creations happen to be language machines, language objects; and we create these identities, we create these poems. And I think that an intense part of my common life is to be surrounded constantly by the kind of scatterd symbologies and frameworks that Charles talks about.

STERN: So was Wordsworth.

JAY: Yeah.

STERN: I want to remind everybody that so was Aristotle and so was Wordsworth.

JAY: I think that history changes here, Gerry.

STERN: It's important to say that. I want . . .

SIMPSON: Who isn't saying that?

JAY: Gerry, I think that history changes.

STERN: An implication of Marjorie's statement about the freeway—I say this with friendship and respect—that there was implications that that happens in 1983 or '84, but it didn't happen in 1983 B.C. If that *is* the implication—forgive me if I'm reading that into your . . .

PERLOFF: No, no, it is.

STERN: If that is the implication, I will argue, respectfully, with Marjorie that that's an incorrect perception. There may not have been an ambulance or a tape recorder, but there was something else . . .

JAY: But that something else was different, Gerry.

STERN: There was something else in languages, in the critics or whoever is making special . . . There are, we could all make spe-

209

cial claims for our time, that's true. But, we do not exclude, we do not exclude the past with its special claims.

SIMPSON: Well, I want to ask you to explain something you just said.

JAY: Okay.

SIMPSON: You said we produce the world. Now this seems to me to be a very crucial question for me as a poet. What do you mean by that?

JAY: I mean that the world that we inhabit as human beings, right, is a human world. It's a world that our imaginations, which I take to be a comprehensive term for both feeling and thought, which our imaginations construct insofar as we live in buildings that we have imagined, we live in poems that we've imagined, we have relationships between each other which are not the products of givens but were the products of the hard work of our hearts and our minds. And that to ever take these things as naive certainties that we can simply represent instead of the products whose construction we must explore to see at what cost we've constructed certain things and what we must labor to do in order to construct the things that we imagine.

SIMPSON: I think I'm beginning to see a basic reason we're disagreeing here. You approach the world as a construct which humanity has made, and therefore language is a construct, so you approach experience *through* language. I would argue that for poets experience occurs as a *primary* thing, without language in between. I quoted Dante yesterday to you about visions. We have visions, we have experiences for which there is no language, and our job is to create that into a poem. And that seems to me a radically different point of view.

JAY: Oh, yeah, yeah. We do disagree fundamentally because I don't think that there is any such thing as uninterpreted experience and I don't think we ever have an experience of anything that isn't an interpretation when it arrives to our knowledge.

SIMPSON: I don't believe that for one second. If you had been in an automobile accident, or I could give you even worse examples—if you've ever had somebody shooting at you in a battlefield, where the heck is interpretation coming in there?

JAY: Well, I have to decide whether the bullet's going to hit me or not, Louis.

210

SIMPSON: But what has that got to do with interpretation?

LEVERTOV: If a child dying of cancer is suffering excruciating pain just as if it were a grown-up person who is able to reflect upon its pain, does that mean that it is not experiencing that excruciating pain? Bullshit!

BERNSTEIN: Of course it doesn't mean that. I think, I mean nobody is saying that. I think we're not going to resolve what are essentially philosophical and theological or metaphysical differences, *religious* differences, really, among us. If you had a panel of different religious people representing different religious groups you would, who were trying to *come* to some consensus, you would have some of these same disagreements. I think the problem I have is not so much understanding that people have a different viewpoint than I have—believe me I've been told that many times, [laughter] and I accept that. I do find it a problem that, and I certainly tend to do this too, that we tend to say "poets" think this and "poets" think that—because by doing that we tend to exclude the practices of other people in our society of divergence. And I think it's that practice that leads to the very deplorable situation that Denise Levertov raised and that I tried to bring up in my talk yesterday about the exclusion of the many different types of communities and cultures from our very multicultural, diverse society, of which there is no encompassing center. And my argument against a common voice has to do partly with that, because the idea of a common voice seems to me exclusion. So in that sense I think when we become emotional about some of these issues, it is because these issues of *exclusion* are political, in just the way that Denise raised, and that's *why* we're emotional. And I don't necessarily think that we need to feel totally reprimanding of ourselves for being emotional about that which we do invest our lives in and take to be of great seriousness. And not, certainly, serious in exactly the same way as the larger kinds of political issues such as you raised are, but in a continuum with them. And if one didn't feel, if I didn't feel that what I did and my concern about the exclusion of the multiplicity of types of writing that exist in our society had some continuum with deep political problems in our society as well as in the society of the Soviet Union, for example, a problem that I see in both of those societies, then I wouldn't do my work. That's what I see as the implication. So when I get emotional, what

211

happens to me? I'm accused of being McCarthyist, and that I did find to be, and that I just take as a personal remark, as being unfair.

STERN: I'm the one who accused you of being, I'm the one who said that, so I just, just briefly, it wasn't because you were emotional that I was, that I was saying that your action reminded me of McCarthyism. It wasn't because of your emotion; it was for other reasons.

PERLOFF: Can I come back to the question of emotion? Before, when it was asked about, David said, . . . I wanted to come back to that point. He said, "Well, if poetry is not about emotion, . . . what is it about?" I just want to raise the point here that for thousands of years people *didn't* think that's what poetry is about. Poetry's fiction, that's certainly both Plato and Aristotle's notion; therefore, the poet should tell truth, but he tells lies. In reading *The Odyssey* or *The Iliad,* which certainly also have elements that are common with our experience even though there are no freeways—and I'll agree with Gerry there—but the idea is why, you know, in general, it was thought for thousands of years, for a thousand years more or less, that the people, that the reason people liked *The Iliad* and *The Odyssey*—and they're great books—is *not* particularly because of the expression of individual emotion, but because they're marvelous fictions that give us mythic paradigms for experience. I just reread *The Odyssey* recently and I just couldn't get over it; it sounds silly to say—I couldn't put it down, because I was so excited at what happens with the sirens and especially "The Oxen in the Sun," which is such an amazing chapter.

IGNATOW: You mean it made *you* emotional?

PERLOFF: Yes. And that's a big difference too.

IGNATOW: Maybe we should define what I mean by emotion. It is the source, it's the source of all thought, philosophy; it's the source of a biologist going out to do his experiments—he feels that he has something to contribute, which is an emotional state.

PERLOFF: Well, I don't think poetry is necessarily the expression of individual emotion.

[Everyone talking]

LEVERTOV: But it's not a question about poetry being *about* emotion!

IGNATOW: It's not *about* emotion. Please get it into your ear.

LEVERTOV: It's *blood* flowing through it . . .

212

IGNATOW: Why can't you get it through your head? . . .

LEVERTOV: I'm not *about* my blood, but I wouldn't exist if I didn't *have* blood.

PERLOFF: Would you apply that to Homer for me, just apply that to Homer.

IGNATOW: Of course. When you look on the overall, you see that it's, he's expressing an attitude . . .

PERLOFF: Who he?

IGNATOW: . . . expressing the whole social class attitude towards life . . .

PERLOFF: Ah, okay . . .

IGNATOW: . . . which involves a physical living with the subject, which in itself produces emotion, an emotional attitude to correspond to the physical existence that goes with it. Now that emotion becomes the incentive with which to elaborate, articulate, and create the myth which corresponds to the emotion and the physical experience. It takes emotion, it takes a need, a desire. It's in every poem by Stevens. For god's sakes, what am I saying which is so strange? I'm not talking like a critic; I'm talking like a poet. Try and understand that I'm not a critic.

ALTIERI: Now wait a minute. I think that's ludicrous. I mean, I think [laughter, clapping], I mean I will take the fact that some of my fellow critics have disappointed me in their literary history, but if you take the end of *The Iliad*, I mean as a sense in which that is the articulation of the capacity of emotion to virtually transform the nature of culture. The relation between Priam and Achilles is one that the culture had not previously had available to it, because it was tribal rather than functional, or at least that's the way the text tends to go. Also, I mean in Aristotle the concept of *energeia*, the way in which rhetoric flows through poetry is not, you cannot go back to traditional doctrines in the past, as stated doctrines in order to be a historicist, because there is so much implicit, there are so many other categories flowing, the fact that poetry was not simply poetry then, but overlapped rhetorics, so you've got to take in the whole history of rhetorical statement.

STERN: It was religion, dance . . .

ALTIERI: But the other reason I want to go on is I really want to get back at Greg, Greg Jay, because it seems to me that he, because he went to Buffalo, he'll never represent the kind of empty, filtering of ideology that I think takes place if you go to Yale. [Laughter] On the other hand, and this comes back to the question of politics and maybe to the uselessness of discourse, I think David's poem about mediocrity and about dealing with other people last night, we've proven the value and the function of poetry, it seems to me, since I need that more and more to get through this session. But Greg took up, in relation to Charles's stuff, a certain kind of political language, which is the language of letting the noise of the world through, it seems to me the best way to talk about it, and suggested that that had a kind of contemporary force, both affectively and politically, that other, more traditional modes don't. Now there's a strange way which I want to agree and disagree with that. I want to agree that there's a certain kind of contemporary necessity to do that because of certain kinds of suspicions we have about media generation and about the ways that we lie to ourselves. But I think in a strange way Charles Bernstein's poetry is more aesthetic than, and more elitist than, the poetry of the other people here. I *like* it for that reason, in fact, because I do not feel mediocre listening to that poetry; I feel myself in some sense challenged, demanded, required to see certain very elaborate, formal structures—not structures, formal hologrammatic illusions—in some way taking place. But it seems to me, the reason I wanted to pick up Jay, Greg, is that he applied a kind of political rhetoric which to me cheapens Bernstein's poem. I think Bernstein sometimes applies a political rhetoric that cheapens Bernstein's poetry. And it seems to me that the one thing critics and poets have to have in common is this resistance to mediocrity. Whatever the functions are, and I think that's also got to be an answer to Denise, that the problem with political poetry is that it tends to be linguistically mediocre by *necessity;* you're trying to move large masses of people. That's a tension, that someone has to make choices.

LEVERTOV: No, I don't agree.

ALTIERI: But we have to keep aware of the danger of that kind of emotional . . .

STERN: Charles, do, do you know Hikmet's poem "On a Cucumber"? Do you know Hikmet's poem? I think it's the greatest political poem of the century—a group of men, there's a group of people sitting in a courtyard. I think it's in Moscow, and they're contemplating a cucumber. I wish I could remember that poem.

214

Does anybody have that text? It's a political poem no matter how you want to define it, and it could move thousands of people, and it could move a few people.

IGNATOW: The problem is that Neruda is never discussed among American critics.

PERLOFF: We have discussed Neruda.

IGNATOW: Neruda, he was a great political poet.

PERLOFF: Yes, yes . . .

IGNATOW: Why aren't there long books about the man, about his work? Why don't the American critics take him up?

PERLOFF: There's a lot of material written on Neruda.

IGNATOW: Where? I never see it. And I read a lot of things . . .

VENDLER: Can I say something about that, David? Because I think if I were asked the function of poetry, to this extent, I may be in some agreement with Charles Bernstein. [Laughter] The function of poetry . . .

IGNATOW: We've known that all along . . .

VENDLER: . . . is to make, is to render transparent language opaque, or to make us render, to make us see the materiality and opacity of language. And you have only to see that that's the function of poetry when you take any poem, I don't care what century, and have it read by people who are accustomed to seeing language as transparent. And they read the language in the poem as transparent, thereby producing to their own mind a satisfactory account of the poem, but to the mind of anyone who cares for that poem, a caricature of that poem, because they have not recognized the wish of that particular poem (whether it's an essay, "The Essay on Man" or anything else) to problematize language—that is to say, to make us conscious that you would not write a theodicy in heroic couplets that took fourteen pages. If you were serious about writing a theodicy, you would not write it in the fourteen-page, heroic couplet form, and therefore, the very problematizing of the issues of theodicy that occurs in "The Essay on Man," by the very form it takes, means that if you treat it as an essay in political theory or an essay in theodicy, you make a fool of yourself, without rendering Pope a fool.

So that every wrong reading of poetry is a reading that re-transparentizes language, which is meant to be a question about the kind of language used for any given form of discourse. And this

215

is true of all poems, as far as I'm concerned, in all languages. Because of the very concreteness of the nature of poetic language, because of its play with its own opacity and transparency at once, I don't think that I as a critic can ever write adequately about poetry in a language in which I am not perfectly bilingual. Once in a while I have been seduced into this for some reason, usually because I feel that it's the kind of poetry of which a great deal survives the translation. As it happens, I read Spanish quite well and have known Spanish since my birth, but I am not bilingual in Spanish, and therefore, although I have read Neruda in Spanish, I wouldn't write an essay on Neruda any more than I would write an essay on Miguel Hernández or Machado or any others that I have read. So I think that you can't ask necessarily that the work on Neruda be done by American, English primary language critics, it should be done by people whose primary language is Spanish.

IGNATOW: Then why don't your people, why do European critics write about American poetry?

VENDLER: Have you ever read what they've written? Have you ever read the French on Walt Whitman? I recommend that you read the French on Walt Whitman.

IGNOTOW: Of course I've read it.

LEVERTOV: There is a book on Neruda by an American critic, by John Felstiner, and this is very interesting in relation to what you say, Helen, because he is not truly bilingual even though he's a linguist and translates books from several different languages, but he approaches his account on Neruda through taking you, the reader, through the process of his own translation of *The Heights of Macchu Picchu:* how he first encounters it, why he makes certain choices that other translators didn't make, how the different existing translations compare with one another to his sensibility. And he moves *with* the reader; he takes the reader *with* him through the entire poem; and at the end of the book, you get the Spanish text and his translation together. So you've really learned something about Neruda, about the process of translation, and, more importantly, about the process of poetry, I think, although this man is not a poet except as a translator. He's not even a closet poet. And it's, I think, the most honest way for a poet who is not inside another language—the only honest way, I agree with you—for a poet to write about something written in a language not his or her own.

IGNATOW: In sum, this explains to me why our major American

critics are parochial. They do not absorb and don't care to; they're not adventurous. They're not *daring* enough to go out and grace Chinese poetry, Japanese poetry . . .

PERLOFF/LAZER: They do say that; they do . . .

IGNATOW: The discussion of Wallace Stevens, for example, why isn't he compared to poets in Europe, certain poets in Europe?

PERLOFF: He *is.*

LAZER: He is *constantly,* David.

IGNATOW: I haven't seen any.

LAZER: We'll get you some books . . .

SIMPSON: I think an interesting issue . . .

STERN: . . . if I understood Helen correctly on this point, was the comment about Pope and theodicy. I'm thinking of Neruda's attack on the United Fruit Company, an early poem, and I think that when Neruda wrote that poem, he was passionately attacking the United Fruit Company. He was not writing, he was not doing a useless, he was not doing an idle dance. At the same time of course, he was doing a beautiful dance, and without that beautiful dance the poem would not be, his feeling . . . Two things: The poem would not be appealing to us, nor would he have been in a sacred state. I'll use that word, if you'll forgive me, a sacred state, be permitted to write that poem. But I think it's important, the issue, I think there is that the poet, a poet does two things simultaneously when he attacks the United Fruit Company. Pope may not have been doing two things simultaneously there, and there are different kinds of poetry, I agree, but as far as the issue of political poetry, it has, there has to be two things involved. I guess they are sacred and profane; I guess I would call it that, sacred and profane.

LAZER: So you wouldn't agree with Charlie's notion that political poetry tends to be linguistically mediocre.

STERN: Some of it is, but I don't think, I don't, I certainly, I don't think *mine* is.

[Laughter]

VENDLER: And in that sense, political poetry's no different from any other poetry—love poetry, religious poetry, etc.

[Many voices at once]

ALTIERI: It is a temptation for mediocrity, though, because it is a temptation for your investments to be in class terms. That's all I want to say.

STERN: True, true.

217

VENDLER: Same way with love, same way with religion, I mean, all of those are subject to mediocrity.

PERLOFF: David, when you say, Why aren't the critics doing this, . . . I want to come back to Helen's distinction between reviewers and critics; although here even the reviewers *have* done it. For instance, this year there was published the poems of Aime Cesaire, a great political poet, the black Martiniquean poet. Aime Cesaire, whose work I never knew well until I got that book, and I did write about it. The translation, I think, is somewhat problematic. It's now also being translated by Gregson Davis, who is at Stanford. Here is a poet of incredible—both emotive and political—terribly exciting consciousness, and a wonderful poet of the twentieth century, and people *are* writing about him. And to give something on a positive note, when everybody here keeps saying the critics don't do this, the critics don't do that—the amount of publication that's recently gone on of foreign poets, Russian poets, Polish poets, poets like Aime Cesaire, the Heine translation, one of the great political poets of all time is Heinrich Heine, who is still very unknown in this country, where there's a marvelous translation by Hal Draper, who devoted twenty years of his life to working on that translation. And it did not get the attention that say Richard Howard's Baudelaire got (there, Louis Simpson may be right, that there's a kind of media hype, so that certain things get more attention than others). But just the same it exists, and it's there to read, and you know, we should know these things.

JAY: I think I discern a point of common agreement here. There have been a lot of slams both in print and at this conference against the poetry workshop, and accusations that the poetry workshop has somehow created mediocrity in American poetry. What's gone unspoken, though, is the degree of mediocrity that the English department as a *scholarly* institution has enforced on the study of literature. There'a parochialism of reading which is reinforced by English and American literature departments in the United States, which sometimes comes from the restriction of critical activities to a kind of elucidating service function to a certain canon of English and American poets long dead. And people who adopt an English department of a scholarly or research nature are often dissuaded from writing on poets who are alive, or poets from other countries, or people who work in other languages, and they're often penal-

218

ized for doing that. On the other hand, people who are practicing in research and scholarship, who draw upon say Continental sources of philosophy or psychology or talk about Ashbery and Freud or something, get criticized for going outside the realm of poetry. But in any case, my point is that it does seem to me that we can agree that American letters sometimes suffers today from a terrible kind of parochialism, whether it's the parochialism of the poets or the parochialism of the professors, and that all of us have been guilty to a certain degree of that kind of parochialism in our own way. And I think I've been guilty of it; I think that one thing I've learned a lot from Hank in the last four years is he came up to me and said, "Look, you're some kind of critic—you write about poetry, but you don't read contemporary poetry"—he tells me. And this, you know, he's beaten me over the head with it for four years, and I think I've learned a lot from it.

ALTIERI: It has a use, huh? . . .

JAY: . . . beating me over the head, you mean? . . .

[Many voices at once]

VENDLER: If I could just say something to that. I think that it is different to be a critic or a teacher in a country of two hundred million people from being—or a poet too—from being a critic in, you know, Budapest or in London of the nineteenth century, or whatever, where at most you were dealing with a literary community of two hundred people. And you weren't dealing with fifty states. Trying even to read a sampling of poetry and criticism from America is very different. It's different from when, the time when everything was centralized in Paris or everything was centralized in Vienna, and there weren't, there wasn't the simple weight of production. We're a much too big country to operate as a single literary unit. I would like, I agree entirely with what Greg said about the parochialism of our reading, and one is always distressed by that, and it comes from many sociological and historical sources other than English departments. It comes from, for instance, the education colleges which had a certain notion of what should have been done in high schools, etc., rather than teaching people six languages, the way they teach in Dutch high schools. So then I don't think you can blame the departments of English, at all, for these sociological and historical factors which have influenced American education. But I would like to correct one piece of misinformation and that is that the English departments are encouraging a submersion in the past, because if you look at the statistics of dissertations done and M.A. theses done all across the face of America today, you will find that overwhelmingly they are done in twentieth-century studies, and the past is in danger of being forgotten altogether by the English departments.

[Clapping]

BERNSTEIN: A central function of poetry, not *all* poetry, say the poetry that *I* write, is to resist then the tendencies within the culture as a whole, our culture as a whole, in my lifetime, toward making language seem alien from its users, making language seem as if it's a formal set of rules that are in a computer somewhere, and that people don't have the ultimate control over what's right and wrong, what makes sense and what doesn't make sense, that there's some standard of correctness. And what poetry *can* do and *does* do is to make an intervention within our language practice in a society. And to make that intervention doesn't mean that it has to have a mass audience, or in some ways, any audience at all, as we have certainly many historical instances. But the intervention is made certainly, primarily since it's done by individuals, it has a meaning for those individuals, and then, possibly extends out and has meaning for some other individuals. If somebody's work has meaning for themselves and for two other people that's signi— . . . well, one other person—but significant meaning for them, people will say that it's elitist because it only has meaning for one other person. I say it's elitist to try to think that one has the knowledge, to be as arrogant to think that what one has to say and has to contribute can appeal to huge masses of people in a multicultural world, much less a multicultural society. And, so, I think I would turn the concept of elitism on its head and try to speak to the kinds of concepts that I'm speaking of as political, as an intervention within language practice—*an* intervention—not the only one necessary, and certainly not the most important one. I think people working with literacy and issues of the politics of literacy are in a certain way, from my politics, on the frontline of the politics of language and of verbal discourse. That is to say, people teach people to read and dealing with those dynamics—something that I don't do. In respect to the issue before about history, I think it's very important to ack— . . . to point out that from my perspective, I am trying to resist the

220

inevitabilities and the assumptions of what history is doing, understood as a totality. But that in order to resist history as an individual and in turn try to link up with other people, so that one can make communities of resistance, I think one has to understand the specific situation of the historical moment. So I'm certainly not saying that the poetry that I'm interested in, that I read, or my own work, is determined by history without an act of intervention by individuals. Quite on the contrary, the reason that I've come to do the work that I do is because for me, in my situation, it seems the most powerful way that I can resist historical forces as a general process.

LEVERTOV: I'd like to respond to that. I believe that one does have to look upon language as, not a static, but nevertheless, a fixed set of rules, a nonstatic set of rules, and that language is common property, part of the commonweal made by all people with different manifestations, just as with flowers—there are many different kinds of flowers, but they're all flowers. So there are different languages, there are different language systems, but they all have this in common: that they are made by the people over the passage of time, and that there's consensus about individual words and about syntax, about words' relational, their individual and their relational significances; and one has to respect this and not take language to oneself as *private* property. One recognizes varieties of language within the system; one recognizes the personal voice of each speaker; but language has life: it is a living thing and it's like a coral reef—we are like coral insects who have produced this thing which we call language, with which we communicate with one another, because part of the very nature of human beings is to have communion with one another. Yes, I'm using it, I'm using theological terms, because I believe that way. I think that it's an affirmation of the possibility of human communion and that when anyone takes language and says, "Well, it's not a set of fixed rules, and I can use it in such and such a way. I can put words in relationships to one another that have meaning to *me,* and they have meaning to one other person. And that's good enough." I don't think it's good enough. I think it is arrogant and that's what I find pernicious about this viewpoint. It is making private property out of the public beach.

LAZER: Wouldn't you grant though that new uses of language also hold forth a promise of communion?

LEVERTOV: New uses of language which respect the nature of language, which has in back of it this consensus, which reflects the etymology and the traditions of a syntax . . .

STERN: In other words, you make a distinction between the *kind* of new uses of language—for example, that Wordsworth or Dante . . .

LEVERTOV: Absolutely . . .

STERN: . . . as young poets used, as . . .

LEVERTOV: Yes, because those . . .

STERN: . . . opposed, for example, to Cummings or Eliot or Bernstein . . .

LEVERTOV: . . . because those, although at first they may have certain limits of availability, they had a potential of access by everyone. They have that potential *inherent* in them. But there are some uses of language which I consider to be *misuses,* because they *do not* hold that potential.

PERLOFF: Now suppose—I just want to ask you this—suppose a hundred people came along and said, "But it *does* commune with me. I commune with it. It means something to me; it makes me feel things; and I commune." Then what would you say, that that's a false communion? I mean, in other words, I don't see how one can pose things in a prescriptive way like that . . .

STERN: It depends if they say, "Wow."

PERLOFF: Suppose, suppose a group of people came along and said in an absolutely natural way, "Yes, it says something to me; it means something to me." Then what would you say?

LEVERTOV: I don't really think that that can happen. I think that's as fanciful as . . .

PERLOFF: But it does happen . . .

LAZER: It does. It does and has.

LEVERTOV: I think it's really a fanciful way of looking at it.

[Mumbling, many voices at once]

PERLOFF: I'm just positing it as a question.

LAZER: Louis, let Louis. Louis, go ahead.

SIMPSON: Ah, well, I'm trying to ask you to clarify that . . .

PERLOFF: Yeah.

SIMPSON: Are you saying that because something works and a certain number of people accept it, that it's fine? Whatever happens is okay?

222

PERLOFF: No, I'm not saying that whatever happens is okay. But I'm saying if something speaks to a group, I mean Denise says it has to commune with people, and this is a selfish and a kind of elitist, arrogant way of using language, because it doesn't commune with people. First of all, we would have to find who the communities are. But suppose I found a community, I'm not saying perhaps now I have, but let's pose it hypothetically. Suppose in fact the community right out here told us, "Yes, it does speak to me." Then would you tell them they're wrong?

STERN: Let me ask . . . excuse me . . .

SIMPSON: Suppose you found some people who were using bad money and thought it was good money. Would you be mistaken to point out to them that it is all forged?

[Laughter]

ALTIERI: What about . . . I think that I . . . is going . . . it's the wrong tack for what Charles is doing—it's the wrong tack . . .

STERN: No, no, it's a good question.

VARIOUS VOICES: . . . It's the wrong tack . . . Wait a minute— why is it the wrong tack? . . . I don't think it is the wrong tack.

ALTIERI: Because Marjorie is using an empirical measure, and the right, the right job for the critic is to try to show the possibilities in the method. It seems to me what Denise is saying is you have to hold syntax common in language, so that the other things can vary. What Charles is doing is saying, "Let's hold some other things constant in language, so that the other things can vary." This is not simply a linguistic point. This is the reason why I want to raise it, and it gets back to the whole notion of narcissism. It seems to me . . .

STERN: Why did you point to me when you said that?

[Laughter]

ALTIERI: Because you raised the point . . . it wasn't intended at you. No. It seems to me that the danger of lyric emotion is always the sense that there is a single syntax that has to be held common while certain kinds of content changes. And part of the crucial role of criticism and of experiment in poetry is to say everything can be varied as long as something else can be held constant. And in a certain sense in your psyche you have to be able to move through the possibility of negating any of your deepest investments. This is, to me, crucial.

223

_ LOUIS, respond to that. Louis, . . .

_IMPSON: No, I, I'm trying to follow you, but I gather that this is what I meant last night when I put it badly—that it's infinitely manipulatable. But for poets it is *not*.

ALTIERI: *Some* poets!

PERLOFF: Let me get back to your money. Can I get back to your money analogy?

SIMPSON: Yes, please.

PERLOFF: I think the money analogy doesn't work in this sense. You would have to tell people that they're using bad money, because if they paid with it, right, something finally would happen. They'd go to jail, or their checks would bounce, or whatever it is— it wouldn't work. But I'm saying that when you prescriptively say the purpose of poetry is to create a communion with others, and then if those others would say, "But we *are* having that communion; we feel we're having it," are you then going to come back and say— forget now about Language poetry or any specific school—are you then going to come back and say, "No, that's a false communion. You have to have the true communion . . ."

ALTIERI: As a *teacher* I am. Sure I am, as a teacher . . .

PERLOFF: . . . which is, which is my communion.

STERN: What if all the major cities in America which have symphony orchestras would, by some act of caprice and madness, replace those symphony orchestras with rock bands. Would that therefore make that good music?

PERLOFF: I don't think you define good and bad in that way. I really don't.

STERN: I do.

IGNATOW: This is ironic, very ironic. Critics are calling for avant, avant-garde writing, and the poets are . . .

[Everyone talking at once]

LAZER: Let's put David on. Let's let David respond . . .

IGNATOW: I'm all for Charles's experimenting as much as he wants. It's okay; it's fine; there's something to be learned from it.

LAZER: Let's end on that note.

[Laughter]

STERN: Really?

LAZER: Yeah, let's give them a hand.

[Clapping]

224

[Several people still talking at once . . .]
ONE VOICE TRAILING OFF: I *know* you don't; I *know* you don't . . .

✦

Immediately after the panel discussion had concluded, Kenneth Burke came up to me and said that he was sorry that he did not have a chance to read the following poem as a conclusion to our panel discussion:

On Putting Things in Order

File this, throw out that.
Alert the Secretariat
In re each claim and caveat
To better serve the Cause of Alphabet.
Throw out this, file that.

File this, throw that out,
We know beyond all doubt
how Perfect Order reconciles—

And now throw out the files.

(From Kenneth Burke, *Collected Poems 1915–1967* [Berkeley: University of California Press, 1968].) With its irony and humor—a touch of Burke's comic frame—I add his poem as a conclusion or postscript to the panel discussion.

ADDITIONAL ESSAYS

Donald Hall

POETRY AND AMBITION

1. I see no reason to spend your life writing poems unless your goal is to write great poems.

An ambitious project—but sensible, I think. And it seems to me that contemporary American poetry is afflicted by modesty of ambition—a modesty, alas, genuine . . . if sometimes accompanied by vast pretense. Of course the great majority of contemporary poems, in any era, will always be bad or mediocre. (Our time may well be characterized by more mediocrity and less badness.) But if failure is constant, the types of failure vary, and the qualities and habits of our society specify the manners and the methods of our failure. I think that we fail in part because we lack serious ambition.

---

2. If I recommend ambition, I do not mean to suggest that it is easy or pleasurable. "I would sooner fail," said Keats at twenty-two, "than not be among the greatest." When he died three years later, he believed in his despair that he had done nothing, the poet of "Ode to a Nightingale" convinced that his name was "writ in water." But he was mistaken, he was mistaken. . . . If I praise the ambition that drove Keats, I do not mean to suggest that it will ever be

rewarded. We never know the value of our own work, and everything reasonable leads us to doubt it; for we can be certain that few contemporaries will be read in a hundred years. To desire to write poems that endure—we undertake such a goal certain of two things: that in all likelihood we will fail, and that if we succeed we will never know it.

Every now and then I meet someone certain of personal greatness. I want to pat this person on the shoulder and mutter comforting words: "Things will get better! You won't always feel so depressed! Cheer up!"

But I just called high ambition sensible. If our goal in life is to remain content, *no* ambition is sensible. . . . If our goal is to write poetry, the only way we are likely to be *any* good is to try to be as great as the best.

---

3. But for some people it seems ambitious merely to set up as a poet, merely to write and to publish. Publication stands in for achievement—but to accept such a substitution is modest indeed, for publication is cheap and easy. In this country we publish more poems (in books and magazines) and more poets read more poems aloud at more poetry readings than ever before; the increase in thirty years has been tenfold.

So what? Many of these poems are often *readable,* charming, funny, touching, sometimes even intelligent. But they are usually brief, they resemble each other, they are anecdotal, they do not extend themselves, they make no great claims, they connect small things to other small things. Ambitious poems usually require a certain length for magnitude; one need not mention monuments like *The Canterbury Tales, The Faerie Queen, Paradise Lost,* or *The Prelude;* "Epithalamion," "Lycidas," and "Ode: Intimations of Immortality" are sufficiently extended, not to mention "The Garden" or "Out of the Cradle." Not to mention the poet like Yeats whose briefer works make great connections.

I do not complain that we find ourselves incapable of such achievement; I complain that we seem not even to entertain the desire.

---

4. Where Shakespeare used "ambitious" of Macbeth, we would say "overambitious"; Milton used "ambition" for the unscrupulous

overreaching of Satan; the word describes a deadly sin like "pride." Now when I call Milton "ambitious" I use the modern word, mellowed and washed of its darkness. This amelioration reflects capitalism's investment in social mobility. In more hierarchical times pursuit of honor might require revolutionary social change, or murder; but Protestantism and capitalism celebrate the desire to rise.

Milton and Shakespeare, like Homer, acknowledge the desire to make words that live forever; ambitious enough, and fit to the *OED*'s first definition of *ambition* as "eager desire of honor"— which will do for poets and warriors, courtiers and architects, diplomats, members of Parliament, and kings. Desire need not imply drudgery. Hard work enters the definition at least with Milton, who is ready "to scorn delights, and live laborious days," to discover fame, "the spur, that last infirmity of noble minds." We note the infirmity, who note that fame results only from laborious days' attendance upon a task of some magnitude: when Milton invoked the Heavenly Muse's "aid to my adventurous song," he wanted merely to "justify the ways of God to men."

If the word *ambitious* has mellowed, *fame* has deteriorated enough to require a moment's thought. For us, fame tends to mean Johnny Carson and *People* magazine. For Keats as for Milton, for Hector as for Gilgamesh, it meant something like universal and enduring love for the deed done or the song sung. The idea is more classic than Christian, and the poet not only seeks it but confers it. Who knows Achilles's valor but for Homer's tongue? But in the 1980s—after centuries of cheap printing, after the spread of mere literacy and the decline of qualified literacy, after the loss of history and the historical sense, after television has become mother of us all—we have seen the decline of fame until we use it now as Andy Warhol uses it, as the mere quantitative distribution of images. . . . We have a culture crowded with people who are famous for being famous.

---

5. True ambition in a poet seeks fame in the old sense, to make words that live forever. If even to entertain such ambition reveals monstrous egotism, let me argue that the common alternative is petty egotism, which spends itself in small competitiveness, which measures its success by quantity of publication, by blurbs on jack-

ets, by small achievement: to be the best poet in the workshop, to be published by Atheneum, to win the Pulitzer or the Nobel. . . . The grander goal is to be as good as Dante.

Let me hypothesize the developmental stages of the poet.

At twelve, say, the American poet-to-be is afflicted with generalized ambition. (Robert Frost wanted to be a baseball pitcher and a United States senator; Oliver Wendell Holmes said that *nothing* was so commonplace as the desire to appear remarkable; the desire may be common but it is at least essential.) At sixteen the poet reads Whitman and Homer and wants to be immortal. Alas, at twenty-four the same poet wants to be in *The New Yorker.*

There is an early stage when the poem becomes more important than the poet; one can see it as a transition from the lesser egotism to the greater. At the stage of lesser egotism, the poet keeps a bad line or an inferior word or image because *that's the way it was; that's what really happened.* At this stage the frail ego of the author takes precedence over art. The poet must develop, past this silliness, to the stage where the poem is altered for its own sake, to make it better art, not for the sake of its maker's feelings but because decent art is the goal. Then the poem lives at some distance from its creator's little daily emotions; it can take on its own character in the mysterious place of satisfying shapes and shapely utterance. The poem freed from its precarious utility as ego's appendage may possibly fly into the sky and become a star permanent in the night air.

Yet, alas, when the poet tastes a little fame, a little praise. . . . Sometimes the poet who has passed this developmental stage will forget duty to the art of poetry and again serve the petty egotism of the self. . . .

Nothing is learned once that does not need learning again. The poet whose ambition is unlimited at sixteen and petty at twenty-four may turn unlimited at thirty-five and regress at fifty. But if everyone suffers from interest, everyone may pursue disinterest.

Then there is a possible further stage: When the poet becomes an instrument or agency of art, the poem freed from the poet's ego may entertain the possibility of grandeur. And this grandeur, by a familiar paradox, may turn itself an apparent 180 degrees to tell the truth. Only when the poem turns wholly away from the petty ego, only when its internal structure fully serves art's delicious purposes, may it serve to reveal and envision. "Man can *embody* truth," said Yeats (my italics), "he cannot *know* it." Embodiment is art and artfulness.

When Yeats was just south of fifty he wrote that he "sought an image not a book." Many aging poets leave the book behind to search for the diagram and write no more poetry than Michael Robartes who drew geometrical shapes in the sand. The turn toward wisdom—toward gathering the whole world into a book—often leaves poetry behind as a frivolity. And though these prophets may delight in abstract revelation, we cannot follow them into knowing, who followed their earlier embodiments. . . . Yeats's soul knew an appetite for invisibility—the temptation of many—but the man remained composite, and although he sought and found a vision he continued to write a book.

---

6. We find our models of ambition mostly from reading.

We develop the notion of art from our reading. When we call the poem more important than ourselves, it is not that we have confidence in *our* ability to write it; we believe in *poetry*. We look daily at the great monuments of old accomplishment, and we desire to add to their number, to make poems in homage to poems. Old poems that we continue to read and love become the standard we try to live up to. These poems, internalized, criticize our own work. These old poems become our Muse, our encouragement to song and our discouragement of comparison.

Therefore it is essential for all poets, all the time, to read and reread the great ones. Some lucky poets make their living by publicly reacquainting themselves in the classroom with the great poems of the language. Alas, many poets now teach nothing but creative writing, read nothing but the words of children . . . (I will return to this subject).

It is also true that many would-be poets lack respect for learning. How strange that the old ones read books. . . . Keats stopped school when he was fifteen or so; but he translated the *Aeneid* in order to study it and worked over Dante in Italian and daily sat at the feet of Spenser, Shakespeare, and Milton. ("Keats studied the old poets every day / Instead of picking up his M.F.A.") Ben Jonson was learned and, in his cups, looked down at Shakespeare's relative ignorance of ancient languages—but Shakespeare learned more

233

language and literature at his Stratford grammar school than we acquire in twenty years of schooling. Whitman read and educated himself with vigor; Eliot and Pound continued their studies after stints of graduate school.

On the other hand, we play records all night and write unambitious poems. Even talented young poets—saturated in S'ung, suffused in Sufi—know nothing of Bishop King's "Exequy." The syntax and sounds of one's own tongue, and that tongue's four-hundred-year-old ancestors, give us more than all the classics of all the world in translation.

But to struggle to read the great poems of another language—*in* the language—that is another thing. We are the first generation of poets not to study Latin; not to read Dante in Italian. Thus the puniness of our unambitious syntax and limited vocabulary.

When we have read the great poems we can study as well the lives of the poets. It is useful, in the pursuit of models, to read the lives and letters of the poets whose work we love. Keat's letters, heaven knows.

---

7. In all societies there is a template to which its institutions conform, whether or not the institutions instigate products or activities that suit such a pattern. In the Middle Ages the Church provided the model, and guilds and secret societies erected their colleges of cardinals. Today the American industrial corporation provides the template, and the university models itself on General Motors. Corporations exist to create or discover consumers' desires and fulfill them with something that satisfies briefly and needs frequent repetition. CBS provides television, as Gillette supplies disposable razors—and, alas, the universities turn out degree-holders equally disposable; and the major publishers of New York City (most of them less profitable annexes of conglomerates peddling soap, beer, and paper towels) provide disposable masterpieces.

The United States invented mass quick-consumption, and we are very good at it. We are not famous for making Ferraris and Rolls Royces; we are famous for the people's car, the Model T, the Model A—"transportation," as we call it: the particular abstracted into the utilitarian generality—and two in every garage. Quality is all very well but it is *not* democratic; if we insist on hand-building Rolls

Royces, most of us will walk to work. Democracy demands the interchangeable part and the worker on the production line; Thomas Jefferson may have had other notions but de Tocqueville was our prophet. Or take American cuisine: it has never added a sauce to the world's palate, but our fast-food industry overruns the planet.

Thus, our poems, in their charming and interchangeable quantity, do not presume to the status of "Lycidas"—for that would be elitist and un-American. We write and publish the McPoem—*ten billion served*—which becomes our contribution to the history of literature as the Model T is our contribution to a history which runs from bare feet past elephant and rickshaw to the vehicles of space. Pull in any time day or night, park by the busload, and the McPoem waits on the steam shelf for us, wrapped and protected, indistinguishable, undistinguished, and reliable—the good old McPoem identical from coast to coast and in all the little towns between, subject to the quality control of the least common denominator.

And every year, Ronald McDonald takes the Pulitzer.

To produce the McPoem, institutions must enforce patterns, institutions within institutions, all subject to the same glorious dominance of unconscious economic determinism, template and formula of consumerism.

The McPoem is the product of the workshops of Hamburger University.

---

8. But before we look into the workshop, with its training program for junior poets, let us take a look at models provided by poetic heroes of the American present. The university does not invent the stereotypes; it provides technology for mass reproduction of a model created elsewhere.

Question: If you manufacture Pac-Man, or a car called Mustang, and everyone suddenly wants to buy what you make, how do you respond? Answer: You add shifts, pay overtime, and expand the plant in order to saturate the market with your product. . . . You make your product as quickly as you can manufacture it; notions of quality control do not disturb your dreams.

When Robert Lowell was young he wrote slowly and painfully and very well. On his wonderful Library of Congress LP, before he recites his early poems about "Falling Asleep over the Aeneid," he tells how the poem began when he tried translating Virgil but produced only eighty lines in six months, which he found disheartening. Five years elapsed between his Pulitzer book *Lord Weary's Castle,* which was the announcement of his genius, and its underrated successor *The Mills of the Kavanaghs. For the Union Dead* was spotty, *Near the Ocean* spottier, and then the rot set in.

Now, no man should be hanged for losing his gift, most especially a man who suffered as Lowell did. But one can, I think, feel annoyed when quality plunges as quantity multiplies: Lowell published six bad books of poems in those disastrous last eight years of his life.

(I say "bad books" and would go to the stake over the judgment, but let me hasten to acknowledge that each of these dreadful collections—dead metaphor, flat rhythm, narcissistic self-exploitation—was celebrated by leading critics on the front page of the *Times* and *The New York Review of Books* as the greatest set of uniformly great emanations of great poetical greatness, greatly achieved. . . . But one wastes one's time in indignation. Taste is always a fool.)

John Berryman wrote with difficult concentration his difficult, concentrated *Mistress Bradstreet;* then he eked out *77 Dream Songs.* Alas, after the success of this product he mass-produced *His Toy His Dream His Rest,* 308 further dream songs—quick improvisations of self-imitation, which is the true identity of the famous "voice" accorded late Berryman-Lowell. Now Robert Penn Warren, our current grand old man, accumulates another long book of poems every year or so, repeating himself instead of rewriting the same poem until it is right—hurry, hurry, hurry—and the publishing tribe celebrates these sentimental, crude, trite products of our industrial culture.

Not all poets overproduce in a response to eminence: Elizabeth Bishop never went on overtime; T. S. Eliot wrote bad plays at the end of his life but never watered the soup of his poems; nor did Williams nor Stevens nor Pound. Of course everyone writes some inferior work—but these poets did not gush out bad poems late in their lives when they were famous and the market required more products for selling.

Mind you, the workshops of Hamburger University turned out

cheap, ersatz Bishop, Eliot, Williams, Stevens, and Pound. All you want. . . .

---

9. Horace, when he wrote the *Ars Poetica,* recommended that poets keep their poems home for ten years; don't let them go, don't publish them until you have kept them around for ten years: by that time, they ought to stop moving on you; by that time, you ought to have them right. Sensible advice, I think—but difficult to follow. When Pope wrote "An Essay on Criticism" seventeen hundred years after Horace, he cut the waiting time in half, suggesting that poets keep their poems for five years before publication. Henry Adams said something about acceleration, mounting his complaint in 1912; some would say that acceleration has accelerated in the seventy years since. By this time, I would be grateful—and published poetry would be better—if people kept their poems home for eighteen months.

Poems have become as instant as coffee or onion soup mix. One of our eminent critics compared Lowell's last book to the work of Horace, although some of its poems were dated the year of publication. Anyone editing a magazine receives poems dated the day of the postmark. When a poet types and submits a poem just composed (or even shows it to spouse or friend), the poet cuts off from the poem the possibility of growth and change; I suspect that the poet *wishes* to forestall the possibilities of growth and change, though of course without acknowledging the wish.

If Robert Lowell, John Berryman, and Robert Penn Warren publish without allowing for revision or self-criticism, how can we expect a twenty-four-year-old in Manhattan to wait five years—or eighteen months? With these famous men as models, how should we blame the young poet who boasts in a brochure of over four hundred poems published in the last five years? Or the publisher, advertising a book, who brags that his poet has published twelve books in ten years? Or the workshop teacher who meets a colleague on a crosswalk and buffs the backs of his fingernails against his tweed as he proclaims that, over the last two years, he has averaged "placing" two poems a week?

---

10. Abolish the M.F.A.! What a ringing slogan for a new Cato: *Iowa delenda est!*

237

The workshop schools us to produce the McPoem, which is "a mold in plaster, / Made with no loss of time," with no waste of effort, with no strenuous questioning as to merit. If we attend a workshop we must bring something to class or we do not contribute. What kind of workshop could Horace have contributed to, if he kept his poems to himself for ten years? No, we will not admit Horace and Pope to our workshops, for they will just sit there, holding back their work, claiming it is not ready, acting superior, a bunch of *elitists*. . . .

When we use a metaphor, it is useful to make inquiries of it. I have already compared the workshop to a fast-food franchise, to a Ford assembly line. . . . Or should we compare Creative Writing 401 to a sweatshop where women sew shirts at an illegally low wage? Probably the metaphor refers to none of the above, because the workshop is rarely a place for starting and finishing poems; it is a place for repairing them. The poetry workshop resembles a garage to which we bring incomplete or malfunctioning home-made machines for diagnosis and repair. Here is the homemade airplane for which the crazed inventor forgot to provide wings; here is the combustion engine all finished except that it lacks a carburetor; here is the rowboat without oarlocks, the ladder without rungs, the motorcycles without wheels. We advance our non-functional machine into a circle of other apprentice inventors and one or two senior Edisons. "Very good," they say. "It *almost* flies. . . . . How about, uh . . . how about *wings*?" Or, "Let me just show you how to build a carburetor. . . ."

Whatever we bring to this place, we bring it too soon. The weekly meetings of the workshop serve the haste of our culture. When we bring a new poem to the workshop, anxious for praise, others' voices enter the poem's metabolism before it is mature, distorting its possible growth and change. "It's only when you get far enough away from your work to begin to be critical of it yourself," Robert Frost said, "that anyone else's criticism can be tolerable. . . ." Bring to class only, he said, "old and cold things. . . ." Nothing is old and cold until it has gone through months of drafts. Therefore work-shopping is intrinsically impossible.

It is from workshops that American poets learn to enjoy the embarrassment of publication—too soon, too soon—because *making public* is a condition of workshopping. This publication

238

exposes oneself to one's fellow poets only—a condition of which poets are perpetually accused and frequently guilty. We learn to write poems that will please not the Muse but our contemporaries, thus poems that resemble our contemporaries' poems—thus the recipe for the McPoem. . . . If we learn one thing else, we learn to publish promiscuously: these premature ejaculations count on number and frequency to counterbalance ineptitude.

Poets who stay outside the circle of peers—like Whitman, who did not go to Harvard; like Dickinson, for whom there was no tradition; like Robert Frost, who dropped out of two colleges to make his own way—these poets take Homer for their peer. To quote Frost again: "The thing is to write better and better poems. Setting our heart when we're too young on getting poems appreciated lands us in the politics of poetry which is death." Agreeing with these words from Frost's dour middle age, we need to add: and "setting our heart" when we are old "on getting our poems appreciated" lands us in the same place.

---

11. At the same time, it's a big country. . . .

Most poets need the conversation of other poets. They do not need mentors: they need friends, critics, people to argue with. It is no accident that Wordsworth, Coleridge, and Southey were friends when they were young; if Pound, H. D., and William Carlos Williams had not known each other when young, would they have become William Carlos Williams, H. D., and Pound? There have been some lone wolves but not many. The history of poetry is a history of friendships and rivalries, not only with the dead great ones but with the living young. My four years at Harvard overlapped with the undergraduates Frank O'Hara, Adrienne Rich, John Ashbery, Robert Bly, L. E. Sissman, and Kenneth Koch. (At the same time Galway Kinnell and W. S. Merwin attended Princeton.) I do not assert that we resembled a sewing circle, that we often helped each other overtly, or even that we *liked* each other. I do assert that we were lucky to have each other around for purposes of conversation.

We were not in workshops; we were merely attending college. Where else in this country would we have met each other? In France there is an answer to this question, and it is Paris. Europe goes in for capital cities. Although England is less centralized than

239

France or Romania, London is more capital than New York, San Francisco, or Washington. While the French poet can discover the intellectual life of his times at a cafe, the American requires a degree program. The workshop is the institutionalized cafe.

The American problem of geographical isolation is real. Any remote place may be the site of poetry—imagined, remembered, or lived in—but for almost every poet it is necessary to live in exile before returning home—an exile rich in conflict and confirmation. Central New Hampshire or the Olympic Peninsula or Cincinnati or the soybean plains of western Minnesota or the lower East Side may shine at the center of our work and our lives; but if we never leave these places we are not likely to grow up enough to do the work. There is a terrible poignancy in the talented artist who fears to leave home—defined as a place *first* to leave and *then* to return to.

So the workshop answers the need for a cafe. But I called it the *institutionalized* cafe, and it differs from the Parisian version by instituting requirements and by hiring and paying mentors. Workshop mentors even make assignments: "Write a persona poem in the voice of a dead ancestor." "Make a poem containing these ten words in this order with as many other words as you wish." "Write a poem without adjectives, or without prepositions, or without content. . . ." These formulas, everyone says, are a whole lot of fun. . . . They also reduce poetry to a parlor game; they trivialize and make safe-seeming the real terrors of real art. This reduction-by-formula is not accidental. We play these games *in order* to reduce poetry to a parlor game. Games serve to democratize, to soften, and to standardize; they are repellent. Although in theory workshops serve a useful purpose in gathering young artists together, workshop practices enforce the McPoem.

This is your contrary assignment: Be as good a poet as George Herbert. Take as long as you wish.

---

12. I mentioned earlier the disastrous separation, in many universities, of creative writing and literature. There are people writing poetry—teaching poetry, studying poetry—who find reading *academic*. Such a sentence sounds like a satiric invention; alas, it is objective reporting.

Our culture rewards specialization. It is absurd that we erect a barrier between one who reads and one who writes, but it is an absurdity with a history. It is absurd because in our writing our standards derive from what we have read, and its history reaches back to the ancient war between the poets and the philosophers, exemplified in Plato's "Ion" as the philosopher condescends to the rhapsode. In the thirties, poets like Ransom, Tate, and Winters entered the academy under sufferance, condescended to. Tate and Winters especially made themselves academically rigorous. They secured the beachheads; the army of their grandchildren occupies the country: often grandsons and daughters who write books but do not read them.

The separation of the literature department from the writing department is a disaster; for poet, for scholar, and for student. The poet may prolong adolescence into retirement by dealing only with the products of infant brains. (If the poet, as in some schools, teaches literature, but only to writing students, the effect is better but not much better. The temptation exists then to teach literature as craft or trade; Americans don't need anyone teaching them trade.) The scholars of the department, institutionally separated from the contemporary, are encouraged to ignore it. In the ideal relationship, writers play gadfly to scholars, and scholars help writers connect to the body of past literature. Students lose the writer's special contribution to the study of literature. Everybody loses.

---

13. It is commonplace that, in the English and American tradition, critic and poet are the same person—from Campion to Pound, from Sidney to Eliot. This tradition started with controversies between poets over the propriety of rhyme and English meter, and with poets' defense of poetry against Puritan attack. It flourished, serving many purposes, through Dryden, Johnson, Coleridge, Wordsworth, Keats in his letters, Shelley, Arnold. . . . Although certain poets have left no criticism, there are *no* first-rate critics in the English tradition who are not also poets—except for Hazlitt. The poet and the critic have been almost continuous, as if writing poetry and thinking about it were not discrete activities.

When Roman Jakobson—great linguist, Harvard professor— was approached some years ago with the suggestion that Vladimir Nabokov might be appointed professor of Slavic, Jakobson was skeptical; he had nothing against elephants, he said, but he would not appoint one professor of zoology.

Oh, dear.

241

The analogy compares the elegant and stylish Nabokov—novelist in various languages, lepidopterist, lecturer, and critic—to the great, gray, hulking pachyderm, intellectually noted *only* for memory. . . . By jokes and analogies we reveal ourselves. Jakobson condescends to Nabokov—just as Plato patted little Ion on his head, just as Sartre makes charitable exception for poets in *What is Literature?*, just as men have traditionally condescended to women and imperialists to natives. The points are clear: (1) "Artists are closer to nature than thinkers; they are more instinctive, more emotional; they are childlike." (2) "Artists like bright colors; artists have a natural sense of rhythm; artists screw all the time." (3) "Don't misunderstand. We *like* artists . . . in their place, which is in the zoo, or at any rate outside the Republic, or at any rate outside tenured ranks."

(One must admit, I suppose, that poets often find themselves in tenured ranks these days. But increasingly they enter by the zoo entrance, which in our universities is the department of creative writing.)

Formalism, with its dream of finite measurement, is a beautiful arrogance, a fantasy of materialism. When we find what's to measure and measure it, we should understand style-as-fingerprint, quantifying characteristic phonemic sequence . . . or whatever. But it seems likely that we will continue to intuit qualities, like degree of intensity, for which objective measure is impossible. Then hard-noses will claim that only the measurable exists—which is why hard-nose usually means soft-head.

Once I audited a course of Jakobson's, for which I am grateful; the old formalist discoursed on comparative prosody, witty and energetic and learned, giving verbatim examples from Urdu and fifty other languages, exemplifying the multiplicity of countable noise. The journey was marvelous, the marvel diminished only a little by its terminus. The last lecture, pointed to for some weeks, turned out to be a demonstration, from an objective and untraditional approach, of how to scan (and the scansion was fine, and it was the way one scanned the poem when one was sixteen) of Edgar Poe's "The Raven."

---

14. A product of the creative writing industry is the writerly newsletter which concerns itself with publications, grants, and

jobs—with nothing serious. If poets meeting each other in 1941 discussed how much they were paid a line, now they trade information about grants; left wing and right united; to be Establishment is to have received an NEA grant; to be anti-Establishment is to denounce the NEA as a conspiracy. . . . Like Republicans and Democrats, all belong to the same capitalist party.

Poets and Writers publishes *Coda,* with chatty articles about self-publication, with lists of contests and awards. It resembles not so much a trade journal as a hobbyist's bulletin, unrelievedly cheerful, relentlessly trivial. The same organization issues the telephone book, *A Directory of American Poets,* "Names and addresses of 1,500 poets. . . ." The same organization offers T-shirts and book bags labeled "Poets and Writers."

Associated Writing Programs publishes *A.W.P. Newsletter,* which includes one article each issue—often a talk addressed to an A.W.P. meeting—and adds helpful business aids: the December 1982 issue includes advice on "The 'Well Written' Letter of Application," lists of magazines requesting material ("The editors state they are looking for 'straightforward but not inartistic work'"), lists of grants and awards ("The annual HARRY SMITH BOOK AWARD is given by COSMEP to . . ."), and notices of A.W.P. competitions and conventions. . . .

Really, these newsletters provide illusion; for jobs and grants go to the eminent people. As we all know, eminence is arithmetical: it derives from the number of units published times the prestige of the places of publication. People hiring or granting do not judge quality—it's so subjective!—but anyone can multiply units by the prestige index and come off with the *product.* Eminence also brings readings. Can we go uncorrupted by such knowledge? I am asked to introduce a young poet's volume; the publisher will pay the going rate; but I did not know that there was a going rate. . . . Even blurbs on jackets are commodities. They are exchanged for pamphlets, for readings; reciprocal blurbs are only the most obvious exchanges. . . .

---

15. Sigh.

If it seems hopeless, one has only to look up in perfect silence at the stars . . . and it *does* help to remember that poems are the stars, not poets. Of most help is to remember that it is possible for people to take hold of themselves and become better by thinking. It is also necessary, alas, to *continue* to take hold of ourselves—if we are to pursue the true ambition of poetry. Our disinterest must discover that last week's nobility was really covert rottenness, et cetera. One is never free and clear; one must work continually to sustain, to recover. . . .

When Keats in his letters praised disinterestedness—his favorite moral idea, destroyed when it is misused as a synonym for lethargy (on the same day I found it misused in the *New York Times, Inside Sports,* and the *American Poetry Review*)—he lectured himself because he feared that he would lose it. (Lectures loud with moral advice are always self-addressed.) No one is guiltless of temptation, but it is possible to resist temptation. When Keats worried over his reputation, over insults from Haydon or *The Quarterly,* over Shelley's condescension or Wordsworth's neglect, he reminded himself to cultivate disinterest; to avoid distraction and to keep his eye on the true goal, which was to become one of the English Poets.

Yeats is responsible for a number of the stars in the sky, and when we read his letters we find that the young man was an extraordinary trimmer—soliciting reviews from Oscar Wilde and flattering Katherine Tynan, older and more established on the Celtic turf. One of the *OED*'s definitions of ambition, after "eager desire of honor," is "personal solicitation of honor." When he wrote, "I seek an image not a book," he acknowledged that as a young man he had sought a book indeed. None of us, beseeching Doubleday or Pittsburgh, has ever sought with greater fervor.

And Whitman reviewed himself, and Roethke campaigned for praise like a legislator at the state fair, and Frost buttered Untermeyer on both sides. . . . (Therefore let us abjure the old saw that self-promotion and empire-building mean bad poetry. Most entrepreneurs are bad poets—but then, so are most poets.) Self-promotion remains a side issue of poetry and ambition. It *can* reflect a greed or covetousness which looks on the life lived only as a source of poems: "I got a poem out of it." Or it can show only the trivial side of someone who, on other occasions, makes great art. At any rate, we should spend our time worrying not about other people's bad characters, but our own.

Finally, of course, I speak of nothing except the modest topic:

244

How shall we lead our lives? I think of a man I admire as much as anyone, the English sculptor Henry Moore, eighty-four as I write these notes, eighty when I spoke with him last. "Now that you are eighty," I asked him, "would you tell me the secret of life?" Being a confident and eloquent Yorkshireman, Moore would not deny my request. He told me:

"The greatest good luck in life, for *anybody,* is to have something that means *everything* to you . . . to do what you want to do, and to find that people will pay you for doing it . . . *if* it's unattainable. It's no good having an objective that's attainable! That's the big thing: you have an ideal, an objective, and that objective is unreachable. . . ."

---

16. There is no audit we can perform on ourselves, to assure that we work with proper ambition. Obviously it helps to be careful: to revise, to take time, to put the poem away: to pursue distance in the hope of objective measure. We know that the poem, to satisfy ambition's goals, must not express mere personal feeling or opinion—as the moment's McPoem does. It must by its language make art's new object. We must try to hold ourselves to the mark; we must not write to publish or to prevail. Repeated scrutiny is the only method general enough for recommending. . . .

And of course repeated scrutiny is not foolproof; and we will fool ourselves. Nor can the hours we work provide an index of ambition or seriousness. Although Henry Moore laughs at artists who work only an hour or two a day, he acknowledges that sculptors can carve sixteen hours at a stretch for years on end—tap-tap-tap on stone— and remain lazy. We can revise our poems five hundred times; we can lock poems in their rooms for ten years—and remain modest in our endeavor. On the other hand, anyone casting a glance over biography or literary history must acknowledge: Some great poems have come without noticeable labor.

But as I speak I confuse realms. Ambition is not a quality of the poem but of the poet. Failure and achievement belong to the poet, and if our goal remains unattainable, then failure must be standard. To pursue the unattainable for eighty-five years, like Henry Moore, may imply a certain temperament. . . . If there is no method of work that we can rely on, maybe at least we can encourage in ourselves a temperament that is not easily satisfied. Sometime

245

when we are discouraged with our own work, we may notice that even the great poems, the sources and the standards, seem inadequate: "Ode to a Nightingale" feels too limited in scope, "Out of the Cradle" too sloppy, "To His Coy Mistress" too neat, and "Among Schoolchildren" padded. . . .

Maybe ambition is appropriately unattainable when we acknowledge: *No poem is so great as we demand that poetry be.*

Hank Lazer

CRITICAL THEORY AND CONTEMPORARY AMERICAN POETRY

Each person
Has one big theory to explain the universe
But it doesn't tell the whole story
And in the end it is what is outside him
That matters . . .

—John Ashbery, "Self-Portrait in a Convex Mirror"

We have still not come face to face, have not yet
come under the sway of what intrinsically desires
to be thought about in an essential sense.
Presumably the reason is that we human beings do
not yet sufficiently reach out and turn toward what
desires to be thought.

—Martin Heidegger, *What Is Called Thinking?*

Some time ago, T. S. Eliot impatiently (and correctly) declared that "criticism is as inevitable as breathing." Perhaps the contemporary equivalent would be the proclamation that theorizing is as inevitable as breathing. Indeed, a quick glance at MLA job lists or ads for new books of literary criticism quickly convinces us that all "serious" English departments must have specialists in critical theory and that graduate students and literary scholars must have training in critical theory. My intent is not to trace the rise of critical theory in current academic curricula, but to ask about a different relationship: What is, or what ought to be, the relationship between critical theory and contemporary American poetry? For it is my observation, albeit based on limited experience, that although there is a great deal of interdisciplinary study resulting from the current interest in critical theory, there remain certain thorny oppositions within English departments and literary studies that deserve attention and questioning. Indeed, there are certain entrenched prejudices which, for the sake of both critical theory and contemporary American poetry, require some discussion.

For example, most English departments, through their sense of teaching positions, specializations, and course content, maintain a strict segregation between "creative" writers and literary critics. Even readers and teachers who are sympathetic to Geoffrey Hartman's desire, stated at the beginning of *Criticism in the Wilderness,* "to view criticism, in fact, as within literature, not outside of it looking in" (CW, 1) would not dare to pursue the institutional and pedagogical consequences of such a desire. In my own department, M.F.A. students complain about the "irrelevant" academic courses they are required to take. They profess not to care what works of literature mean; they want more courses in technique. And though the training for poets and critics remains separate, certain shared conclusions and assumptions about writing have, in recent years, begun to emerge. After several prefatory detours, I would like to state and explore several such shared assumptions. To do so is to examine the uneasy relationship between poetry and critical theory, or between poetry and philosophy. Or, to state it more succinctly, to do so is to examine the relationship between poetry and thought.

At one extreme, we have the poet Karl Shapiro in "What Is Not Poetry?," an essay in *In Defense of Ignorance* (1960), declaring that:

> My favorite essay is Longinus' "On the Sublime," but philosophical essays in general are beyond me. I cannot retain a philosophical concept in my head for more than five minutes and I suspect any poet who can. If poetry has an opposite it is philosophy. Poetry is a materialization of experience; philosophy the abstraction of it. (DI, 264)

248

Though Shapiro is no longer regarded as one of the "stars" of contemporary American poetry, his attitude regarding a split between poetry and philosophy remains a commonly accepted one. Similar remarks can be found in the essays and interviews of poets such as Robert Bly, Louis Simpson, Philip Levine, and countless others. In "A Wrong Turning in American Poetry" (1963), a seminal essay for American poetry of the sixties and seventies, Robert Bly, while advocating an inward, spiritual turn in American poetry, takes potshots at the overly philosophical poetry of his immediate predecessors. He attacks Eliot for working up "the poem as an idea" (RB, 18) and criticizes "the Metaphysical Generation," the American poets of the twenties and thirties, because "not only were these poets . . . profoundly influenced by the English metaphysical poets, but their basic attitude was detached, doctrinaire, 'philosophical'" (RB, 28).

Suffice it to say that the contemporary poet's suspicion of philosophy and his desire to rule out philosophy is simply the mirror image of an earlier philosopher's banishment of poetry from the realm of serious thinking. In the *Republic,* Plato's Socrates decides that it would be best to banish the poet from the philosopher's ideal city:

> Thus we are justified at once in refusing to let him [the poet] into a city which is to be ordered well; because he arouses and fosters and strengthens this [inferior] part of the soul, and destroys the rational part, just as in a city, when by putting bad men in power one hands over the city to them and ruins the finer people. (Book X)

The contemporary poet is just as eager to throw out the philosopher or theorist from the city of creative writing. Usually, when a contemporary poet refers to another poet's work as "philosophical" and "abstract," he means "bad" and "wrong-headed."

But there are varying degrees of this mutual dislike and suspicion between poetry and philosophy. While less suspicious of "philosophical" thinking than Shapiro or Bly, Czesław Miłosz, in an essay on Pasternak, simultaneously grants the importance of thought to poetry and warns of the dangers posed by abstract thinking:

249

> . . . for us a lyrical stream, a poetic idiom liberated from the chaos of discourse was not enough, the poet should also be a *thinking creature;* yet in our efforts to build a poem as an "act of mind" we encountered an obstacle: speculative thought is vile and cunning, it eats up the internal resources of a poet from the inside. (EE 66–67)

Most recently, in the first of his Charles Eliot Norton Lectures 1981–82, Miłosz alludes to the competition between poetry and theory or poetics:

> Many learned books on poetry have been written, and they find, at least in the countries of the West, more readers than does poetry itself. This is not a good sign, even if it may be explained both by the brilliance of their authors and by their zeal in assimilating scientific disciplines which today enjoy universal respect. A poet who would like to compete with those mountains of erudition would have to pretend he possesses more self-knowledge than poets are allowed to have. Frankly, all my life I have been in the power of a daimonion, and how the poems dictated by him came into being I do not quite understand. That is the reason why, in my years of teaching Slavic literatures, I have limited myself to the history of literature, trying to avoid poetics. (WP, 3)

Besides acknowledging a competition between poets and theorists, Miłosz raises a key issue that I will return to: the readership of contemporary poetry.

I wonder if it would be possible to find a well-respected poet who also admits to reading and enjoying theory. Even John Ashbery, the darling of current sophisticated critics and theorists of contemporary American poetry (and a favorite of *this* author), in two recent interviews denies the influence of current critical theory on his own poetry. In an interview with Richard Jackson (included in *Acts of Mind: Conversations with Contemporary Poets*), the following exchange takes place:

> JACKSON: In "And UT PICTURA POESIS Is Her Name" you deconstruct, as Derrida would say, traditional poetics "so that understanding / May begin, and in doing so be undone." And in "Flowering Death," you write, "We must first trick the idea / Into being, then dismantle it, / Scattering the pieces on the wind." I think

also of "Five Pedantic Pieces," in which you write, "The poem of these things takes them apart." The poem tends to take apart or undo what they refer to in a way that reminds me of the writings of such contemporary thinkers as Derrida, Foucault, and Lacan.

ASHBERY: I think that it is probably not a coincidence that we've been addressing ourselves to similar problems and that these sorts of things tend to happen simultaneously in history from certain causes. I know, for example, that Raymond Roussel, who has been characterized as a kind of primitive Mallarmé, was asked in a letter about his opinion of Mallarmé, and he replied that he was unfortunately not familiar enough with the poet to give a serious estimation. So, while I am not very familiar with these authors, you may have a point in mentioning them. (AM, 71)

In an interview conducted by John Koethe in the spring of 1982 (and recently published in *SubStance*), Ashbery again addresses the issue of his poetry's relationship to current theory:

KOETHE: Many of those who are interested in your poetry seem to be interested in it in connection with theoretical ideas, particularly French theoretical ideas, like those of Jacques Derrida. Do you ever read works by such theorists, or do their views influence you secondhand, or do you ever use them in any way?

ASHBERY: No. I think I'm very good subject matter for people who are trying to elaborate new theories of criticism. Perhaps it would be better for me if I didn't know anything about them because then I might consciously try to write stuff that would fit their theories. (SS, 181–82)

Despite his denial of familiarity with Derrida and others, Ashbery's remarks interest me because they begin to hint at a conceptual milieu shared by contemporary poetry and critical theory.

Tempting as it may be, to dismiss the question I raised earlier—what might be the relationship between contemporary poetry and theory?—simply because poetry and theory are viewed as two distinct specialties is to fall victim to bigoted, inaccurate characterizations that we have inherited from Plato and subsequently reenforced ourselves. Like it or not, the current interest in critical theory will inevitably have significant effects on the way contemporary poetry is read, studied, and reviewed. It is my contention that contemporary critical theory, particularly that of Derrida and his American assimilators, can be of great value to poets and to readers of contemporary poetry because of several key assertions and actions: the emphasis given to play in poetry; the study of Heidegger's remarks on poetry; redefinitions of thinking found in Heidegger's work and in Richard Rorty's term "edifying philosopher"; discussions of the indeterminacy or instability of signification; the study of and praise for John Ashbery's poetry; a reaction against an anti-intellectualism rampant in American poetry of the sixties and seventies; a rejection of the notion that literary criticism must always play a subordinate, handmaiden role in relation to "primary" texts; and a rejection of the assumption that poetry and philosophy are antithetical, and hence separate, modes of thinking. And though these assertions may provide the framework for a less antagonistic relationship between poetry and theory, I do not wish to be identified as an uncritical partisan of deconstructive thought. For it is also my contention that recent critical theory retains traces of hostility to (and competition with) the poetry of its time, and that current theory privileges a certain kind of poetry: complex, abstract, ambiguous, indeterminate, poly-vocal, and ironic. Such privileging threatens to ignore, exclude, or underestimate American poetry of the plain style, a major poetic legacy too vital and accomplished to be downgraded because of its differing assumptions about language and representation. Finally, I remain skeptical about whether current critical theory will in any way enhance the readership for contemporary poetry.

But the form of skepticism which I will resort to again and again is one that questions the habit of separating poetry and thought. In so doing, I wish to emulate Paul Valéry, who begins his lecture "Poetry and Abstract Thought" with the following observations:

> The idea of Poetry is often contrasted with that of Thought, and particularly "Abstract Thought." People say "Poetry and Abstract Thought" as they say Good and Evil, Vice and Virtue, Hot and Cold. Most people, without thinking any further, believe that the analytical work of the intellect, the efforts of will and precision in which it

implicates the mind, are incompatible with that freshness of inspiration, that flow of expression, that grace and fancy which are the signs of poetry and which reveal it at its very first words. . . . This opinion may possibly contain a grain of truth, though its simplicity makes me suspect it to be of scholarly origin. I feel we have learned and adopted this antithesis without reflection, and that we now find it firmly fixed in our mind, as a verbal contrast, as though it represented a clear and real relationship between two well-defined notions. . . . At all events, this classic contrast, crystallized, as it were, by language, has always seemed to me too abrupt, and at the same time too facile, not to provoke me to examine the things themselves more closely. (PV, 136–37)

✦

In his preface to *On Deconstruction: Theory and Criticism after Structuralism,* Jonathan Culler attempts a brief explanation of what all this "theory" business is about:

> To put it another way, what distinguishes the members of this genre is their ability to function not as demonstrations within the parameters of a discipline but as redescriptions that challenge disciplinary boundaries. The works we allude to as "theory" are those that have had the power to make strange the familiar and to make readers conceive of their own thinking, behavior, and institutions in new ways. (C, 9)

But there is no unified entity called "critical theory": such a term is merely an evasion or a necessary fiction which I am forced to practice in an essay attempting to address two large, unstable entities, poetry and theory. As Culler wryly observes, "Once upon a time it might have been possible to think of criticism as a single activity practiced with different emphases. The acrimony of recent debate suggests the contrary: the field of criticism is contentiously constituted by apparently incompatible activities" (C, 17). Within the academic / critical community the more energetic debates have centered (forgive me) on the relative merits and demerits of deconstruction. Though my own purpose is not to explain or evaluate deconstruction, one of Culler's descriptions proves helpful:

> . . . deconstruction does not elucidate texts in the traditional sense of attempting to grasp a unifying content or theme; it investigates the work of metaphysical oppositions in their arguments and the ways

in which textual figures and relations, such as the play of the supplement in Rousseau, produce a double, aporetic logic. (C, 109)

Loosely, that is what I also mean by "theory": an investigation of the
nature and structure of signification, meaning, and representation.
As Culler observes about deconstruction, it "is not a theory that
defines meaning in order to tell you how to find it" (C, 131). And so
the purpose of recent critical theory is not to provide a new list of
themes nor to create a new method of explication. Instead, current
theory may involve speculation regarding the nature of language,
writing, and thought.

With the exception of Richard Jackson's excellent collection *Acts
of Mind: Conversations with Contemporary Poets,* poets have
rarely commented with any depth or consideration on developments in contemporary theory. In interviews or essays most poets
will, often in obvious ignorance, merely dismiss current trends in
theory as something irrelevant to their own pursuits. Yet, as the
University of Michigan's ever-expanding Poets on Poetry series indicates, the poets are not the least bit shy about expressing their
theories of poetry. Clearly, our poets are not allergic to exposition
nor to poetics. Among literary critics, the debate often focuses on
Derrida and deconstruction. From different bunkers, William
Pritchard and John R. Searle lob their carefully aimed bombs at the
encroaching encampment of deconstructionists. Though Searle's
attack (in the twentieth-anniversary issue of *The New York Review of
Books*) on Culler, Derrida, and deconstruction is the more polite of
the two, by the end of the essay, after his carefully reasoned philosophical objection, Searle makes it quite clear how annoying he
finds deconstruction: "One last question: granted that deconstruction has rather obvious and manifest intellectual weaknesses,
granted that it should be fairly obvious to the careful reader that the
emperor has no clothes, why has it proved so influential among
literary theorists?" (JS, 78). After a swipe at deconstruction for
making everything "just a free play of signifiers," Searle concludes,
"The upper limit, and I believe the *reductio ad absurdum*, of this
'sense of mastery' conveyed by deconstruction, is in Geoffrey
Hartman's claim that the prime creative task has now passed from
the literary artist to the critic" (JS, 79). If we believe Searle (and his
distortions of Hartman and others), these deconstructionists are a
dangerous gang indeed.

From a humanist outpost (in *The Hudson Review*), Pritchard offers this advice:

> I think rather that noncooperation is the proper response to decon.
> If they keep insisting how *hard* reading is—virtually impossible,
> Harold Bloom has declared—then it is time to emphasize the ease,
> the grace, the pleasure of reading. All one needs is an active mind, a
> good chair and a lot of time to sit in it: now get at those Trollopes
> you've been meaning to get at for years! Further suggestions: if
> possible never refer to a "text," but use the word "book" (or poem or
> novel or play) without apology. If somebody tells you that you really
> can't talk about an "author," just say, why of course I can, and proceed
> to. Do not argue the point, but be prepared to speak boldly of what,
> as you see it, Frost or Stevens was "getting at " in this or that poem,
> and maintain that a good poem is one in which that intention, that
> meaning, is vibrantly, originally, beautifully stated. Eschew the
> word "problematic" (almost as much as "problematics"), as well as
> "valorize," "recuperate," "binary opposition," "slippage" (except
> when talking about hydraulics or trouble on the ice) and all words
> ending with "centric" (logo, phono, and phallo). . . . Finally, and
> more gravely: do not speak of English studies as if it were a phe-
> nomenon of the past merely. (HR, 548)

Pritchard is not merely an out-of-it Archie Bunker shrewdly (or naively) satirizing the rhetorical excesses of deconstruction. The last sentence I quote from his essay points to the reason for the heat of his argument. The stakes in the current debate over the impor- tance of deconstruction (and of critical theory in general) are high. What is at issue is institutional power and institutional control. For that reason alone it would be foolish for poets, who after years of exclusion from the academic community now occupy hundreds of creative writing positions throughout the country, to ignore the debate. To put it crudely, what will emerge from the fights will be control of various English departments, curricula, academic presses, and journals, not to mention the effects on canon forma- tion, habits of literary judgment, reviews, awards, and the training of a generation of readers.

Though there are several fine contemporary poetry critics who practice and demonstrate various kinds of theoretical sophistica- tion—I am thinking specifically of Marjorie Perloff, Cary Nelson, Harold Bloom, Charles Molesworth, and Charles Altieri—I would like to focus briefly on an important essay by Altieri to point out

255

some of the dangerous judgments and attitudes toward contemporary poetry that can be found in such criticism. In "From Experience to Discourse: American Poetry and Poetics in the Seventies," Altieri posits "an unresolvable dichotomy":

> Either poets recover religious dimensions of experience by invoking an immediacy that fails to voice the full ironic and self-reflective play of mind or they dramatize their mastery as reflective, judging sensibilities by reducing the subject matter and scope of our lyric traditions. Religion comes to appear trivial or delusive and mature judgment to lack the impassioned self-dramatization of our most compelling lyric voices. (ALT, 191)

I wish to call attention to Altieri's devaluing of lyric / religious poetry, while privileging "the full ironic and self-reflexive play of mind." In studying the aesthetics and standards of judgment informing Altieri's essay, a relatively consistent pattern emerges. In describing the poetics of younger poets who "turn away from a romantic poetics of experience to older models of the poem as intelligent and subtle discourse" (193), Altieri tells us "we must concentrate on the different implications involved in emphasizing tone rather than image as 'technique of discovery'" (192). Altieri explains that younger poets such as Plumly, Hass, Glück, Charles Wright, Goldbarth, Dubie, and St. John, who follow and react against the generation of Bly, Kinnell, and James Wright, "insist that the poem is less transparent act of perception than act of discourse using the rhetorical potential of language to make complex reflections on ordinary perceptions" (193). When Altieri criticizes the poems of the preceding generation, presumably that "naive" poetry of immediacy, he takes to task Bly's poem "Surprised by Evening" because "its diffuse emotion is not tempered by sharp recognitions or verbal wit, leaving only the passive associations of fancy masking as active imagination" (200), and Kinnell's *The Book of Nightmares* fares no better, for "Kinnell ultimately has no significant ideas, only the verbal gestures of intense emotion grafted onto conventional romantic gestures" (203). Kinnell's long poem gets characterized by Altieri as "a lyric masquerade for thought" (204). But the more generalized villain (in Altieri's mind) lurking behind these "impoverished" poems by Bly and Kinnell is plain style. For

Altieri, "this plain style so slackens the cognitive pressures on the poem's details and ways of developing relationships that it renders consciousness as too passive and narrow to enact or act upon any moments of insight the poem might bring" (204). If the results of plain style are so woefully limited and limiting, we might do well to ask what Altieri proposes in its place. Altieri praises those younger poets who are "attempting to work out both fresh rhetorical strategies and different sets of thematic and aesthetic emphases in order to place the mind in a position to perform acts of self-conscious scrutiny" (206). Instead of the image or the directness of plain style, Altieri chooses to place greater emphasis (and promise) in the poem on tone. He explains:

> Tone, on the other hand, allows the cognitive pressure on the poem to derive from the self-conscious judgments of the poet rather than the working of deeper forces that may be mere illusions. Tone puts the emphasis on quality of judging voice rather than on vision. (210)

While I must admit that Altieri is one of the brightest critics of contemporary poetry, and one of a handful of intelligent, demanding critics who actually gives evidence of reading widely in contemporary poetry and who seems to do so with joy, intensity, and care, I find the drift of his argument in "From Experience to Discourse: American Poetry and Poetics in the Seventies" to be both alarming and narrow. His emphasis on "tone," "complex reflections," "verbal wit," "acts of self-conscious scrutiny," and "self-conscious judgments," adds up to a set of values remarkably like those which led to the rebellion headed by Robert Bly in the late fifties and early sixties. The aesthetic which Altieri traces and advocates sounds like a rehash of the prevailing standards for American verse in the early fifties, complete with a love of wit, irony, complexity (of voice and theme both), and acute self-consciousness. Unfortunately, or fortunately indeed, we don't need a return to this academic nostalgia for the good old complexities of Modernism, for, as we are all well aware, such a narrow view of poetry leaves out too much: William Carlos Williams for starters, and more recently, Bly, James Wright, Louis Simpson, Kinnell, and so on. My point is not that everything Altieri has to say is wrong, but that lurking behind his judgments is a binary opposition—between plain style and, for a lack of a better

257

term, playful style—and a narrowness of taste that does not bode
well for the reading of contemporary poetry. I will argue for a more
inclusive critical framework based on a broadened definition of
thinking. I merely single out Altieri's essay as representative of an
emerging critical temperament, which, while it may applaud the
complexities of a John Ashbery (or a W. S. Merwin or a Robert
Duncan), creates this applause at the expense of an equally vital and
valuable kind of poetry.

◆

To return to the more theoretical aspects of critical theory, what
is often frustrating (for the uninitiated) about reading this theoretical writing is that its goal is not necessarily to clarify the meaning of
a particular poem or poet's work. Geoffrey Hartman explains
rather abruptly that "the critical spirit, to conclude, does not auto-
matically place itself on the side of reason, enlightenment, or de-
mystification" (CW, 40). In sentences stylistically more typical of
recent critical writing, Hartman adds: "But contemporary criticism
aims at a hermeneutics of indeterminacy. It proposes a type of
analysis that has renounced the ambition to master or demystify its
subject (text, psyche) by technocratic, predictive, or authoritarian
formulas" (CW, 41). Many poets and critics may find this indeterminacy (and, as Pritchard and others have observed, its accom-
panying cumbersome jargon) disturbing, but Hartman has a brief,
direct description of one function of such criticism: "To keep a
poem in mind is to keep it there, not to resolve it into available
meanings" (CW, 274). But I don't think that it is the indeterminacy
or the jargon that has kept poets and theorists apart. Hartman calls
our attention to an interesting contemporary phenomenon: "A
curious reversal may therefore occur in the world of letters. Often
poems seem to be less demanding than essays. To be precise,
poems, especially today, are there as identity marks, written because to write is part of the contemporary heraldry of identity" (CW,
197). In comparison to much of our current poetry, Hartman argues that "the essays of the more intellectual practitioners of the art
of literary or philosophical criticism make greater demands on the
reader" (CW, 197). Perhaps for my own generation of poets, raised
on Bly's attack on intellect and educated in the workshop atmosphere where poems are read once or twice and then critiqued,
the level of sustained thinking called for in theoretical essays is too

rigorous. Such a lessening of intellectual capacity is serious for the reason that Hartman points out: "Too many consider philosophical questions impractical—obfuscating, not life-related. This is a misunderstanding of understanding" (CW, 297).

It is a crucial "misunderstanding of understanding" because it blocks out from consideration the very activity *shared* by poetry and theory: "Even in the absence of a competent theory, however, we should recognize the fact that with the Symbolist poets, from Mallarmé and Rimbaud to Hofmannsthal, Yeats and Valèry, a reflection on language accompanies explicitly the writing of poetry" (CW, 266–67). Certainly Perloff's *The Poetics of Indeterminacy: Rimbaud to Cage* begins to articulate such a theory. But where Hartman is especially accurate about Symbolist and post-Symbolist poets is when, quoting from Iris Murdoch, he argues:

> "Their attention is fixed upon language itself to the point of obsession, and their poems are thing-like, non-communicative, nontransparent to an unprecedented degree; they are independent structures, either outside the world or containing the world." This, then, is part of the context in which literary criticism moves at the present time. The poets were there before Saussure. (CW, 267)

I would now like to turn to several aspects of this shared context, where poetry and theory meditate on the nature of thinking and language. In *Acts of Mind,* Richard Jackson asks W. S. Merwin about a recurring vocabulary in Merwin's poetry of the sixties and seventies:

> JACKSON: And yet there is a sense in the poems of a distrust of the language, a sense of how it always fails us, and a sense of how this failure is what motivates, generates narratives, explanations. In *The Lice* you explain lives like "I who always believed too much in words" and in *The Carrier of Ladders,* "It has taken me this long / To know what I cannot say." But despite this distrust, things are always said—"I sing to drown the silence of far flowers," you say. There's an insistent vocabulary that defines each book and is developed from book to book, a vocabulary of things that can't be said yet are. I mean words like emptiness, distance, window, door, silence, mirror, echo, and the like. This vocabulary provides a certain resonance, a feel to the language, a sense of the language's being able to *presence* what it can't accurately name.

259

> MERWIN: I think you're describing well the way I've come to feel about language. There's a sense in which language is always inadequate. . . . The more you use language imaginatively, the more you try to describe what's unique about something, the more you realize the inadequacies of language. . . . So there is a simultaneous reverence and distrust of language. (AM, 49–50)

If we follow up Jackson's interview with Merwin's comments on silence (in an interview with Cary Nelson and Ed Folsom in *The Iowa Review*):

> And I've come to believe that existence—and by that I don't mean just human existence, I mean existence as a whole—has always got, basically, these two aspects to it, one which is relative, and the other which is not relative at all. The second, of course, is the teacher who is not dead, the world of silence. But that's also the world in which you can't call upon words. The arrogance comes from saying that that world doesn't exist or is of no importance, when of course in my view it's that world that gives words their real life. (IR, 43)

and juxtapose these with several remarks by Derrida on the relationship between language and silence, we begin to see some evidence of a shared area of concern. In "Cogito and the History of Madness" (in *Writing and Difference*), Derrida tells us that "silence plays the irreducible role of that which bears and haunts language, outside and *against* which alone language can emerge," adding that "like nonmeaning, silence is the work's limit and profound resource" (WD, 54). And when Derrida writes about Edmond Jabès's *Le livre des questions*, we begin to feel that we are reading about a French Merwin:

> . . . *Le livre des questions* is simultaneously the interminable song of absence and a book on the book. Absence attempts to produce itself in the book and is lost in being pronounced; it knows itself as disappearing and lost, and to this extent it remains inaccessible and impenetrable. To gain access to it is to lose it; to show it is to hide it; to acknowledge it is to lie. (WD, 69)

Derrida could also be describing aspects of Merwin's *The Lice,* which opens with an epigraph from Heraclitus which announces the poet's attention to absence, disappearance, and all that escapes our attempt to capture (or name) it:

> All men are deceived by the appearance of things, even Homer himself, who was the wisest man in Greece; for he was deceived by boys catching lice: they said to him, "What we have caught and what we have killed we have left behind, but what has escaped us we bring with us."

But my intent here is *not* to begin a Derridean reading of Merwin, for as Culler reminds us the purpose of deconstruction is not to provide us with a new set of themes which we can then point out in various poems. Though it may be tempting to some to dash off an essay on Merwin's decentered world, or the Derridean view of marginality in Ashbery's poetry, instead I would like to elaborate on the shared concerns of some recent theory and poetry.

From the passages quoted above, one shared area of concern is the nature of representation; that is, the relationship between word and thing, or, if you prefer, between signifier and signified. If there is a degree of arbitrariness and play built into language, if words do not adequately name or represent things, then not just poetry but philosophy too is subject to this imprecision. If philosophical writing, as Derrida argues persuasively in "White Mythology," is also based on figures and metaphors, then indeed Culler is correct in observing that "the philosophical is condemned to be literary in its dependence on figure even when it defines itself by its opposition to figure" (C, 148). Or, put more precisely, Derrida argues:

> On the one hand, it is impossible to get a grip on philosophical metaphor as such from the *outside,* since one is using a concept of metaphor which remains a product of philosophy. Only philosophy itself would seem to have any authority over its metaphorical productions. But on the other hand, and for the same reason, philosophy deprives itself of what it gives. Since its instruments belong to its field of study, it is powerless to exercise control over its general tropology and metaphorics. (WM, 28)

It is this location of philosophy *within* the realm of literature that is a crucial step in reopening the conversation between poets and theorists. As Borges, Barthelme, Calvino, Cortázar, Ashbery, Eco,

261

Gass, O'Hara, Zukofsky, Pound, Williams, and Derrida, Hartman, Barthes, and countless others have made us aware, "The essence of literature is to have no essence, to be protean, undefinable, to encompass whatever might be situated outside it" (C, 182). Or, on the desire of poets and philosophers to be untainted by the other, Culler's city metaphor, borrowed from Plato, and significantly modified, begins to describe the city that I too envision:

> The *pharmakos* may be repeatedly cast out of the city to keep it pure, but casting out metaphors, poetry, the parasitic, the nonserious, is possible only because they already dwell in the heart of the city: and they are repeatedly discovered to dwell there, which is why they can be repeatedly cast out. (C, 148–49)

I would add philosophy, criticism, and theory to the list of city dwellers, noting that there may be suburbs and outskirts, but finally nothing ever gets cast out permanently. Evictions from this city are temporary and amnesiac at best. For if the collective project of recent theoretical writing has been one of redefinition, that act of redescription has both expanded and relaxed our notions of literature, philosophy, and thinking.

Part of Derrida's task has been to offer an interpretation of interpretation. In "Structure, Sign, and Play," he describes two directions of interpretive activity:

> The one seeks to decipher, dreams of deciphering a truth or an origin which escapes play and the order of the sign, and which lives the necessity of interpretation as an exile. The other, which is no longer turned toward the origin, affirms play and tries to pass beyond man and humanism, the name of man being the name of that being, who, throughout the history of metaphysics or of ontotheology—in other words, throughout his entire history—has dreamed of full presence, the reassuring foundation, the origin and the end of play. (WD, 292)

It is this affirmation of play which enrages many who read Derrida and his assimilators. But Derrida is not the villain here. No need to shoot the messenger, especially when plenty of others have arrived at the gates of the city with the same news. I think particularly of Charles Olson's remark in "Projective Verse" (1950), a remark which indicates its grafting upon the observations of Pound and Confucius:

> It is true, what the master says he picked up from Confusion: all the thots men are capable of can be entered on the back of a postage stamp. So, is it not the PLAY of a mind we are after, is not that what shows whether a mind is there at all? (CO, 151)

In order to understand better the current attempts at redefining thinking, and philosophical thinking particularly, one source worth consulting is the philosopher whose work Derrida's most resembles, namely Heidegger. In *What Is Called Thinking?*, a series of university lectures delivered in 1951 and 1952, Heidegger warns that a reconsideration of thinking will require us to put aside a great deal: "Especially we moderns can learn only if we always unlearn at the same time. Applied to the matter before us: we can learn thinking only if we radically unlearn what thinking has been traditionally" (WCT, 8). Citing Hegel, what Heidegger eventually describes is an open-ended, indeterminate variety of thinking:

> And yet, precisely when thinking plies its proper trade, which is to rip away the fog that conceals beings as such, it must be concerned not to cover up the rift. Hegel once expressed the point as follows, though only in a purely metaphysical respect and dimension: "Better a mended sock than a torn one—not so with self-consciousness." Sound common sense, bent on utility, sides with the "mended" sock. On the other hand, reflection on the sphere in which particular beings are revealed—which is for philosophy the sphere of subjectivity—is on the side of the torn condition—the torn consciousness. Through the rift, torn consciousness is open to admit the Absolute. This holds true for thinking: . . . The torn condition keeps the way open into metaphysics. (WCT, 89–90)

Among American philosophers, Richard Rorty (in *Philosophy and the Mirror of Nature*) best makes use of Heidegger's reconsideration of thinking. Though he turns to Gadamer as much as to Heidegger, Rorty's description of another philosophic tradition—edifying philosophy as opposed to systematic philosophy—reopens the realm of thinking in a manner which, I will argue, admits poetry too. The "other tradition" that Rorty proposes substitutes "the notion of *Bildung* (education, self-formation) for that of 'knowledge' as the goal of thinking" (RR, 359). An important conclusion reached by Rorty is that the pursuit of so-called objective truth or objective knowledge is only *one* quest among many:

> The contrast between the desire for edification and the desire for truth is, for Gadamer, not an expression of a tension which needs to be resolved or compromised. If there is a conflict, it is between the Platonic-Aristotelian view that the *only* way to be edified is to know what is out there (to reflect the facts accurately) and the view that the quest for truth is just one among many ways in which to be edified. Gadamer rightly gives Heidegger the credit for working out a way of seeing this search for objective knowledge (first developed by the Greeks, using mathematics as a model) as one human project among others. (RR, 360)

In describing edifying philosophy, Rorty turns our attention to figures such as Goethe, Kierkegaard, Santayana, William James, Dewey, the later Wittgenstein, and the later Heidegger, writers who question and undermine the conceptual frameworks of their day. When Rorty makes the following point, he is beginning to see the kinship I have been implicitly arguing for throughout the essay:

> Edifying philosophers want to keep space open for the sense of wonder which poets can sometimes cause—wonder that there is something new under the sun, something which is *not* an accurate representation of what was already there, something which (at least for the moment) cannot be explained and can barely be described. (RR, 370)

I would argue that one of the most important projects for the humanities in our time is to throw out once and for all certain persistent misconceptions about poetry and philosophy. Poetry is *not* exotic intuition which bears no helpful relationship to serious thinking; philosophy is not the systematic presentation of abstract propositions untainted by metaphorical, figural language. Either narrow description is part of a bigoted city planning, whether the city planner is Plato or Karl Shapiro. Rorty is right to remind us that "Plato defined the philosopher by opposition to the poet" (RR, 370), and that such a definition was motivated by competition, fear, and self-interest. In our own time, when few read poetry and even

264

fewer read philosophy, not only have poets attempted to steer us clear of philosophy (meaning "abstract" thinking), but philosophers, such as Searle, attack and wish to dismiss their indeterminate brethren as not really philosophers: "So argumentative systematic philosophers say of Nietzsche and Heidegger that, whatever else they may be, they are not *philosophers*. This 'not really a philosopher' ploy is also used, of course, by normal philosophers against revolutionary philosophers" (RR, 370). But these revolutionary (or edifying) philosophers, as Rorty argues, play an important cultural role: "to help us avoid the self-deception which comes from believing that we know ourselves by knowing a set of objective facts" (RR, 373).

The pluralistic, open-ended view of thinking which Rorty proposes is that of conversation, a metaphor he picks up from Michael Oakeshott's essay "The Voice of Poetry in the Conversation of Mankind." Rorty argues:

> To see edifying philosophers as conversational partners is an alternative to seeing them as holding views on subjects of common concern. One way of thinking of wisdom as something of which the love is not the same as argument, and of which the achievement does not consist in finding the correct vocabulary for representing essence, is to think of it as the practical wisdom necessary to participate in a conversation. One way to see edifying philosophy *as* the love of wisdom is to see it as the attempt to prevent conversation from degenerating into inquiry, into an exchange of views. Edifying philosophers can never end philosophy, but they can help prevent it from attaining the secure path of a science. (RR, 372)

Before insisting upon poetry's place in such a conversation, I would like to return to Heidegger's lectures on thinking so as to ask what, in part, might this conversation be about. The key question which Heidegger asks about thinking is one that takes us into a religious or spiritual dimension: "What makes a call upon us that we should think and, by thinking, be who we are?" (WCT, 121). Heidegger further opens the mystery of his own question by observing:

> What calls us to think, and thus commands, that is, brings our essential nature into the keeping of thought, needs thinking because what calls us wants itself to be thought about according to its nature. What

265

> calls on us to think, demands for itself that it be tended, cared for, husbanded in its own essential nature, by thought. What calls on us to think, gives us food for thought. . . . The question "what calls for thinking?" asks for what wants to be thought about in the pre-eminent sense: it does not just give us something to think about, nor only itself, but it first gives thought and thinking to us, it entrusts thought to us as our essential destiny, and thus first joins and appropriates us to thought. (WCT, 121)

So far does Heidegger's characterization of thinking remove the activity from its mischaracterization as a tool or instrument for gaining advantage or reaching conclusions, that thinking can no longer be considered as merely a practical activity whereby we process information and solve problems. For Heidegger, thinking becomes a kind of house or temple wherein we exist. It is a domain given to us; literally, we are called to it, called into thinking which is our essential activity. As Heidegger concludes, "Man only *inhabits* the keeping of what gives him food for thought—he does not create the keeping" (WCT, 151). Indeed, a long history, albeit a fragmented and indeterminate one, stands behind Heidegger's description, two such fragments being Heraclitus's eightieth, "All men think," and Parmenides's third, ". . . for to think and to be are one and the same."

In his lectures, Heidegger remarks that "to answer the question 'what is called thinking?' is itself always to keep asking, so as to remain underway" (WCT, 169). It is this always being underway, "The caravan passes on" of Ashbery's "Grand Galop," that characterizes much of the best poetry of our age, a poetry (and thinking) that resists containment and conclusion. Within the metaphor of conversation, Michael Oakeshott gives us a description of an adventure which includes both poetry and philosophy:

> Conversation is not an enterprise designed to yield an extrinsic profit, a contest where a winner gets a prize, nor is it an activity of exegesis; it is an unrehearsed intellectual adventure. It is with conversation as with gambling, its significance lies neither in winning nor in losing, but in wagering. Properly speaking, it is impossible in the absence of diversity of voices: in it different universes of discourse meet, acknowledge each other and enjoy an oblique relationship which neither requires nor forecasts their being assimilated to one another.
> This, I believe, is the appropriate image of human intercourse—

appropriate because it recognizes the qualities, the diversities, and the proper relationships of human utterances. As civilized beings, we are the inheritors, neither of an inquiry about ourselves and the world, nor of an accumulating body of information, but of a conversation, begun in the primeval forests and extended and made articulate in the course of centuries. It is a conversation which goes on both in public and within each of ourselves. Of course there is argument and inquiry and information, but wherever these are profitable they are to be recognized as passages in this conversation, and perhaps they are not the most captivating of the passages. It is the ability to participate in this conversation, and not the ability to reason cogently, which distinguishes the human being from the animal and the civilized man from the barbarian. Indeed, it seems not improbable that it was the engagement in this conversation (where talk is without conclusion) that gave us our present appearance, man being descended from a race of apes who sat in talk so long and so late that they wore out their tails. Education, properly speaking, is an invitation into the skill and partnership of this conversation in which we learn to recognize the voices, to distinguish the proper occasions of utterance, and in which we acquire the intellectual and moral habits appropriate to conversation. (OAK, 198–99)

Such views of philosophy, thinking, and conversation as I have been sketching could go a long way toward breaking down the Platonic method of city planning. The views of Rorty, Oakeshott, and Heidegger suggest an open-ended thinking wherein philosophy and poetry are not both merely included but indeed depend upon one another. What is needed today is not an increasingly specialized view of literature—practical criticism versus theoretical criticism, critical writing versus creative writing, plain style versus playful style—but an educational curriculum and an intellectual environment that accept a broadened notion of thinking, inquiry, and rumination, a frame of mind sufficiently open and flexible to hear the remarks of Derrida, Hartman, Rorty, *and* Ashbery, Merwin, Simpson, and James Wright as part of the same conversation. Or, as Heidegger observes in a speech given in 1955 (and included in *Discourse on Thinking*), "Just as we can grow deaf only because we hear, just as we can grow old only because we were young; so we can grow thought-poor or even thought-less only because man at the core of his being has the capacity to think; has 'spirit and reason' and is destined to think" (DT, 45).

WORKS CITED

I have used the following abbreviations (followed by page number) to indicate my sources:

ALT   Charles Altieri, "From Experience to Discourse: American Poetry and Poetics in the Seventies," *Contemporary Literature* XXI (1980) 2:191–224.

RB   Robert Bly, "A Wrong Turning in American Poetry," (1963), rpt. in *Claims for Poetry,* ed. Donald Hall (Ann Arbor: University of Michigan Press, 1982).

C   Jonathan Culler, *On Deconstruction: Theory and Criticism after Structuralism* (Ithaca, New York: Cornell University Press, 1982).

WM   Jacques Derrida, "White Mythology," *New Literary History* (1974) 6: 5–74.

WD   Jacques Derrida, *Writing and Difference* (Chicago: University of Chicago Press, 1978).

IR   Ed Folsom and Cary Nelson, "'Fact Has Two Faces': An Interview with W. S. Merwin," *The Iowa Review* XIII (1982) 1: 30–66.

CW   Geoffrey Hartman, *Criticism in the Wilderness: The Study of Literature Today* (New Haven: Yale University Press, 1980).

DT   Martin Heidegger, *Discourse on Thinking* (New York: Harper & Row, 1966).

WCT   Martin Heidegger, *What Is Called Thinking?* (New York: Harper & Row, 1968).

AM   Richard Jackson, *Acts of Mind: Conversations with Contemporary Poets* (University, Alabama: The University of Alabama Press, 1983).

SS   John Koethe, "An Interview with John Ashbery," *Sub-Stance* 37/38 (1983): 178-86.

EE   Czesław Miłosz, *Emperor of the Earth: Modes of Eccentric Vision* (Berkeley: University of California Press, 1977).

WP   Czesław Miłosz, *The Witness of Poetry* (Cambridge: Harvard University Press, 1983).

OAK   Michael Oakeshott, "The Voice of Poetry in the Conversation of Mankind," in *Rationalism in Politics and Other Essays* (London: Methuen and Co., 1974), 197–247.

CO   Charles Olson, "Projective Verse" (1950), rpt. in *The Poetics of the New American Poetry*, ed. Donald Allen and Warren Tallman (New York: Grove Press, 1973).

HR   William Pritchard, "Dealing with Decon," *The Hudson Review* XXXVI (1983) 3: 541-48.

RR   Richard Rorty, *Philosophy and the Mirror of Nature* (Princeton: Princeton University Press, 1979).

JS   John R. Searle, "The World Turned Upside Down," *The New York Review of Books* XXX (October 27, 1983) 16: 74–79.

DI   Karl Shapiro, *In Defense of Ignorance* (New York: Random House, 1960).

PV   Paul Valéry, "Poetry and Abstract Thought," in *Paul Valéry: An Anthology* (Princeton: Princeton University Press, 1977), 136–65.

269

Suggestions for Further Reading

What follows is a selective (and necessarily personal) list of books, essays, and journals which may be of interest to readers wishing to explore further questions of poetics in contemporary American poetry. I have selected some recent writings by symposium participants and other (mostly) recent writings of general interest.

Charles Altieri. *Self and Sensibility in Contemporary American Poetry*. Cambridge: Cambridge University Press, 1984.

Bruce Andrews and Charles Bernstein, eds. *The L=A=N=G=U=A=G=E Book*. Carbondale: Southern Illinois University Press, 1984.

Charles Bernstein. *Content's Dream: Essays 1975–1984*. Los Angeles: Sun & Moon Press, 1986.

James E. B. Breslin. *From Modern to Contemporary: American Poetry, 1945–1965*. Chicago: University of Chicago Press, 1984.

Kenneth Burke. *Language as Symbolic Action: Essays on Life, Literature, and Method*. Berkeley: University of California Press, 1966.

Christopher Clausen. *The Place of Poetry*. Lexington: University Press of Kentucky, 1981.

Jacques Derrida. *Writing and Difference*. Chicago: University of Chicago Press, 1978.

Stephen Fredman. *Poet's Prose: The Crisis in American Verse*. Cambridge: Cambridge University Press, 1983.

Donald Hall, ed. *Claims for Poetry*. Ann Arbor: University of Michigan Press, 1982.

Robert Hass. *Twentieth Century Pleasures*. New York: Ecco Press, 1984.

Martin Heidegger. *Poetry, Language, Thought*. New York: Harper & Row, 1971.

David Ignatow. *Open Between Us*. Ann Arbor: University of Michigan Press, 1980.

Richard Jackson. *Acts of Mind: Conversations with Contemporary Poets*. University, Ala.: University of Alabama Press, 1983.

Hank Lazer. "Criticism and the Crisis in American Poetry." *The Missouri Review*, Vol. IX, No. 1 (1986), 201–32.

Denise Levertov. *The Poet in the World*. New York: New Directions, 1973.
———. *Light Up the Cave*. New York: New Directions, 1981.

Audre Lorde. *Sister Outsider: Essays and Speeches*. Trumansburg, N.Y.: The Crossing Press, 1984.

Douglas Messerli, ed. *"Language" Poetries*. New York: New Directions, 1987.

Czesław Miłosz. *The Witness of Poetry*. Cambridge, Mass.: Harvard University Press, 1983.

Cary Nelson. *Our Last First Poets: Vision and History in Contemporary American Poetry*. Urbana: University of Illinois Press, 1981.

Alicia S. Ostriker. *Stealing the Language: The Emergence of Women's Poetry in America*. Boston: Beacon Press, 1986.

Bob Perelman, ed. *Writing/Talks*. Carbondale: Southern Illinois University Press, 1985.

Marjorie Perloff. *The Poetics of Indeterminacy: Rimbaud to Cage*. Princeton: Princeton University Press, 1980.
———. *The Dance of the Intellect: Studies in the Poetry of the Pound Tradition*. Cambridge: Cambridge University Press, 1985.

Ron Silliman. *The New Sentence*. New York: Roof Books, 1987.
———, ed. *In the American Tree*. Orono, Maine: National Poetry Foundation, 1986.

Louis Simpson. *A Company of Poets*. Ann Arbor: University of Michigan Press, 1981.
———. *The Character of the Poet*. Ann Arbor: University of Michigan Press, 1986.

Helen Vendler. *Part of Nature, Part of Us: Modern American Poets*. Cambridge, Mass.: Harvard University Press, 1980.

Robert Von Hallberg. *American Poetry and Culture: 1945–1980*. Cambridge, Mass.: Harvard University Press, 1985.

Alan Williamson. *Introspection and Contemporary Poetry.* Cambridge, Mass.: Harvard University Press, 1984.

The following journals may also be of interest: *The American Book Review, American Poetry, The American Poetry Review, Antaeus, boundary 2, Contemporary Literature, The Georgia Review, How(ever), Hudson Review, The Iowa Review, Ironwood, Jimmy & Lucy's House of "K", The Missouri Review, The Ohio Review, Ottotole, Paper Air, Poetics Journal, Poetry, Poetry Flash, Salmagundi, Sulfur,* and *Temblor.*

Contributors

CHARLES ALTIERI, professor of English and comparative literature at the University of Washington, is the author of two books on contemporary poetry, *Enlarging the Temple: Ontological Themes in American Poetry of the 1960s* and *Self and Sensibility in Contemporary American Poetry,* as well as *Act and Quality: A Theory of Literary Meaning and Humanistic Understanding.* A leading critic of contemporary poetry, Altieri's essays have appeared in *Contemporary Literature, PMLA, College English, Criticism,* and others.

CHARLES BERNSTEIN, the author of eleven books of poetry, including *Islets/Irritations* and *Controlling Interests,* has recently published *Content's Dream: Essays 1975–1984.* With Bruce Andrews, he edited the magazine $L=A=N=G=U=A=G=E$. Recipient of an NEA creative writing fellowship and a Guggenheim fellowship, Bernstein's writing appears in *Sulfur, Poetics Journal, Sagetrieb, Paris Review,* and others. Bernstein lives and works in New York City, where he helps direct The Segue Foundation, a distribution center for books and magazines encouraging new expression in literature.

273

KENNETH BURKE, born May 5, 1897, is one of the great men of American letters. Recipient of the *Dial* Award (1928), the National Institute of Arts and Letters Gold Medal, and the National Medal for Literature, he is the author of numerous books including *The Philosophy of Literary Form, Language as Symbolic Action,* and *Collected Poems: 1915–1967.* Close friend to Malcolm Cowley, William Carlos Williams, Theodore Roethke, and Hart Crane, Burke's writings have been influential in many fields of study, including literary theory, religious studies, speech communications, political science, history, rhetoric, sociology, and philosophy.

GAY CHOW, whose photographs appear in *What Is a Poet?,* is completing a Ph.D. in English at The University of Alabama. He has published an essay on Flannery O'Connor, as well as an autobiographical essay, "A Personal View of the Mississippi Chinese," which appeared in *Reflections of Childhood.*

DONALD HALL is one of America's most influential writers and editors. The author of ten books of poetry, including *The Happy Man, The Alligator Bride: Poems New and Selected,* and *Kicking the Leaves,* he has also written several books of criticism, children's books, biographies of the sculptor Henry Moore and the pitcher Dock Ellis, and such noted textbooks as *Writing Well* and *The Pleasures of Poetry.* He has been poetry editor for *The Paris Review* and the editor of thirteen anthologies, including *New Poets of England and America* (with Robert Pack and Louis Simpson). He is the recipient of the Lamont Award for Poetry and of Guggenheim fellowships.

DAVID IGNATOW, whose first book, *Poems,* was "discovered" and praised by William Carlos Williams, has received the Bollingen Prize for Poetry, the National Institute of Arts and Letters Award, and the Shelley Memorial Award. His *New and Collected Poems, 1970–1985* was recently published. In addition to fourteen other volumes of poetry, he has published *The Notebooks of David Ignatow* and *Open Between Us,* a collection of essays and interviews. James Wright called Ignatow "one of a precious handful of indispensable poets in all of American literature." Ignatow has taught at York College, Columbia University, and New York University.

274

GREGORY JAY, comoderator for the symposium panel discussion, is the author of *T. S. Eliot and the Poetics of Literary History* and of essays on Poe, genre, the Yale critics, and the dispute between Marxism and deconstruction. With David L. Miller, he has coedited *After Strange Texts: The Role of Theory in the Study of Literature.* He teaches critical theory and American literature at the University of Wisconsin at Milwaukee.

HANK LAZER directed The Eleventh Alabama Symposium: What Is a Poet? For the past fourteen years, his poems have appeared in magazines such as *Midstream, The Virginia Quarterly Review, San Jose Studies, Poetry East,* and *The Nation.* Lazer's essays on modern poetry appear in *ELH, The Missouri Review, Ironwood, The Virginia Quarterly Review,* and *Modern Poetry Studies.* Currently, he is editing a collection of reviews and essays on Louis Simpson's poetry for the University of Michigan Press, and he is writing a book on contemporary poetry. He teaches modern poetry and American literature at The University of Alabama.

DENISE LEVERTOV is the author of more than ten books of poetry, including most recently *Oblique Prayers* and *Candles in Babylon.* Levertov has translated the poetry of Guillevic, and she is the author of two books of essays. Recipient of the Morton Dauwen Zabel Prize for poetry, a Guggenheim fellowship, and a grant from the National Institute of Arts and Letters, she currently teaches winter quarter at Stanford University.

MARJORIE PERLOFF, one of America's foremost critics of the poetic avant-garde, is professor of English and comparative literature at Stanford University. She has recently published *The Dance of the Intellect: Studies in the Poetry of the Pound Tradition,* and *The Futurist Moment: Avant-Garde, Avant-Guerre, and the Language of Rupture.* Her previous books include *The Poetics of Indeterminacy: Rimbaud to Cage* and *Frank O'Hara: Poet Among Painters.*

LOUIS SIMPSON is the author of ten books of poetry, most recently *The Best Hour of the Night* and *People Live Here: Selected Poems 1949–1983.* The recipient of the Pulitzer Prize for Poetry, the Prix

275

de Rome fellowship, two Guggenheim fellowships, and Columbia University's Medal for Excellence, Simpson, a professor of English at the State University of New York at Stony Brook, has also written a novel, a book of autobiography, several books of criticism, and a textbook, *An Introduction to Poetry.*

GERALD STERN, author of six books of poetry, most recently *Paradise Poems,* has received the Academy of American Poets' Lamont Poetry Award, the Poetry Society of America's Melville Cane Award, prizes from *The Paris Review* and *The American Poetry Review,* as well as fellowships from the NEA and the Guggenheim Foundation. In 1984, Stern was the chair-holder in creative writing at The University of Alabama. He teaches at The Iowa Writers' Workshop.

HELEN VENDLER is poetry critic of *The New Yorker* and professor of English at Harvard University. Among her half-dozen books on poetry, *On Extended Wings: Wallace Stevens' Longer Poems* won the James Russell Lowell Prize and the Explicator Prize, and *Part of Nature, Part of Us: Modern American Poets* won the National Book Critics Circle Award for Criticism. Editor of *The Harvard Book of Contemporary American Poetry* (1985), she is currently writing a book on Shakespeare's sonnets.

276

Permissions

The editor wishes to thank the following editors, authors, and publishers for permission to reprint:

Charles Bernstein's "Blood on the Cutting Room Floor" appears in a shorter version in *Content's Dream: Essays 1975–1984* (Los Angeles: Sun & Moon Press, 1986).

"Poetry and Ambition" by Donald Hall first appeared in *The Kenyon Review,* Fall 1983, and is reprinted here by permission of the author.

"Critical Theory and Contemporary American Poetry," by Hank Lazer, first appeared in *The Missouri Review* (Vol. VII, No. 3, 1984). The author thanks the editors of *The Missouri Review* for permission to reprint the essay.

Marjorie Perloff's "Lucent and Inescapable Rhythms: Metrical 'Choice' and Historical Formation" will appear in a slightly different version in *The Line in Contemporary Poetry,* Henry Sayre, ed. (University of Illinois Press).

Louis Simpson's "The Character of the Poet" also appears in *The Character of the Poet* (University of Michigan Press, 1986).

"Fears of the Eighth Grade," by Toi Derricotte, reprinted by permission of the author.

"Speed of Light," copyright © 1985 by Richard Kenney, from *Orrery*, published by Atheneum Publishers.

277

278

Index

279